IRON FIST

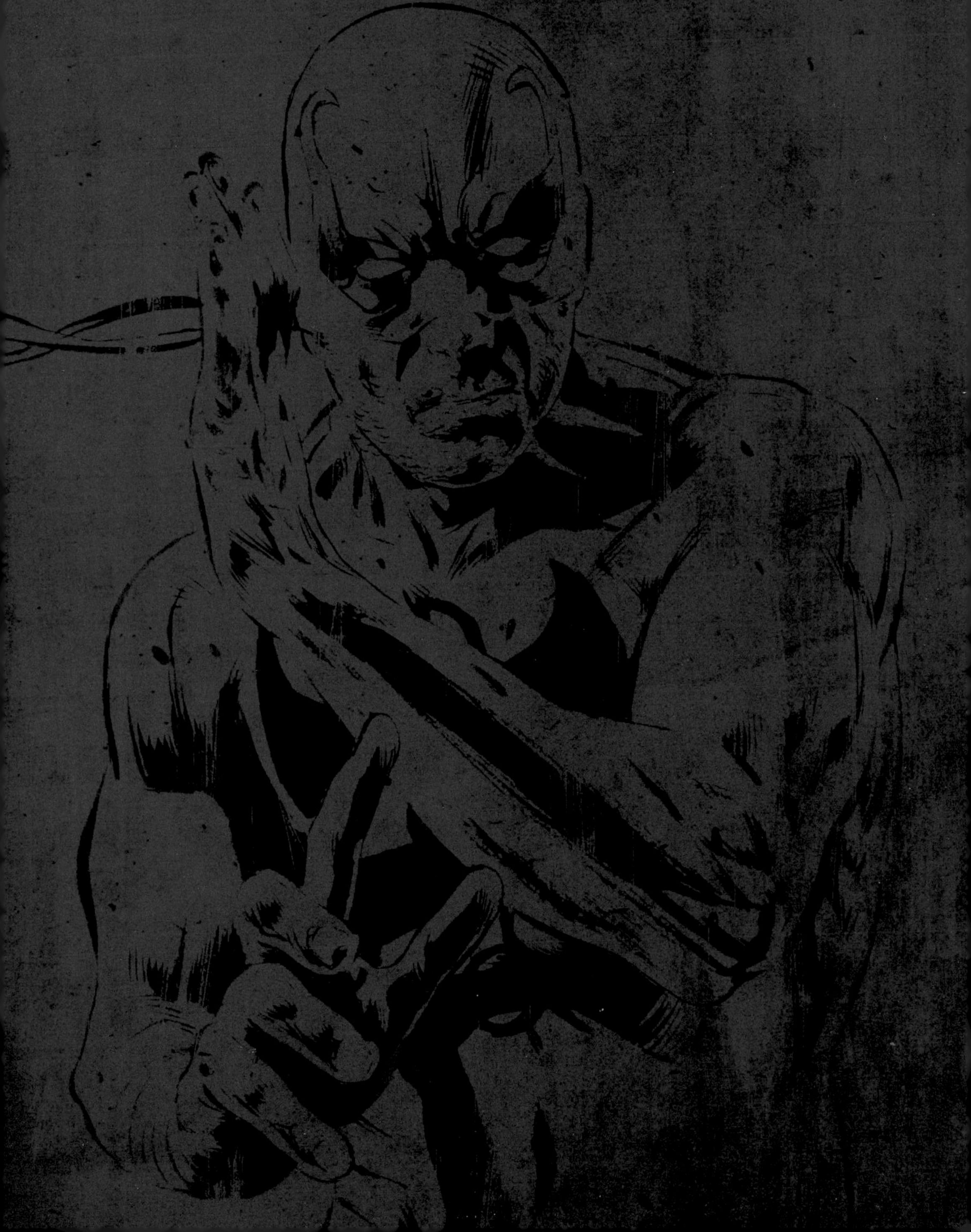

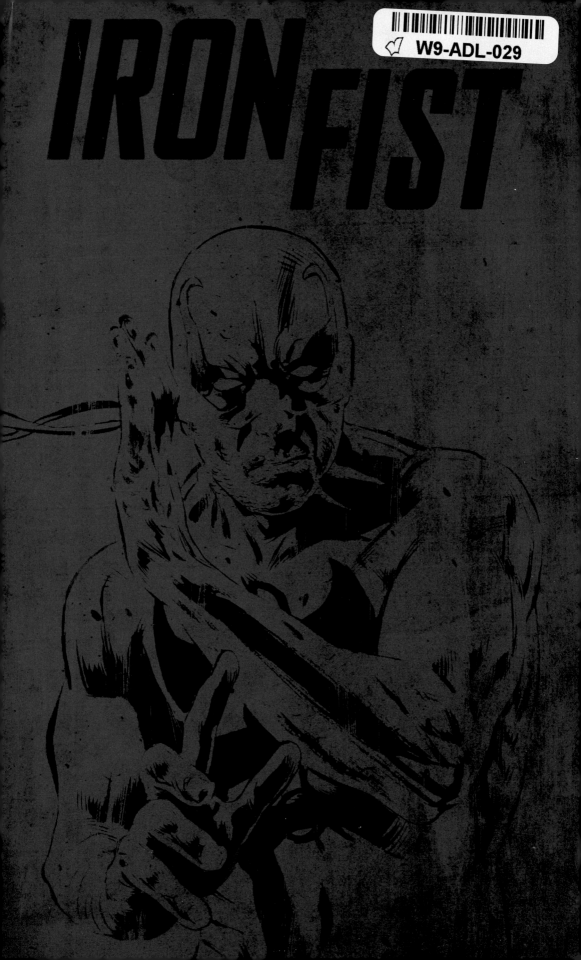

DANIEL RAND was orphaned in the mystical city of **K'UN-LUN** as a child. There, he grew up to conquer a series of trials to become the **IRON FIST**: K'un-Lun's chi-fueled defender of the innocent. Recently, while away from K'un-Lun living his other life as Danny Rand, K'un-Lun was attacked and destroyed, severing his connection to K'un-Lun's chi, and his powers...

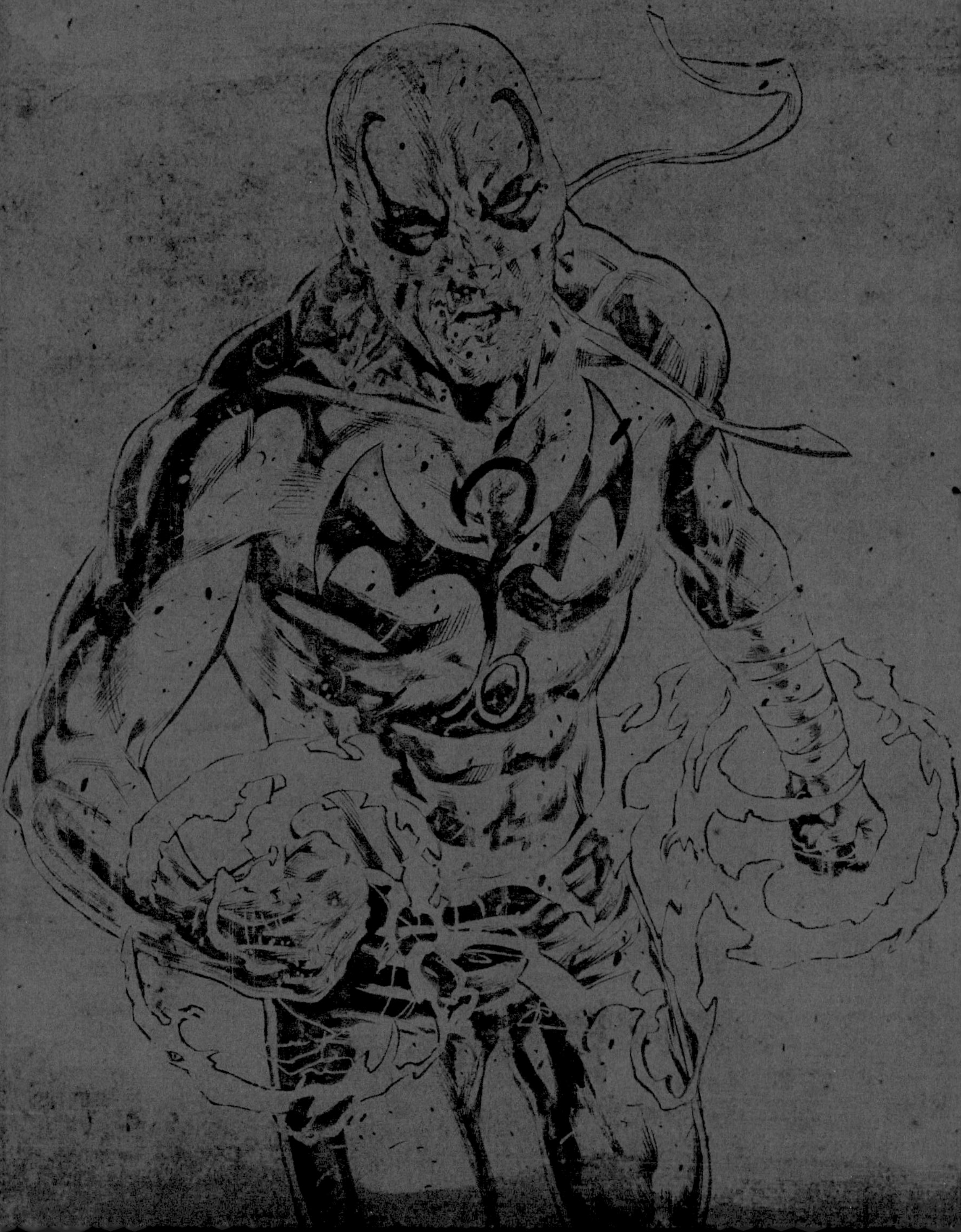

IRON FIST

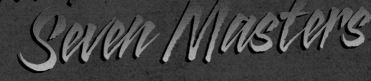

The Trial of the Seven Masters

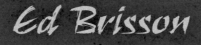

Ed Brisson
writer

Mike Perkins
artist

Andy Troy
color artist

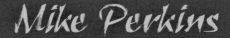

VC's Travis Lanham
letterer

Jeff Dekal
cover art

Kathleen Wisneski
assistant editor

Jake Thomas
editor

collection editor **JENNIFER GRÜNWALD**
assistant editor **CAITLIN O'CONNELL**
associate managing editor **KATERI WOODY**
editor, special projects **MARK D. BEAZLEY**

vp production & special projects **JEFF YOUNGQUIST**
svp print, sales & marketing **DAVID GABRIEL**
book designer **ADAM DEL RE**

editor in chief **AXEL ALONSO**
chief creative officer **JOE QUESADA**
president **DAN BUCKLEY**
executive producer **ALAN FINE**

IRON FIST VOL. 1: THE TRIAL OF THE SEVEN MASTERS. Contains material originally published in magazine form as IRON FIST #1-5. First printing 2017. ISBN# 978-1-302-90776-1. Published by MARVEL WORLDWIDE, INC., a subsidiary of MARVEL ENTERTAINMENT, LLC. OFFICE OF PUBLICATION: 135 West 50th Street, New York, NY 10020.

Printed in the U.S.A. DAN BUCKLEY, President, Marvel Entertainment; JOE QUESADA, Chief Creative Officer; TOM BREVOORT, SVP of Publishing; DAVID BOGART, SVP of Business Affairs & Operations, Publishing & Partnership; C.B. CEBULSKI, VP of Brand Management & Development, Asia; DAVID GABRIEL, SVP of Sales & Marketing, Publishing; JEFF YOUNGQUIST, VP of Production & Special Projects; DAN CARR, Executive Director of Publishing Technology; ALEX MORALES, Director of Publishing Operations; SUSAN CRESPI, Production Manager; STAN LEE, Chairman Emeritus. For information regarding advertising in Marvel Comics or on Marvel.com, please contact Vit DeBellis, Integrated Sales Manager, at vdebellis@marvel.com. For Marvel subscription inquiries, please call 888-511-5480. Manufactured between 7/14/2017 and 8/14/2017 by QUAD/GRAPHICS WASECA, WASECA, MN, USA.

10 9 8 7 6 5 4 3 2 1

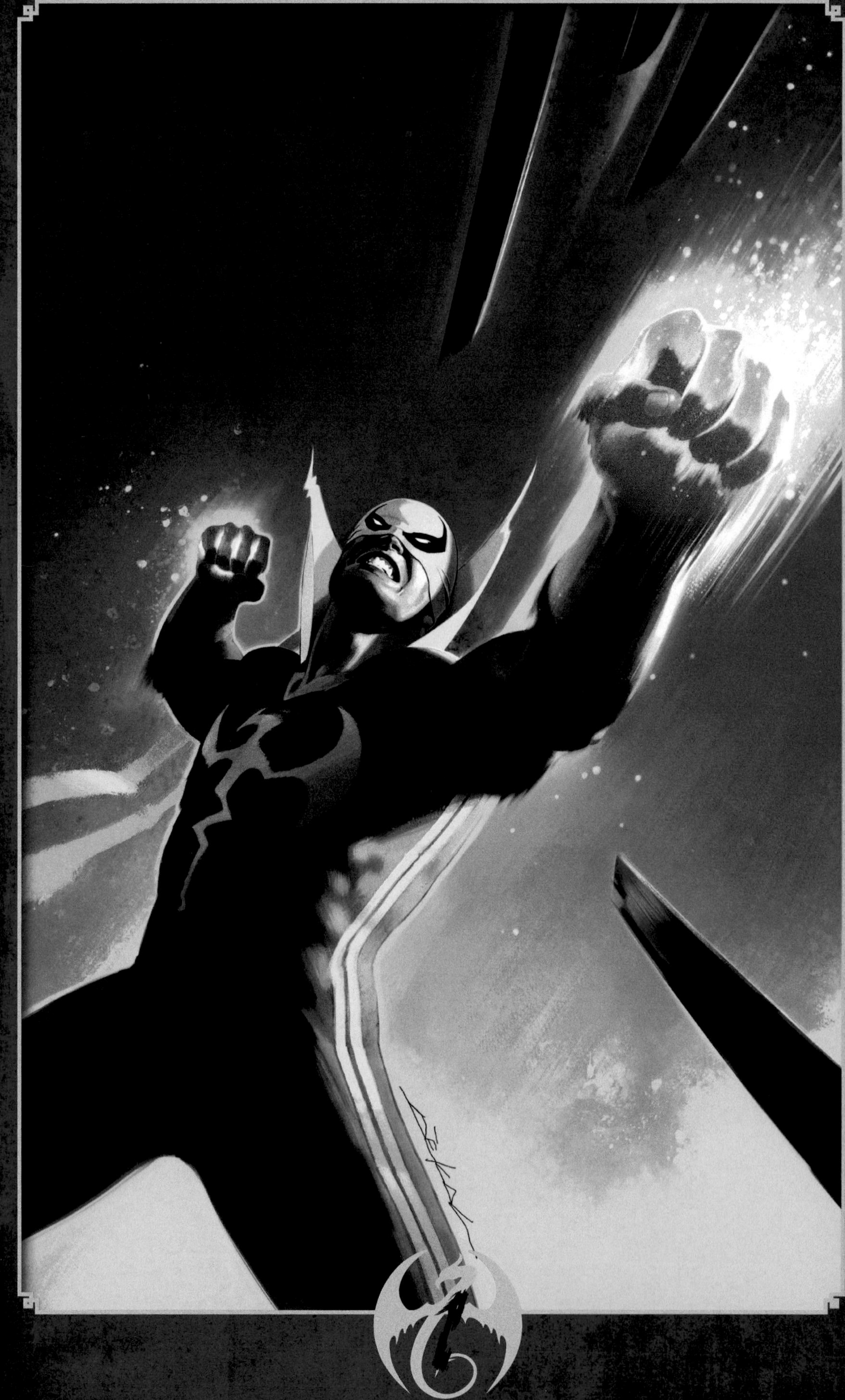

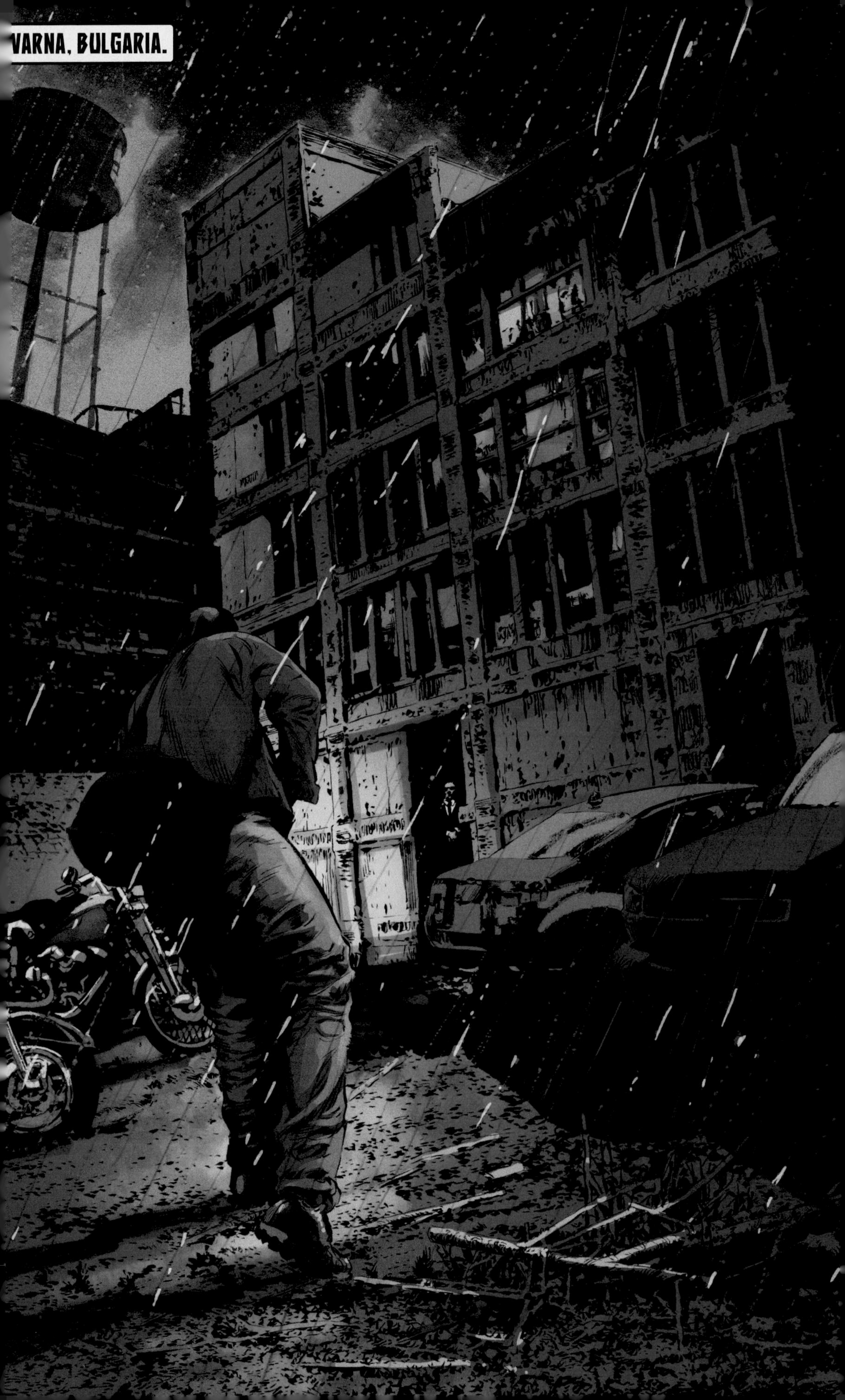
VARNA, BULGARIA.

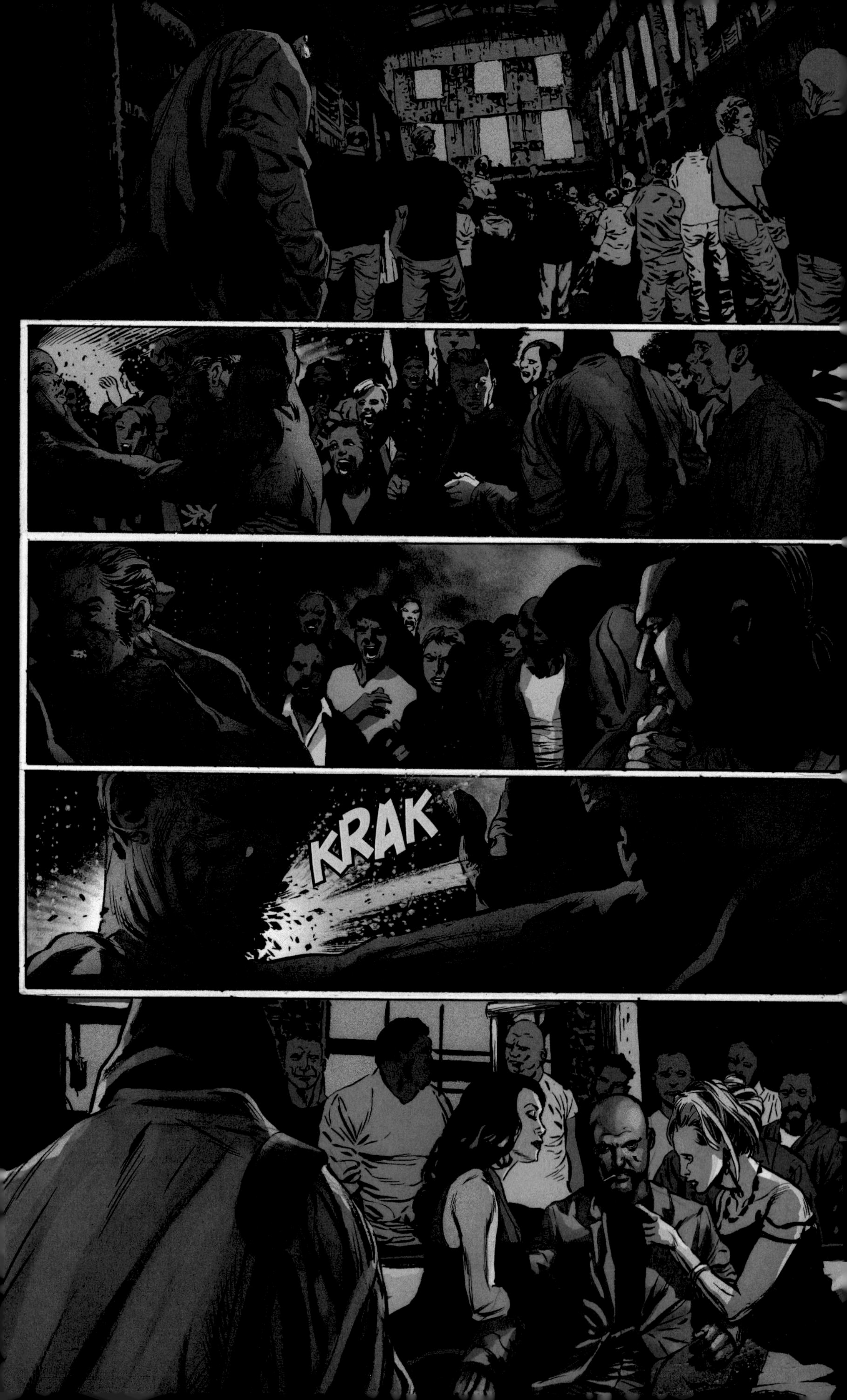
KRAK

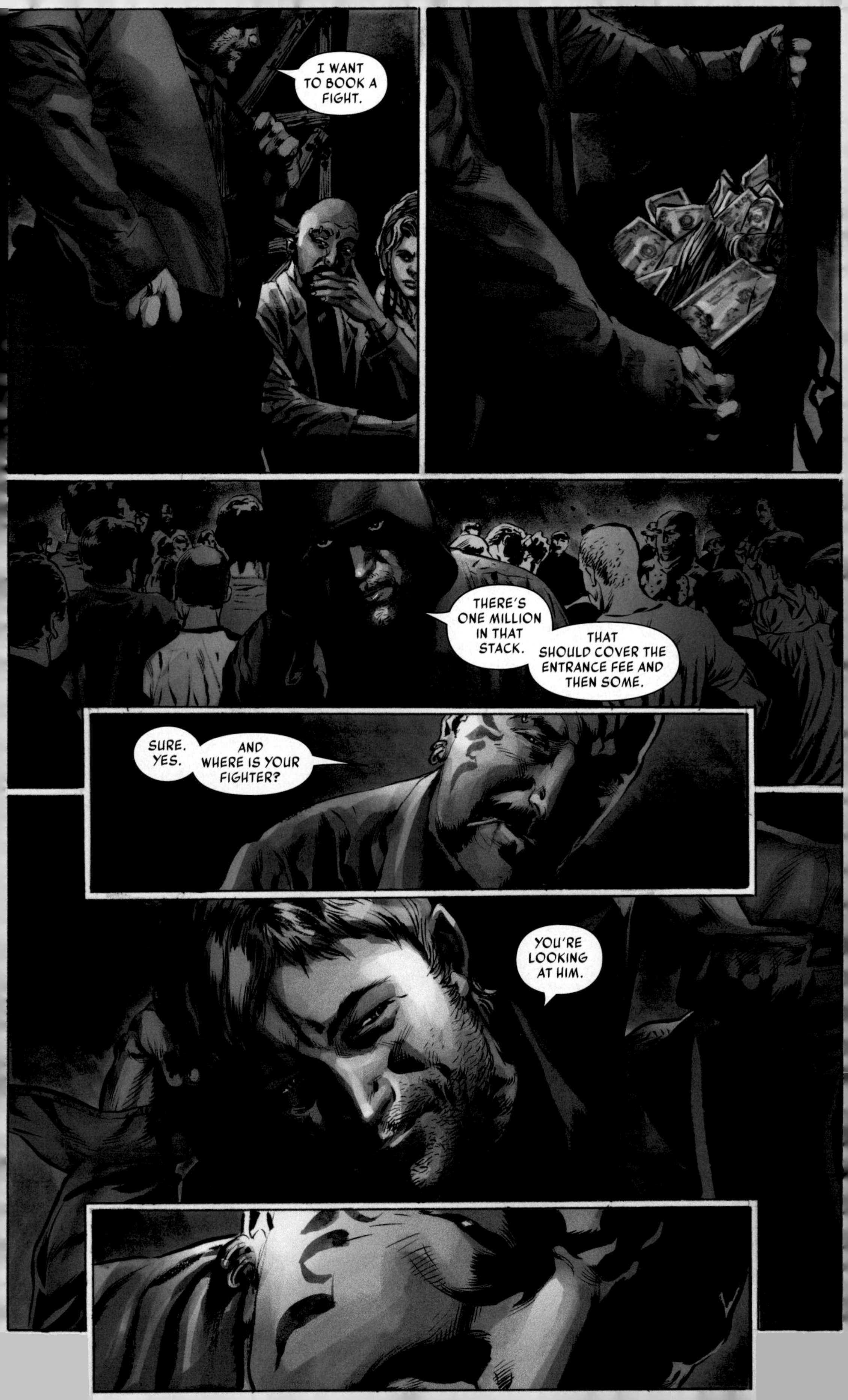
I WANT TO BOOK A FIGHT.
THERE'S ONE MILLION IN THAT STACK.
THAT SHOULD COVER THE ENTRANCE FEE AND THEN SOME.
SURE. YES.
AND WHERE IS YOUR FIGHTER?
YOU'RE LOOKING AT HIM.

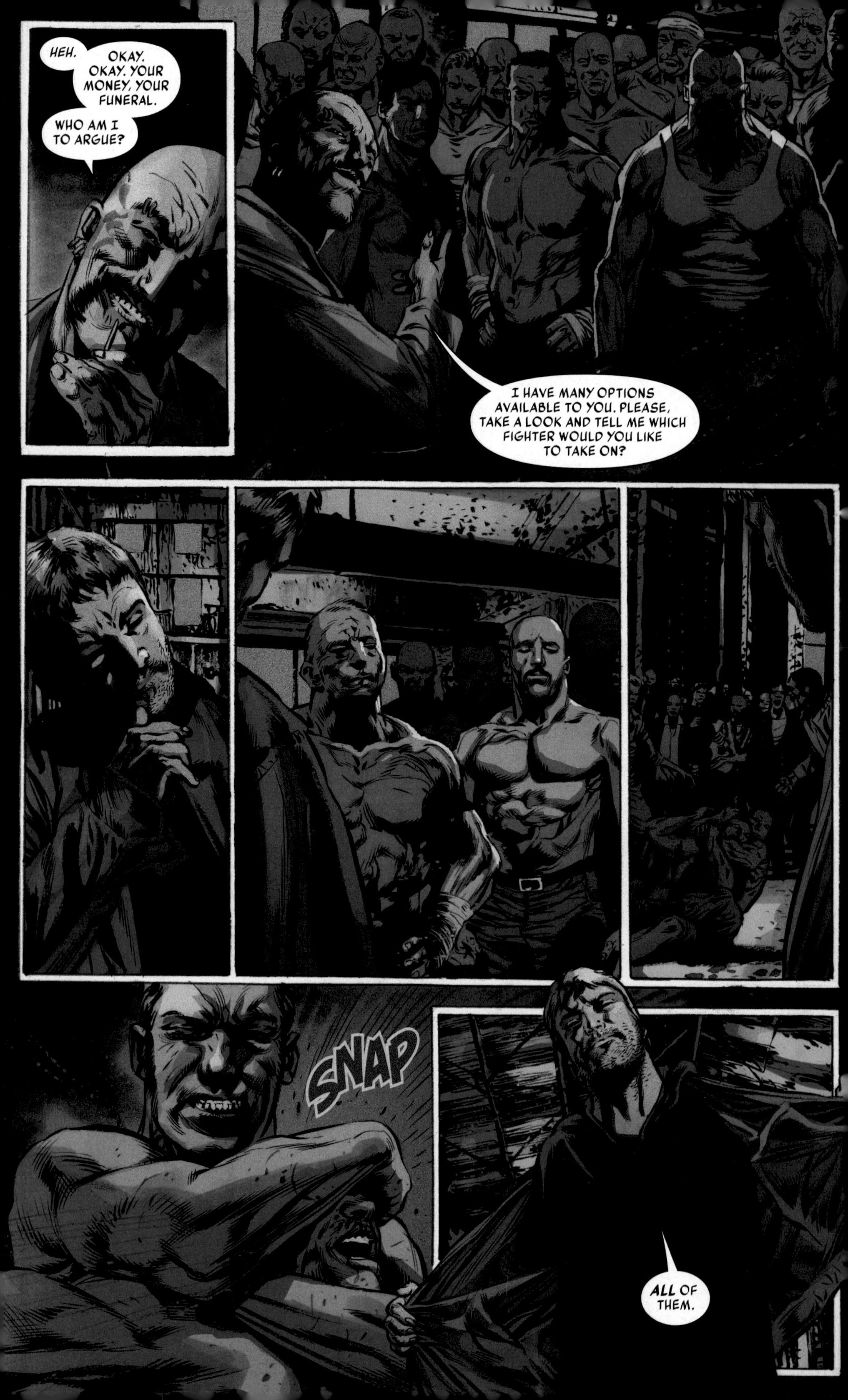
HEH.
OKAY. OKAY. YOUR MONEY, YOUR FUNERAL.
WHO AM I TO ARGUE?
I HAVE MANY OPTIONS AVAILABLE TO YOU. PLEASE, TAKE A LOOK AND TELL ME WHICH FIGHTER WOULD YOU LIKE TO TAKE ON?
SNAP
ALL OF THEM.

"THE TRIAL OF THE SEVEN MASTERS"
PART ONE

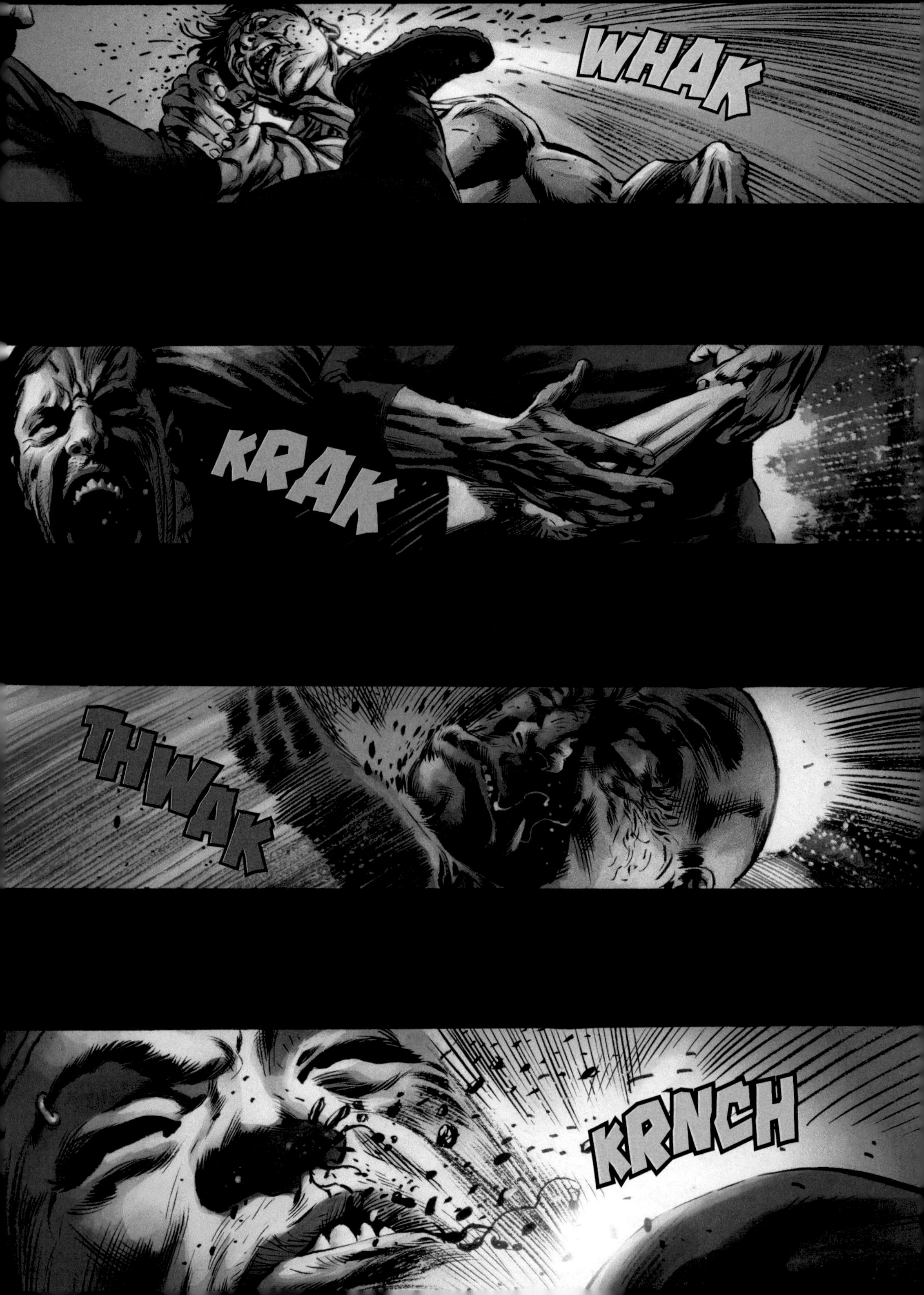

WHAK
KRAK
THWAK
KRNCH

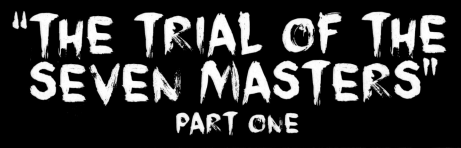

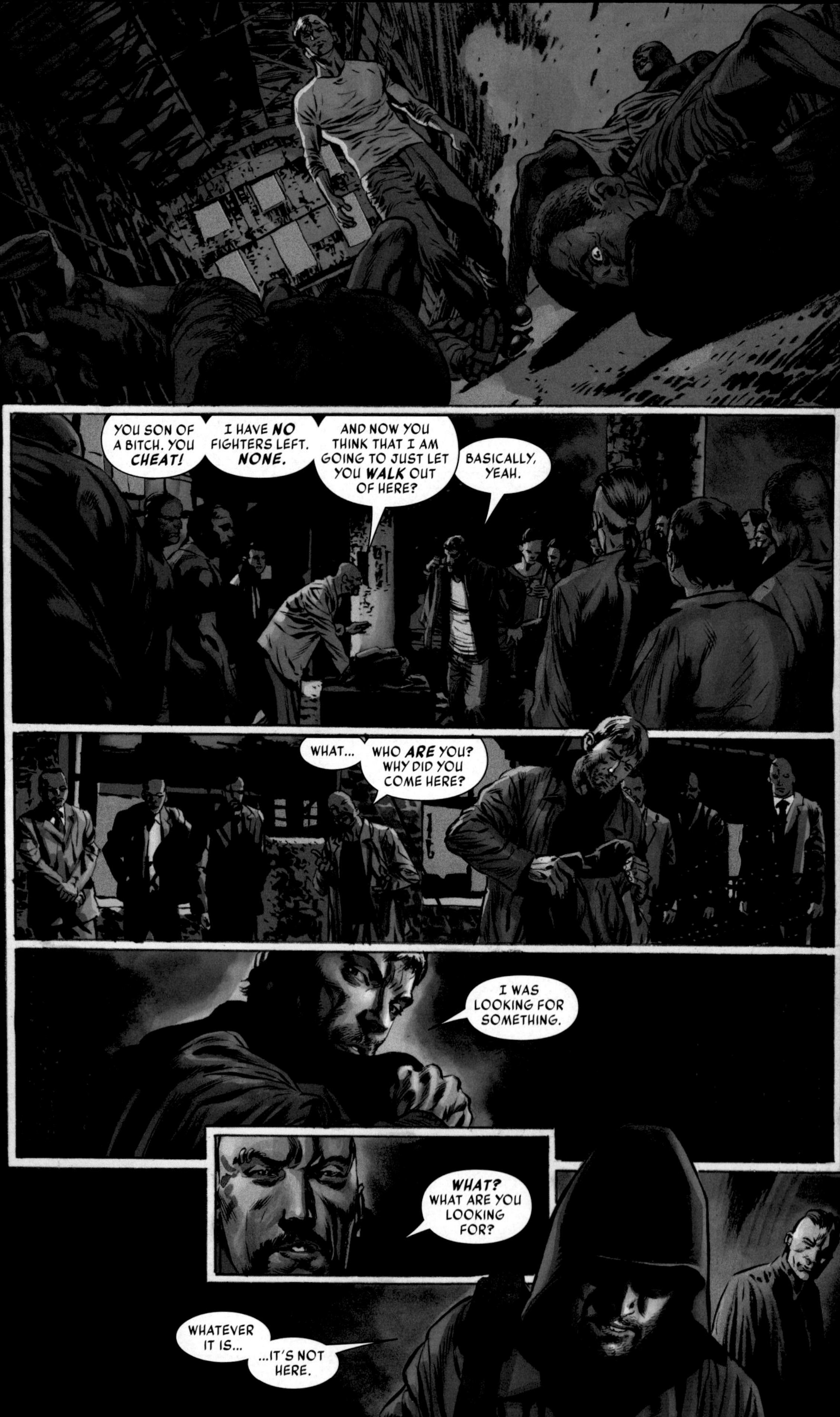
YOU SON OF A BITCH. YOU CHEAT!
I HAVE NO FIGHTERS LEFT. NONE.
AND NOW YOU THINK THAT I AM GOING TO JUST LET YOU WALK OUT OF HERE?
BASICALLY, YEAH.
WHAT...
WHO ARE YOU? WHY DID YOU COME HERE?
I WAS LOOKING FOR SOMETHING.
WHAT? WHAT ARE YOU LOOKING FOR?
WHATEVER IT IS...
...IT'S NOT HERE.

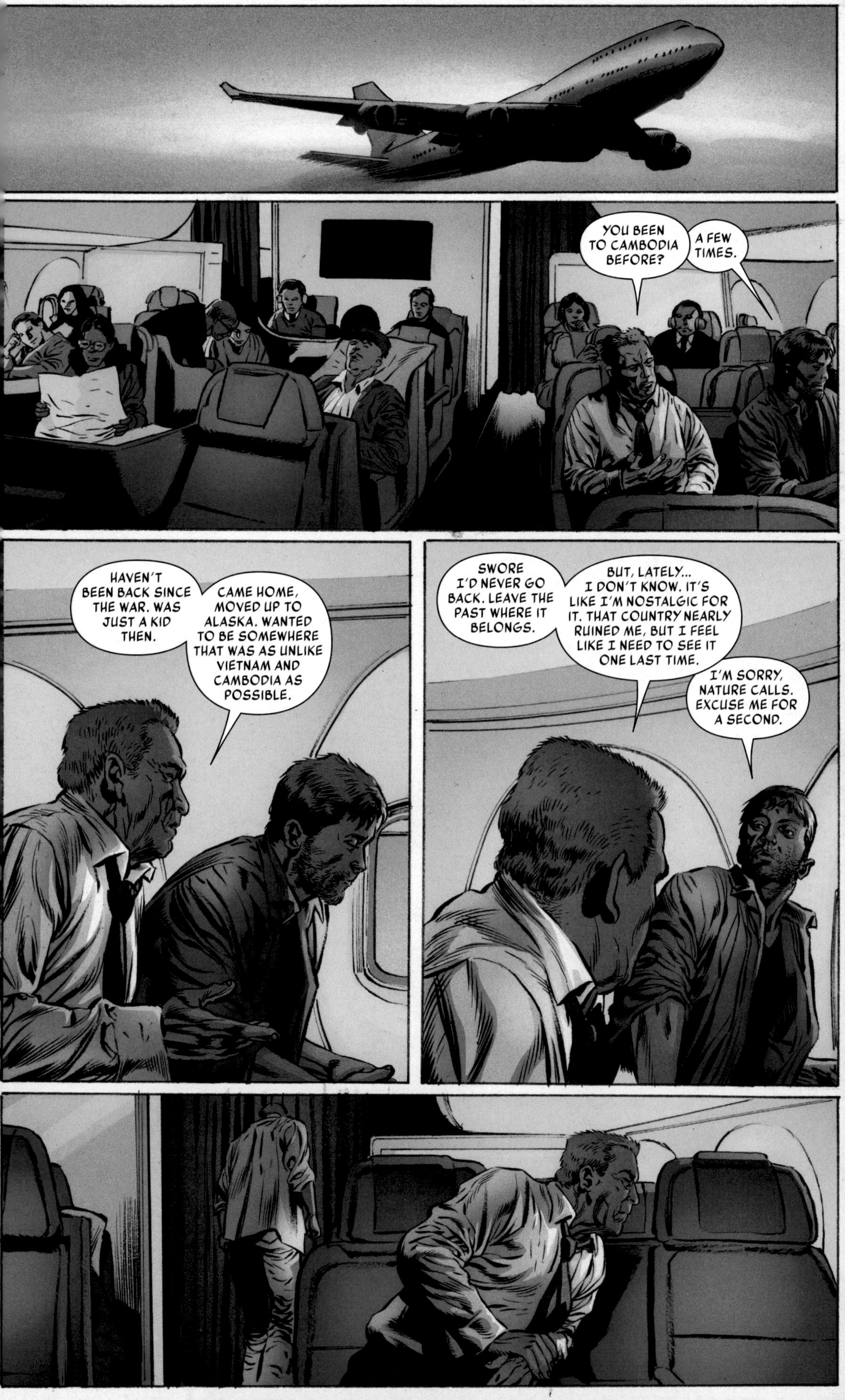
YOU BEEN TO CAMBODIA BEFORE?
A FEW TIMES.
HAVEN'T BEEN BACK SINCE THE WAR. WAS JUST A KID THEN.
CAME HOME, MOVED UP TO ALASKA. WANTED TO BE SOMEWHERE THAT WAS AS UNLIKE VIETNAM AND CAMBODIA AS POSSIBLE.
SWORE I'D NEVER GO BACK. LEAVE THE PAST WHERE IT BELONGS.
BUT, LATELY... I DON'T KNOW. IT'S LIKE I'M NOSTALGIC FOR IT. THAT COUNTRY NEARLY RUINED ME, BUT I FEEL LIKE I NEED TO SEE IT ONE LAST TIME.
I'M SORRY, NATURE CALLS. EXCUSE ME FOR A SECOND.

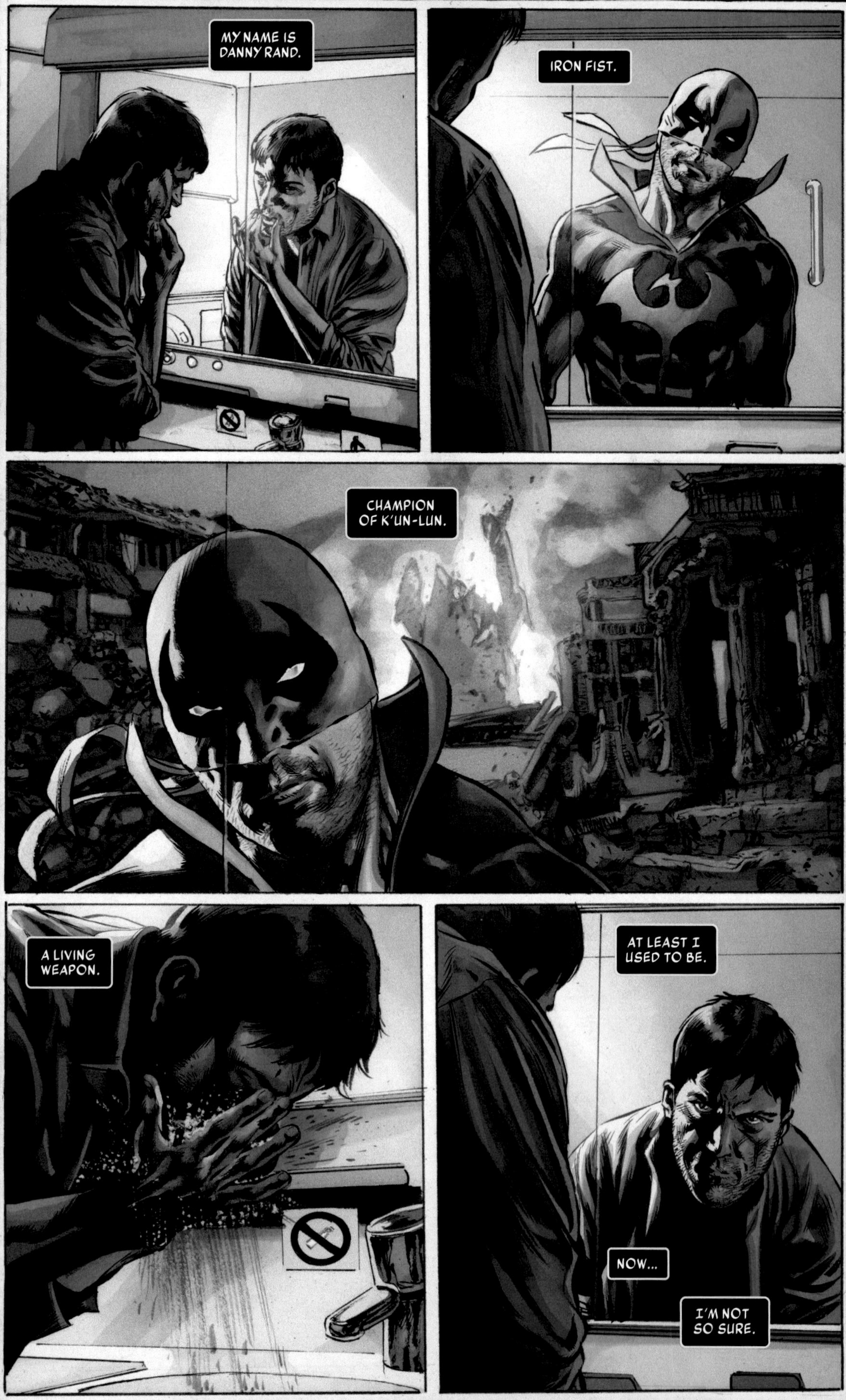
MY NAME IS DANNY RAND.
IRON FIST.
CHAMPION OF K'UN-LUN.
A LIVING WEAPON.
AT LEAST I USED TO BE.
NOW...
I'M NOT SO SURE.

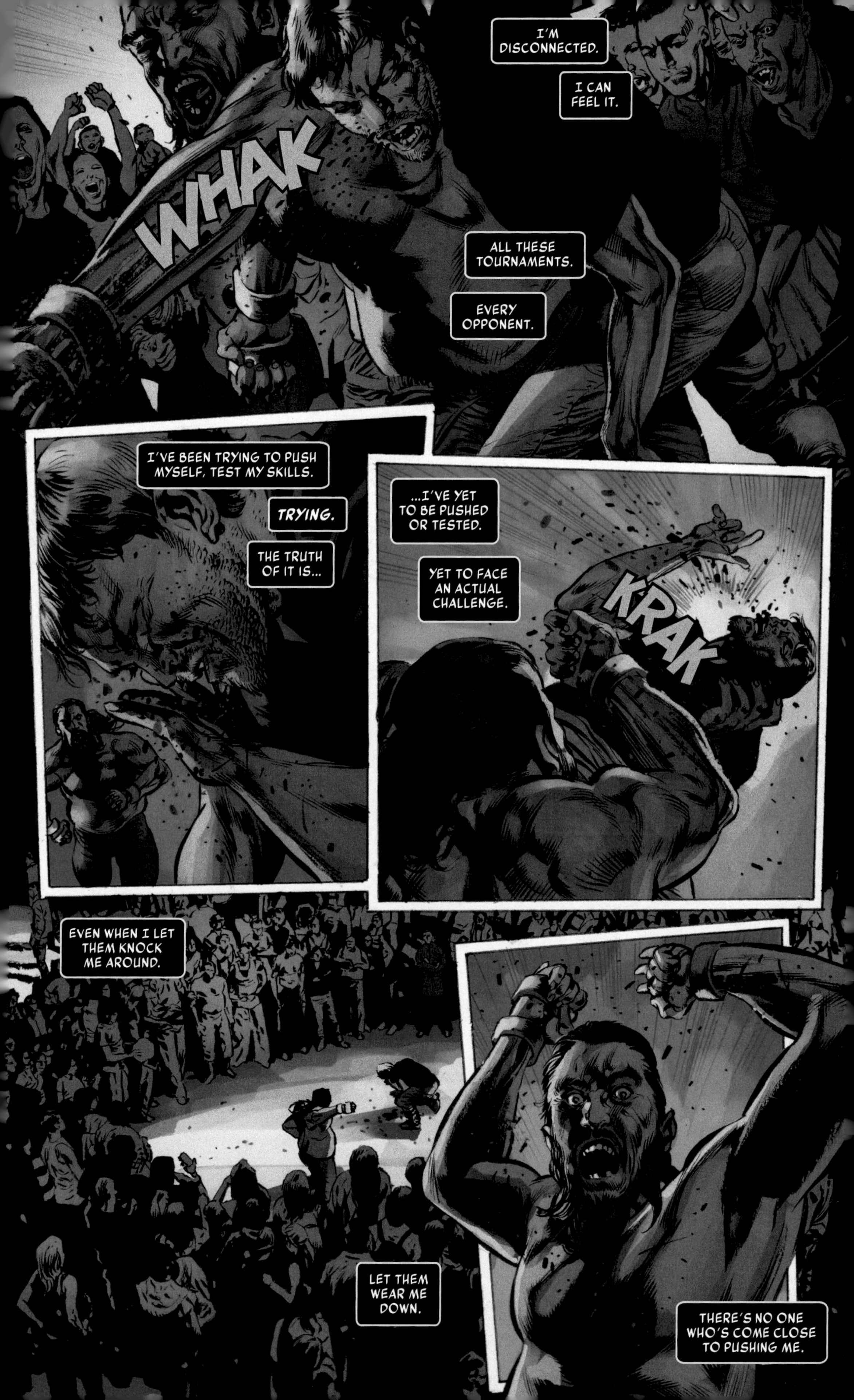
WHAK
I'M DISCONNECTED.
I CAN FEEL IT.
ALL THESE TOURNAMENTS.
EVERY OPPONENT.
I'VE BEEN TRYING TO PUSH MYSELF, TEST MY SKILLS.
TRYING.
THE TRUTH OF IT IS...
...I'VE YET TO BE PUSHED OR TESTED.
YET TO FACE AN ACTUAL CHALLENGE.
KRAK
EVEN WHEN I LET THEM KNOCK ME AROUND.
LET THEM WEAR ME DOWN.
THERE'S NO ONE WHO'S COME CLOSE TO PUSHING ME.

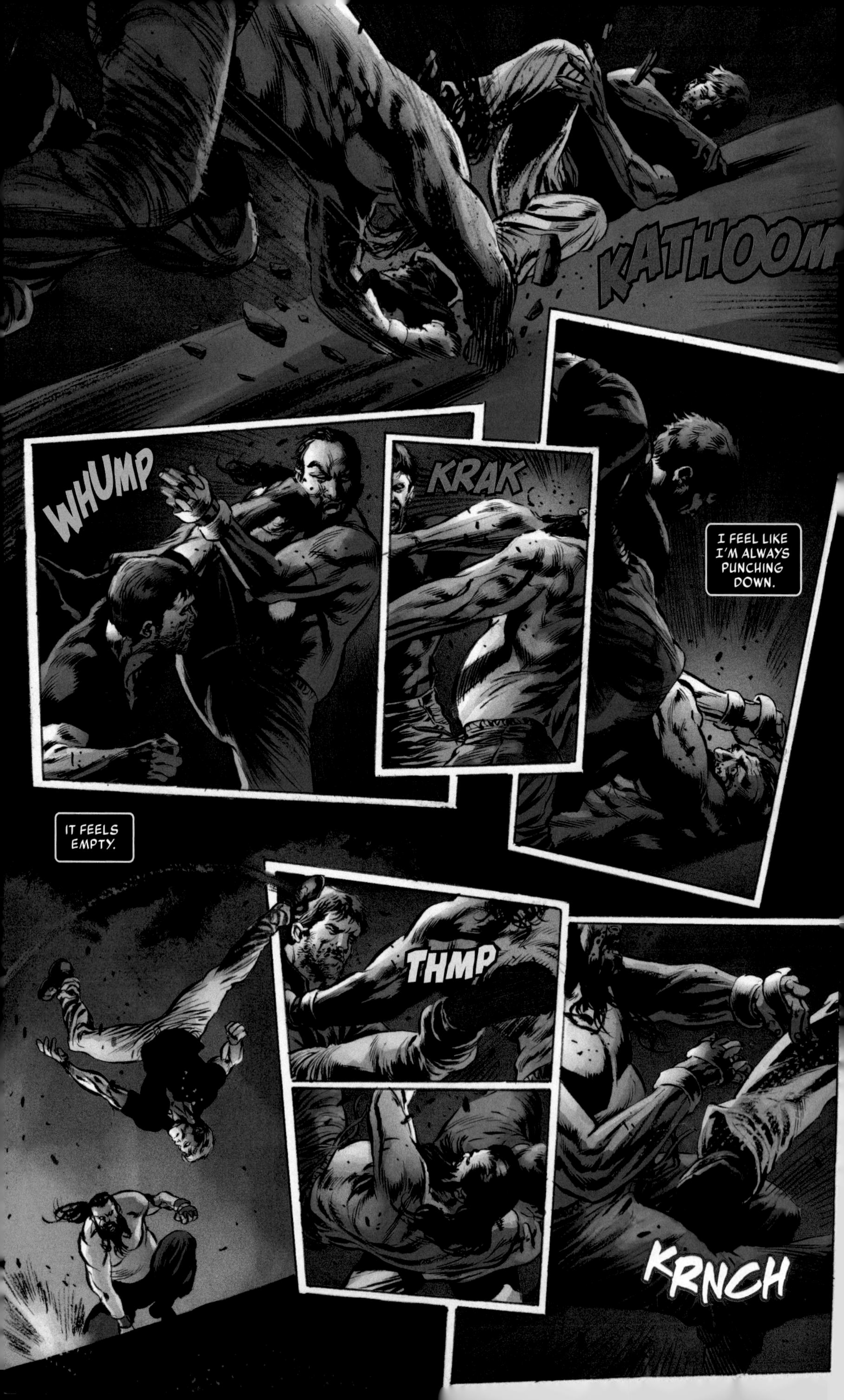
KATHOOM
WHUMP
KRAK
I FEEL LIKE I'M ALWAYS PUNCHING DOWN.
IT FEELS EMPTY.
THMP
KRNCH

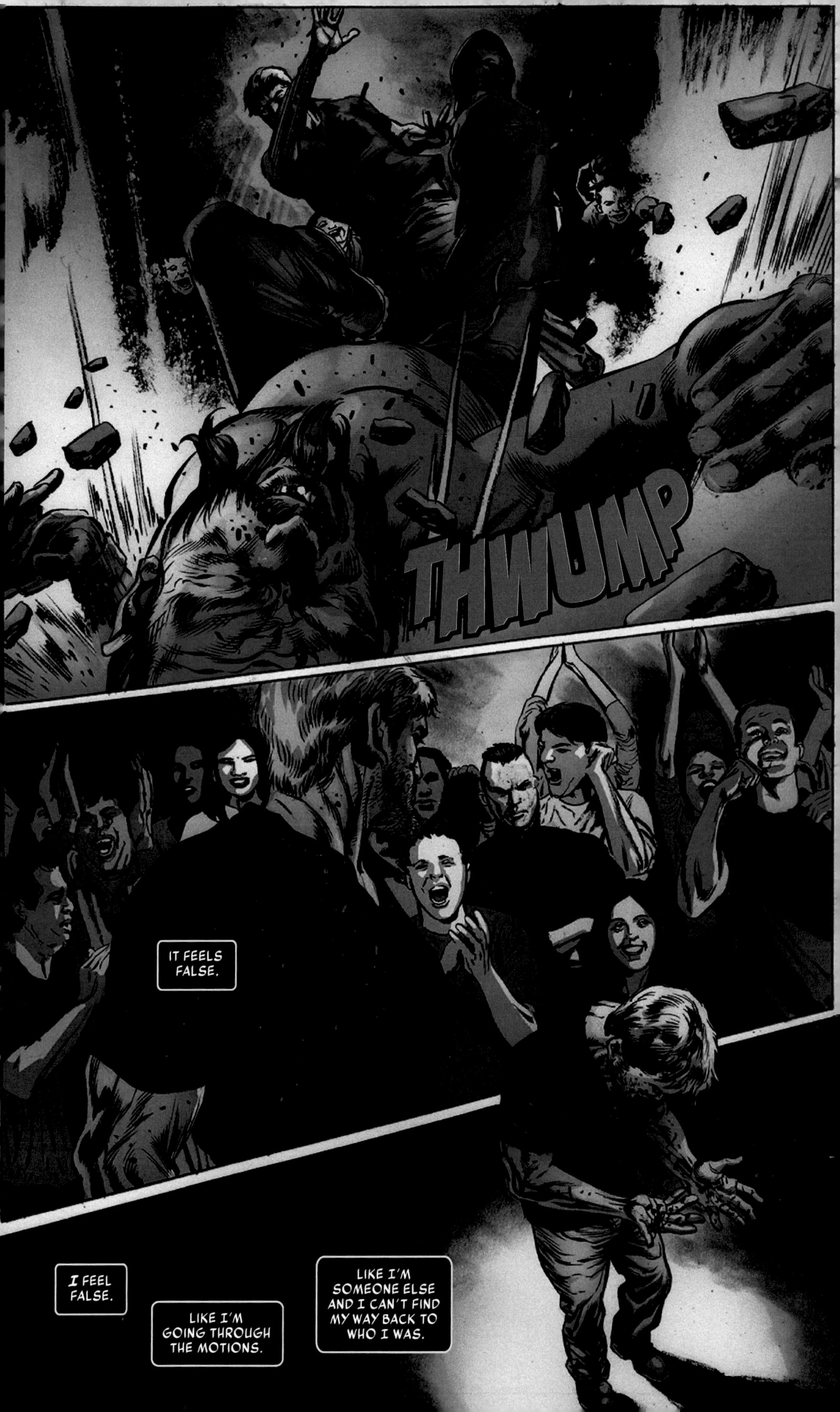
THWUMP
IT FEELS FALSE.
I FEEL FALSE.
LIKE I'M GOING THROUGH THE MOTIONS.
LIKE I'M SOMEONE ELSE AND I CAN'T FIND MY WAY BACK TO WHO I WAS.

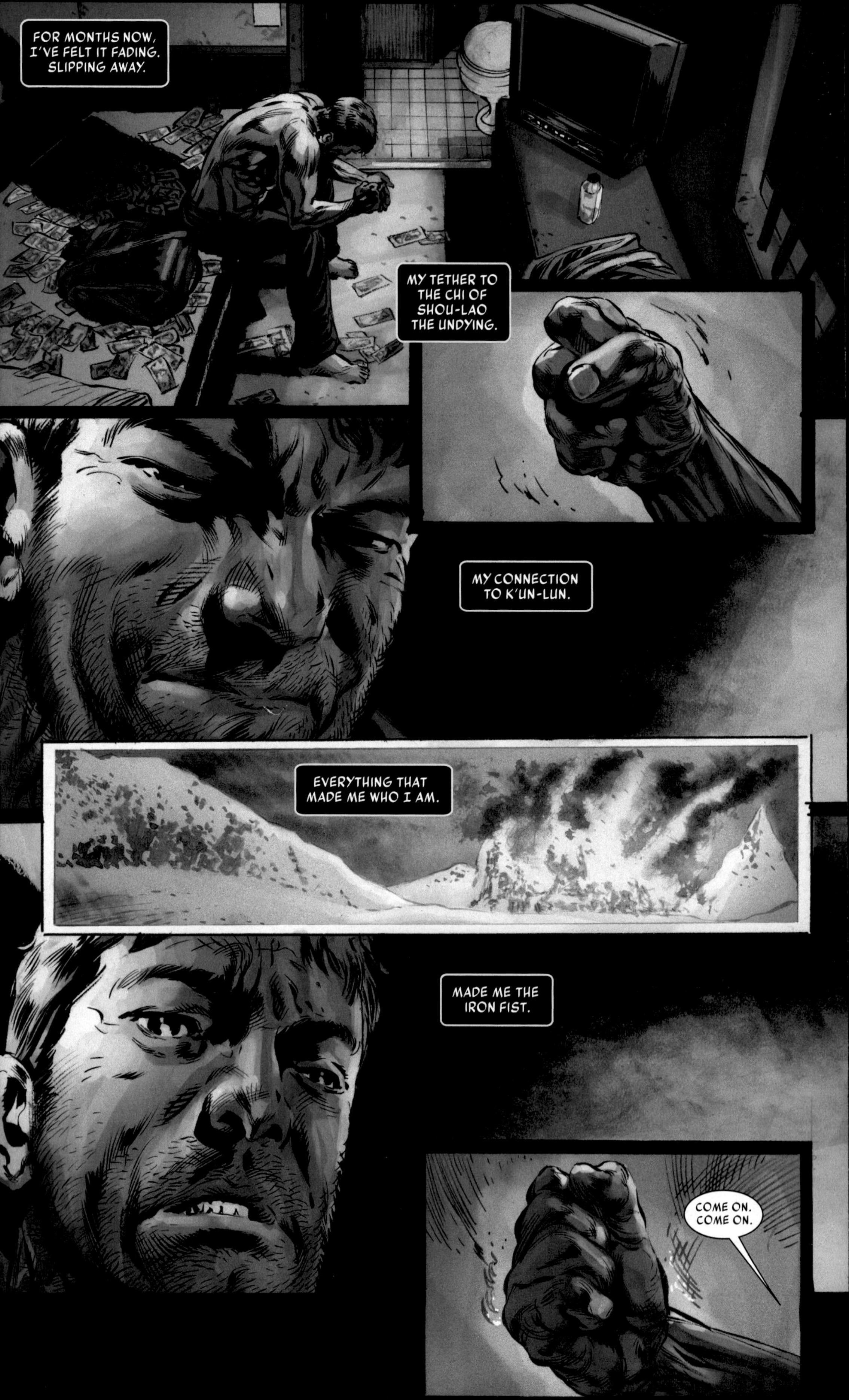
FOR MONTHS NOW, I'VE FELT IT FADING. SLIPPING AWAY.
MY TETHER TO THE CHI OF SHOU-LAO THE UNDYING.
MY CONNECTION TO K'UN-LUN.
EVERYTHING THAT MADE ME WHO I AM.
MADE ME THE IRON FIST.
COME ON. COME ON.

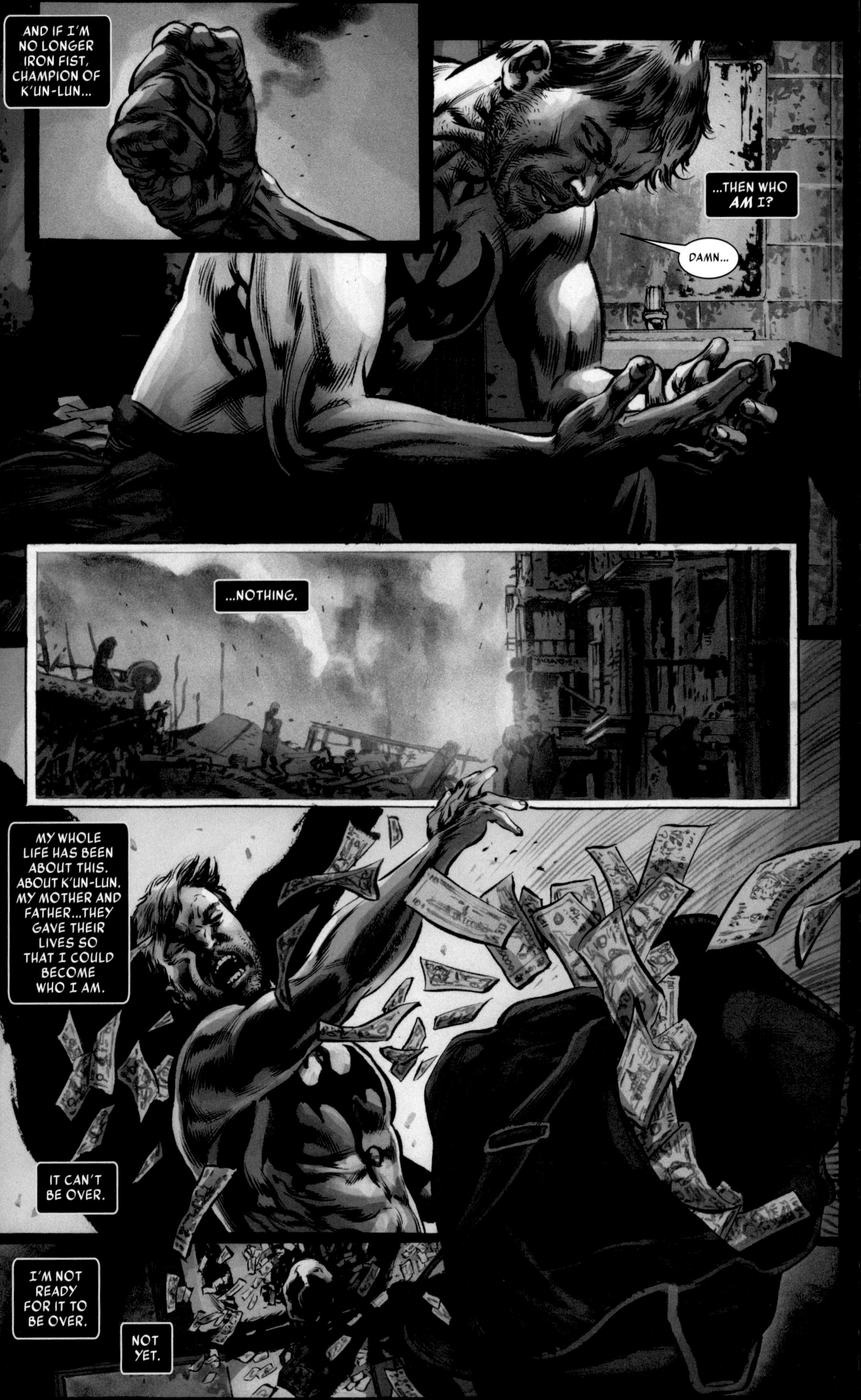
AND IF I'M NO LONGER IRON FIST, CHAMPION OF K'UN-LUN...
...THEN WHO AM I?
DAMN...
...NOTHING.
MY WHOLE LIFE HAS BEEN ABOUT THIS. ABOUT K'UN-LUN. MY MOTHER AND FATHER...THEY GAVE THEIR LIVES SO THAT I COULD BECOME WHO I AM.
IT CAN'T BE OVER.
I'M NOT READY FOR IT TO BE OVER.
NOT YET.

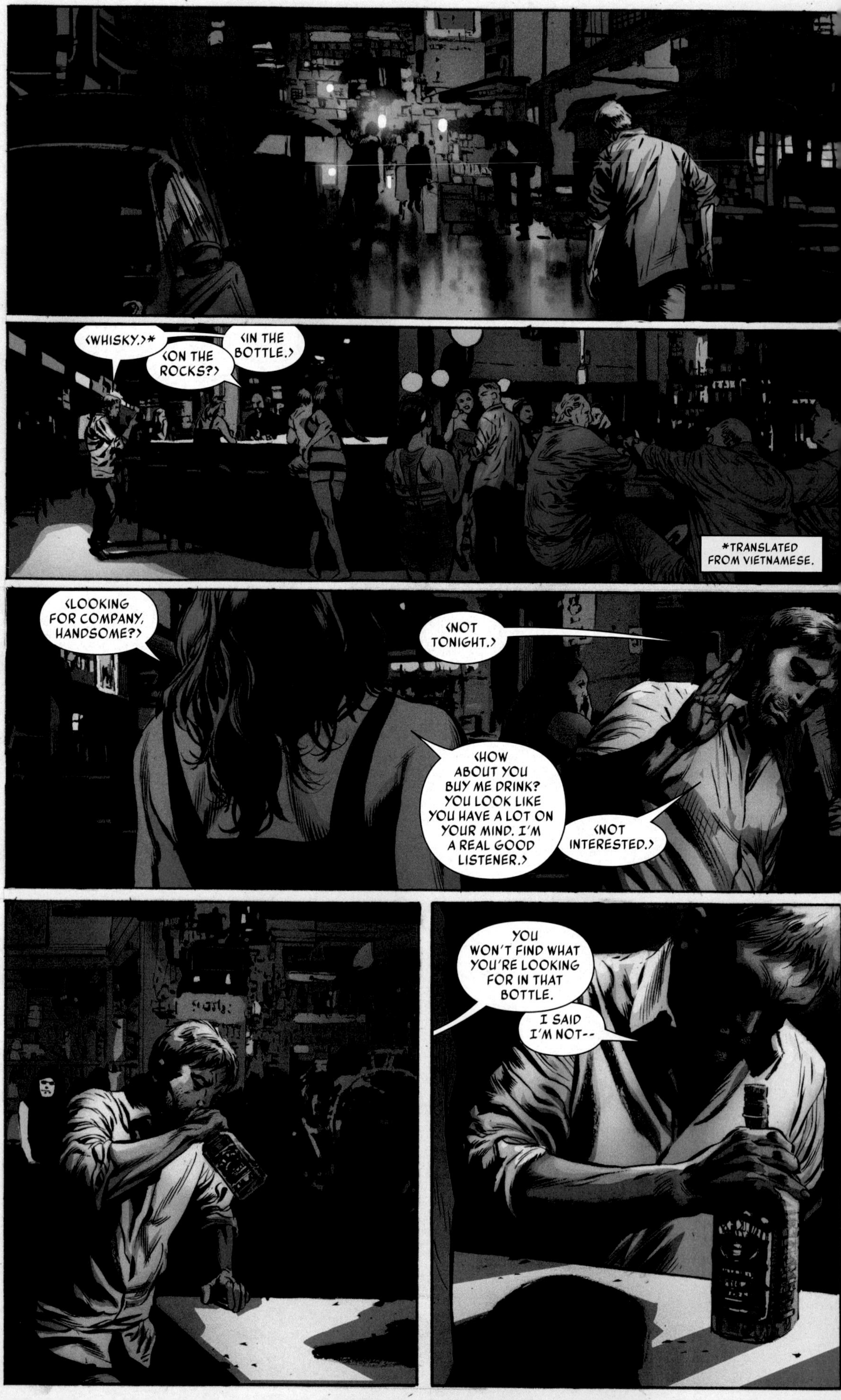
‹WHISKY.›*
‹ON THE ROCKS?›
‹IN THE BOTTLE.›
*TRANSLATED FROM VIETNAMESE.
‹LOOKING FOR COMPANY, HANDSOME?›
‹NOT TONIGHT.›
‹HOW ABOUT YOU BUY ME DRINK? YOU LOOK LIKE YOU HAVE A LOT ON YOUR MIND. I'M A REAL GOOD LISTENER.›
‹NOT INTERESTED.›
YOU WON'T FIND WHAT YOU'RE LOOKING FOR IN THAT BOTTLE.
I SAID I'M NOT--

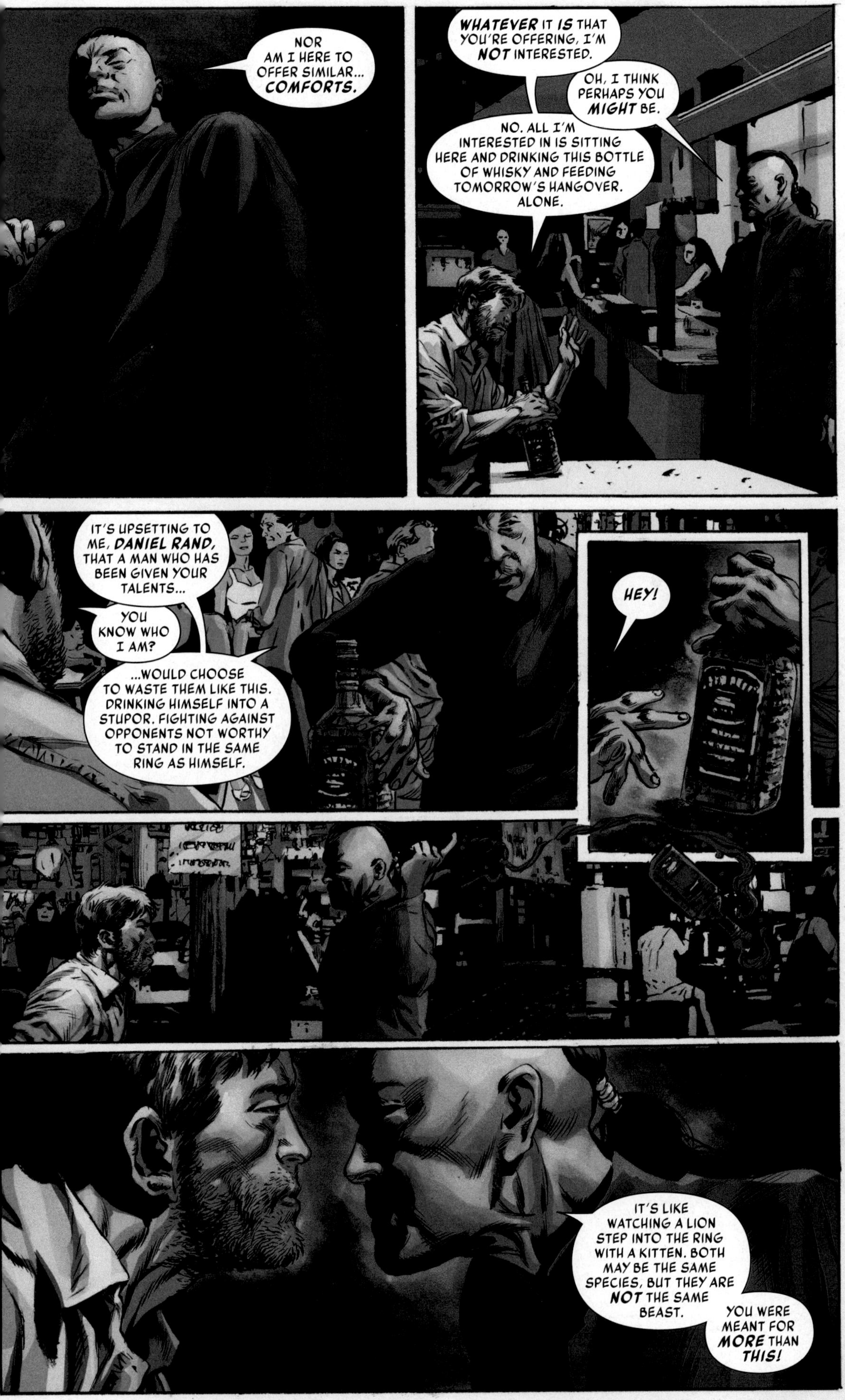
NOR AM I HERE TO OFFER SIMILAR... COMFORTS.
WHATEVER IT IS THAT YOU'RE OFFERING, I'M NOT INTERESTED.
OH, I THINK PERHAPS YOU MIGHT BE.
NO. ALL I'M INTERESTED IN IS SITTING HERE AND DRINKING THIS BOTTLE OF WHISKY AND FEEDING TOMORROW'S HANGOVER. ALONE.
IT'S UPSETTING TO ME, DANIEL RAND, THAT A MAN WHO HAS BEEN GIVEN YOUR TALENTS...
YOU KNOW WHO I AM?
...WOULD CHOOSE TO WASTE THEM LIKE THIS. DRINKING HIMSELF INTO A STUPOR. FIGHTING AGAINST OPPONENTS NOT WORTHY TO STAND IN THE SAME RING AS HIMSELF.
HEY!
IT'S LIKE WATCHING A LION STEP INTO THE RING WITH A KITTEN. BOTH MAY BE THE SAME SPECIES, BUT THEY ARE NOT THE SAME BEAST.
YOU WERE MEANT FOR MORE THAN THIS!

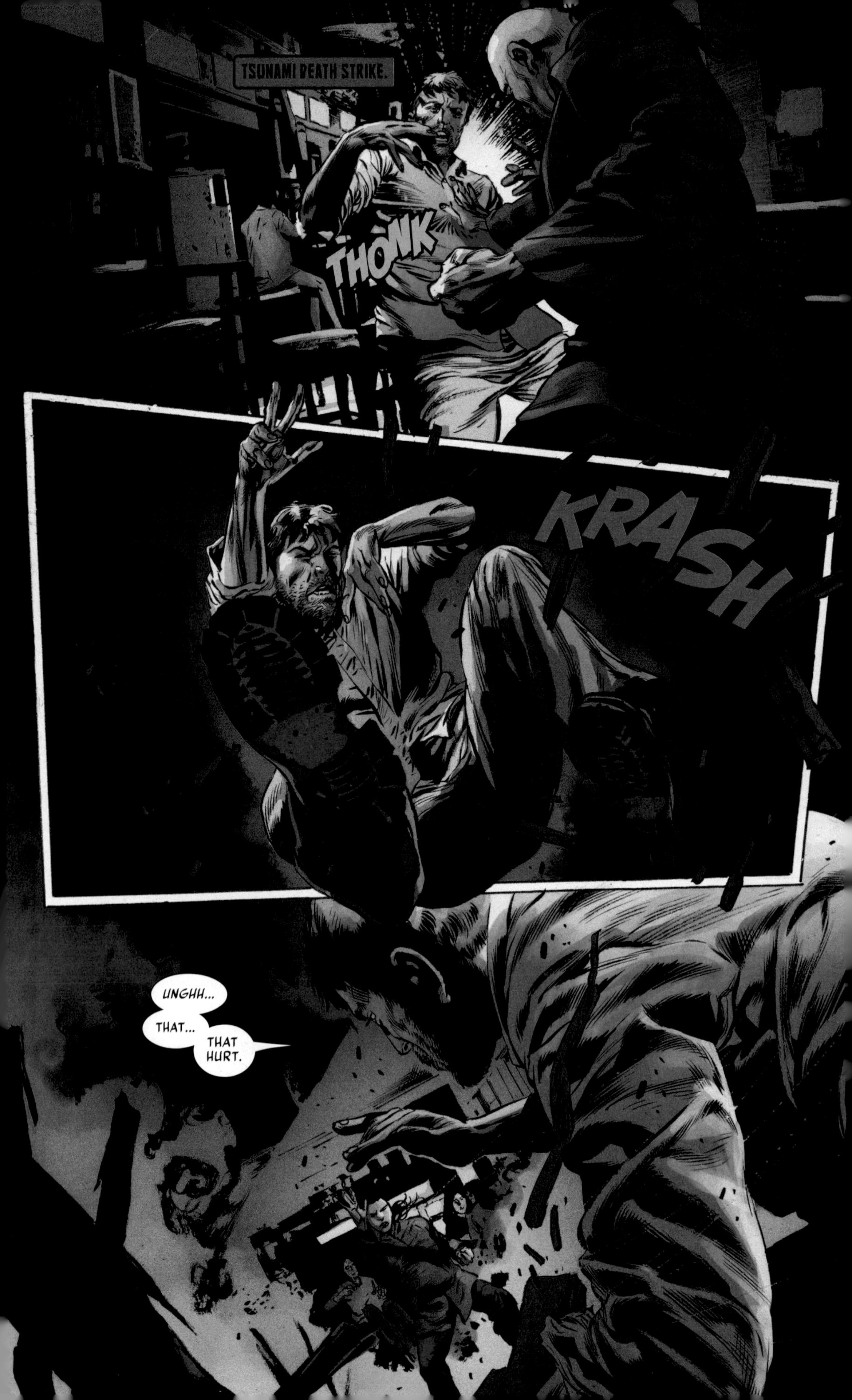
TSUNAMI DEATH STRIKE.
THONK
KRASH
UNGHH...
THAT...
THAT HURT.

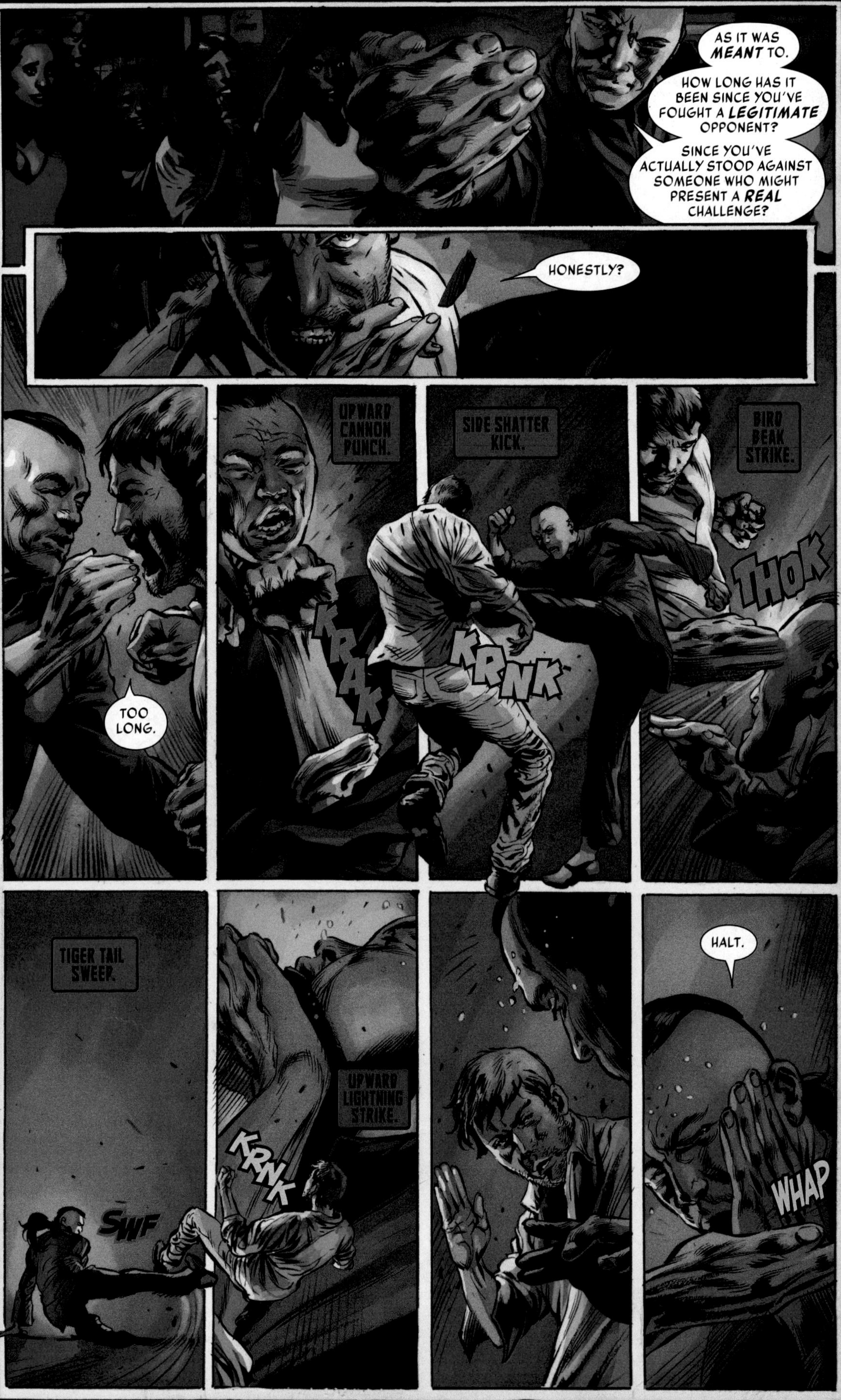
AS IT WAS MEANT TO.
HOW LONG HAS IT BEEN SINCE YOU'VE FOUGHT A LEGITIMATE OPPONENT?
SINCE YOU'VE ACTUALLY STOOD AGAINST SOMEONE WHO MIGHT PRESENT A REAL CHALLENGE?
HONESTLY?
TOO LONG.
UPWARD CANNON PUNCH.
KRAK
SIDE SHATTER KICK.
KRNK
BIRD BEAK STRIKE.
THOK
TIGER TAIL SWEEP.
SWF
UPWARD LIGHTNING STRIKE.
KRNK
HALT.
WHAP

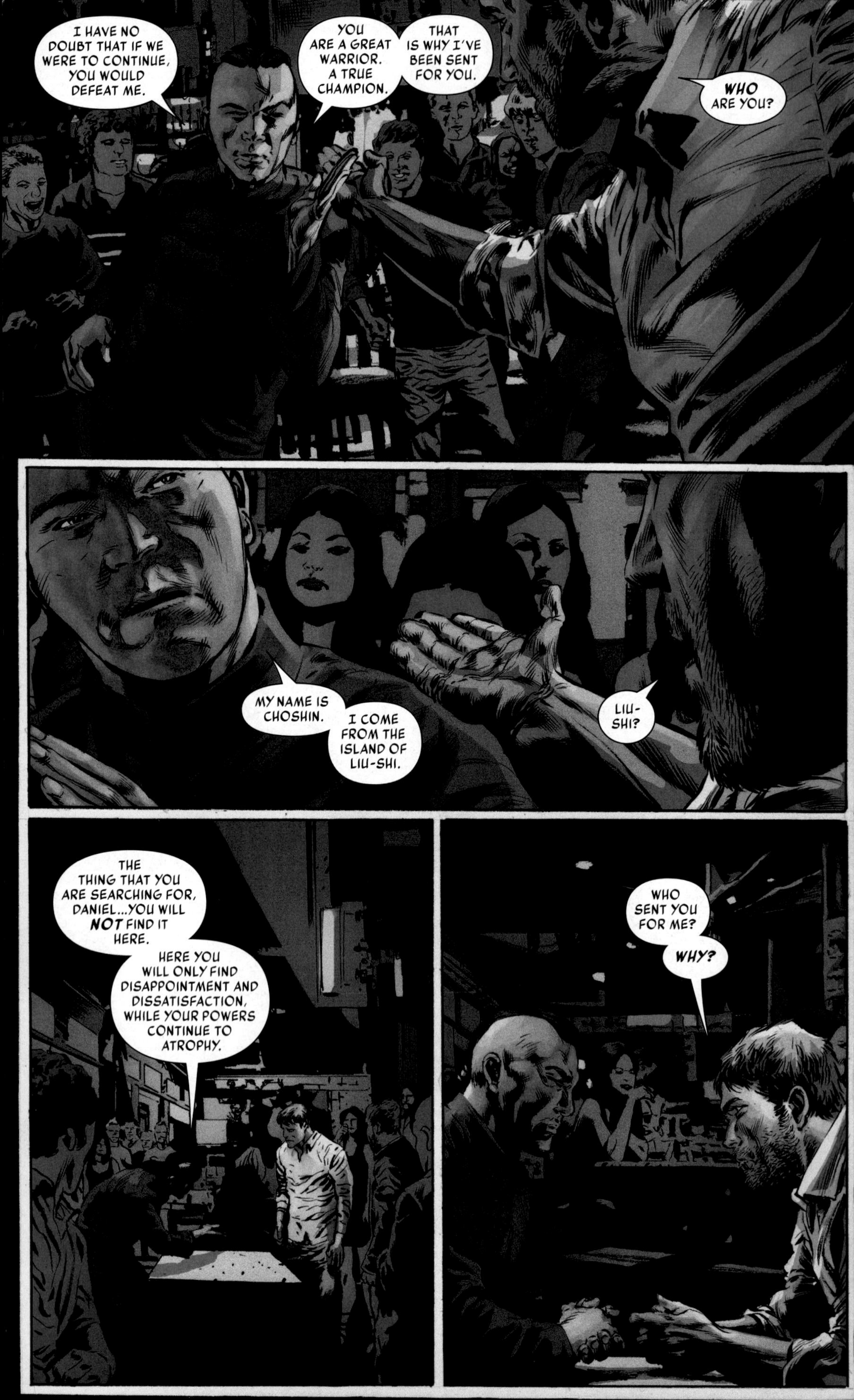
I HAVE NO DOUBT THAT IF WE WERE TO CONTINUE, YOU WOULD DEFEAT ME.
YOU ARE A GREAT WARRIOR. A TRUE CHAMPION.
THAT IS WHY I'VE BEEN SENT FOR YOU.
WHO ARE YOU?
MY NAME IS CHOSHIN.
I COME FROM THE ISLAND OF LIU-SHI.
LIU-SHI?
THE THING THAT YOU ARE SEARCHING FOR, DANIEL...YOU WILL NOT FIND IT HERE.
HERE YOU WILL ONLY FIND DISAPPOINTMENT AND DISSATISFACTION, WHILE YOUR POWERS CONTINUE TO ATROPHY.
WHO SENT YOU FOR ME?
WHY?

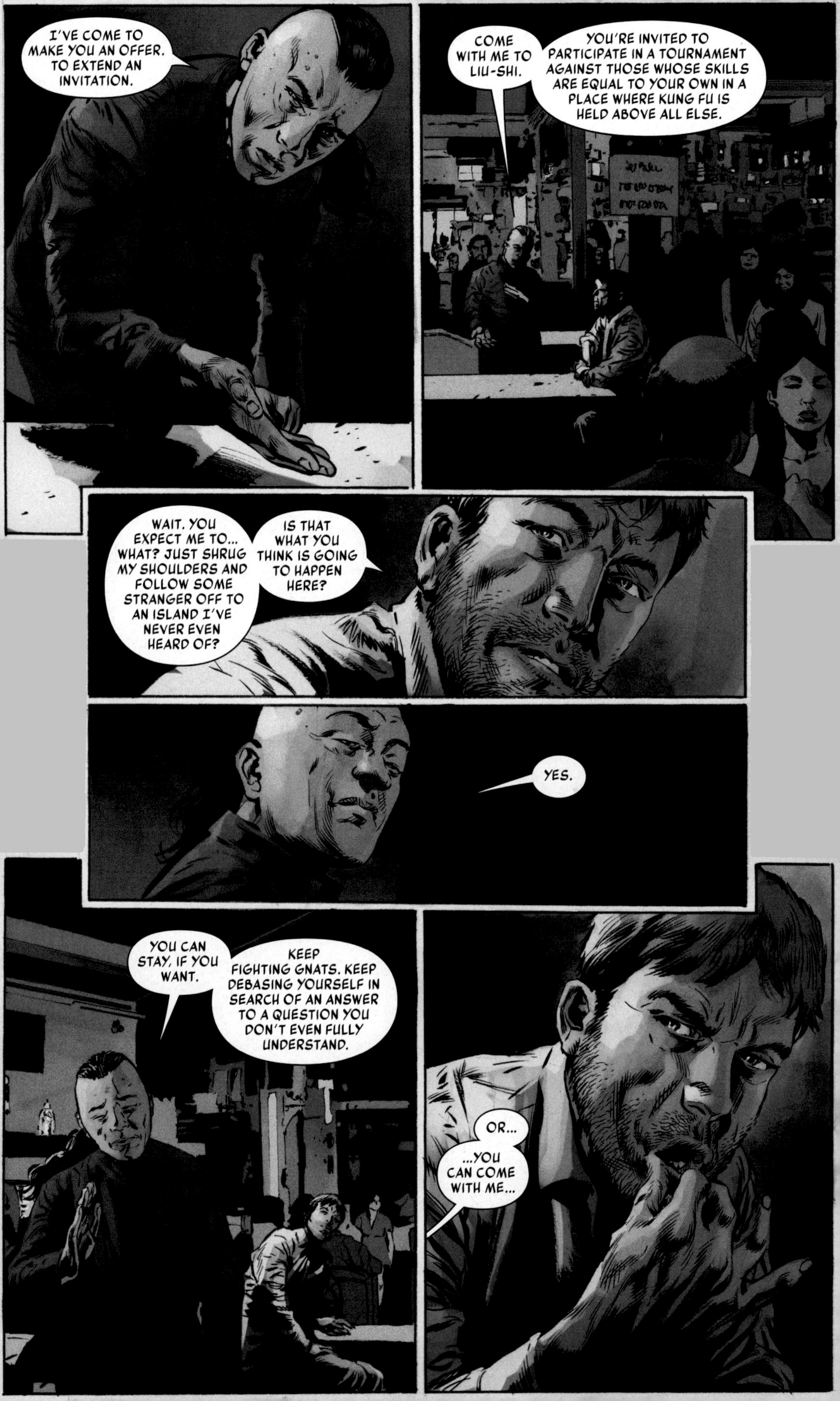
I'VE COME TO MAKE YOU AN OFFER. TO EXTEND AN INVITATION.
COME WITH ME TO LIU-SHI.
YOU'RE INVITED TO PARTICIPATE IN A TOURNAMENT AGAINST THOSE WHOSE SKILLS ARE EQUAL TO YOUR OWN IN A PLACE WHERE KUNG FU IS HELD ABOVE ALL ELSE.
WAIT. YOU EXPECT ME TO... WHAT? JUST SHRUG MY SHOULDERS AND FOLLOW SOME STRANGER OFF TO AN ISLAND I'VE NEVER EVEN HEARD OF?
IS THAT WHAT YOU THINK IS GOING TO HAPPEN HERE?
YES.
YOU CAN STAY, IF YOU WANT.
KEEP FIGHTING GNATS. KEEP DEBASING YOURSELF IN SEARCH OF AN ANSWER TO A QUESTION YOU DON'T EVEN FULLY UNDERSTAND.
OR...
...YOU CAN COME WITH ME...

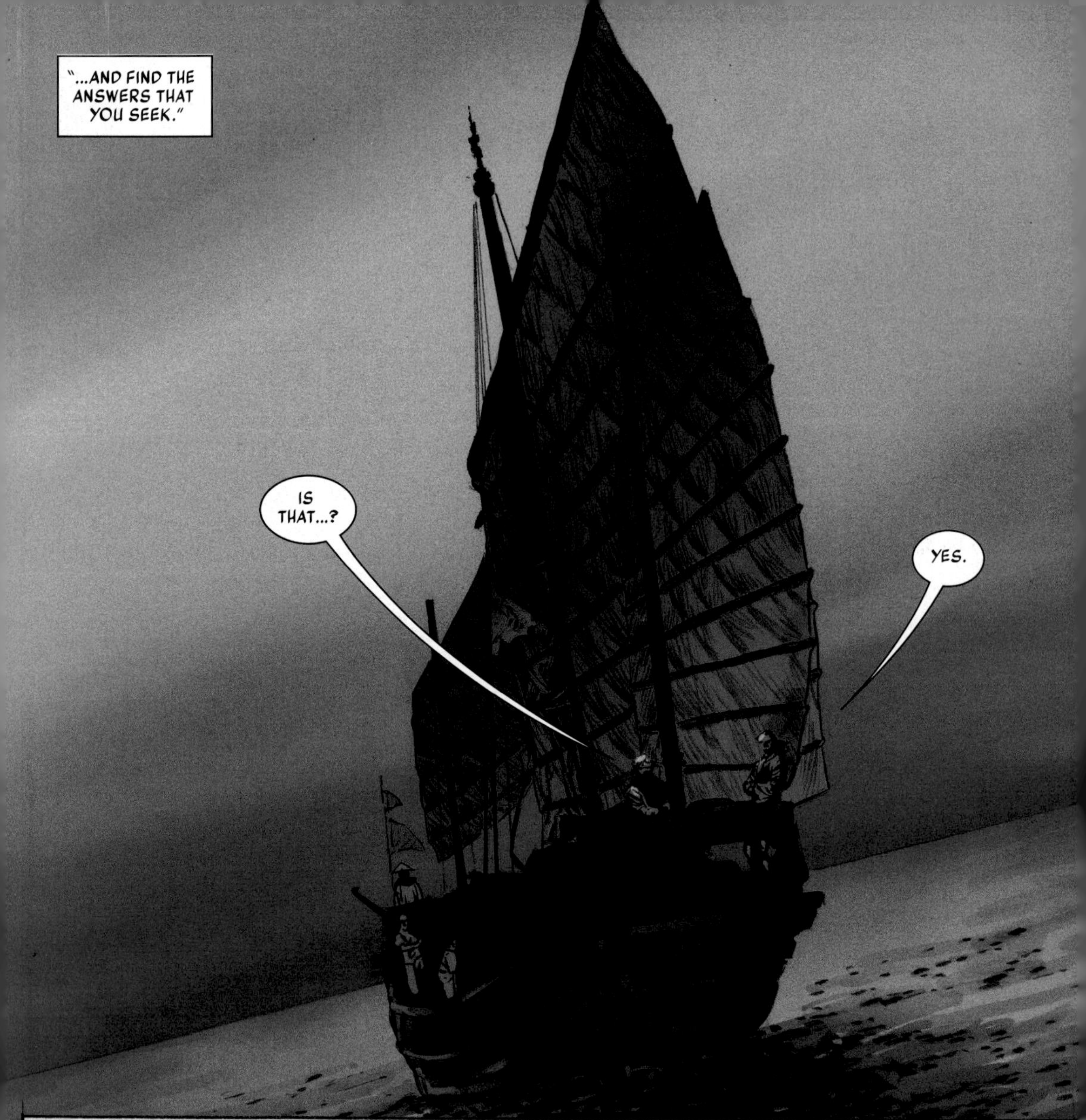
"...AND FIND THE ANSWERS THAT YOU SEEK."
IS THAT...?
YES.

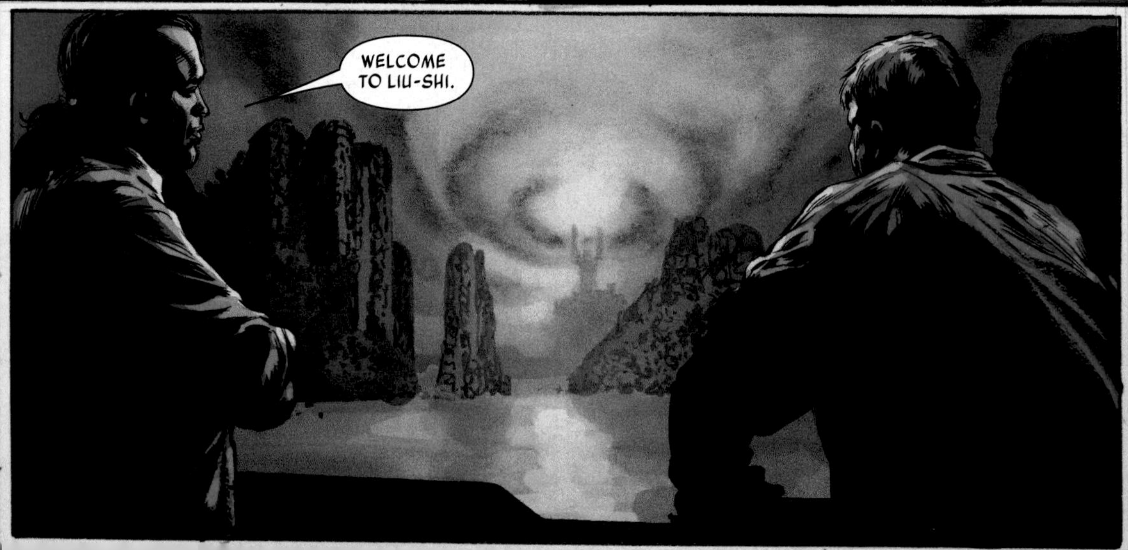
WELCOME TO LIU-SHI.

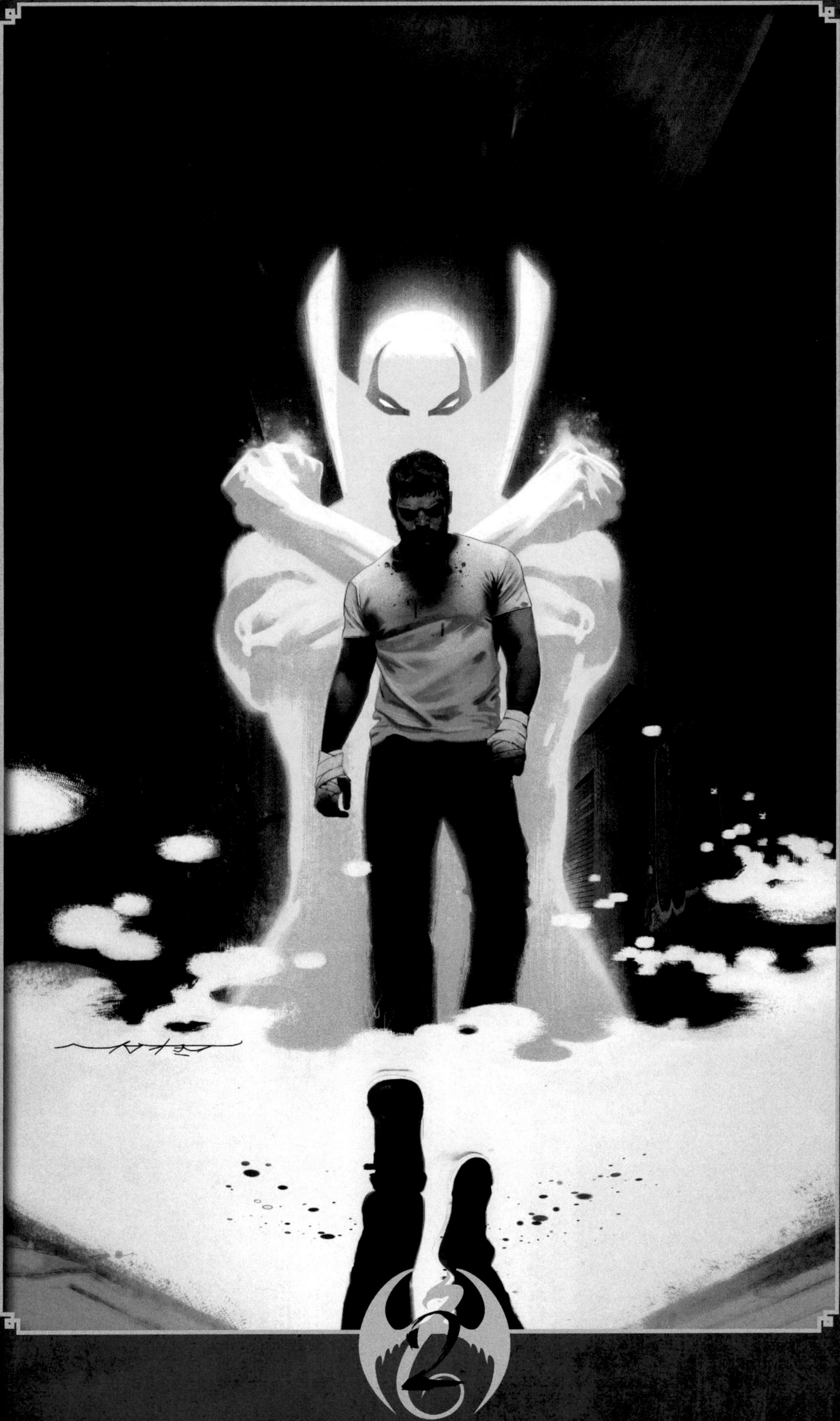
2

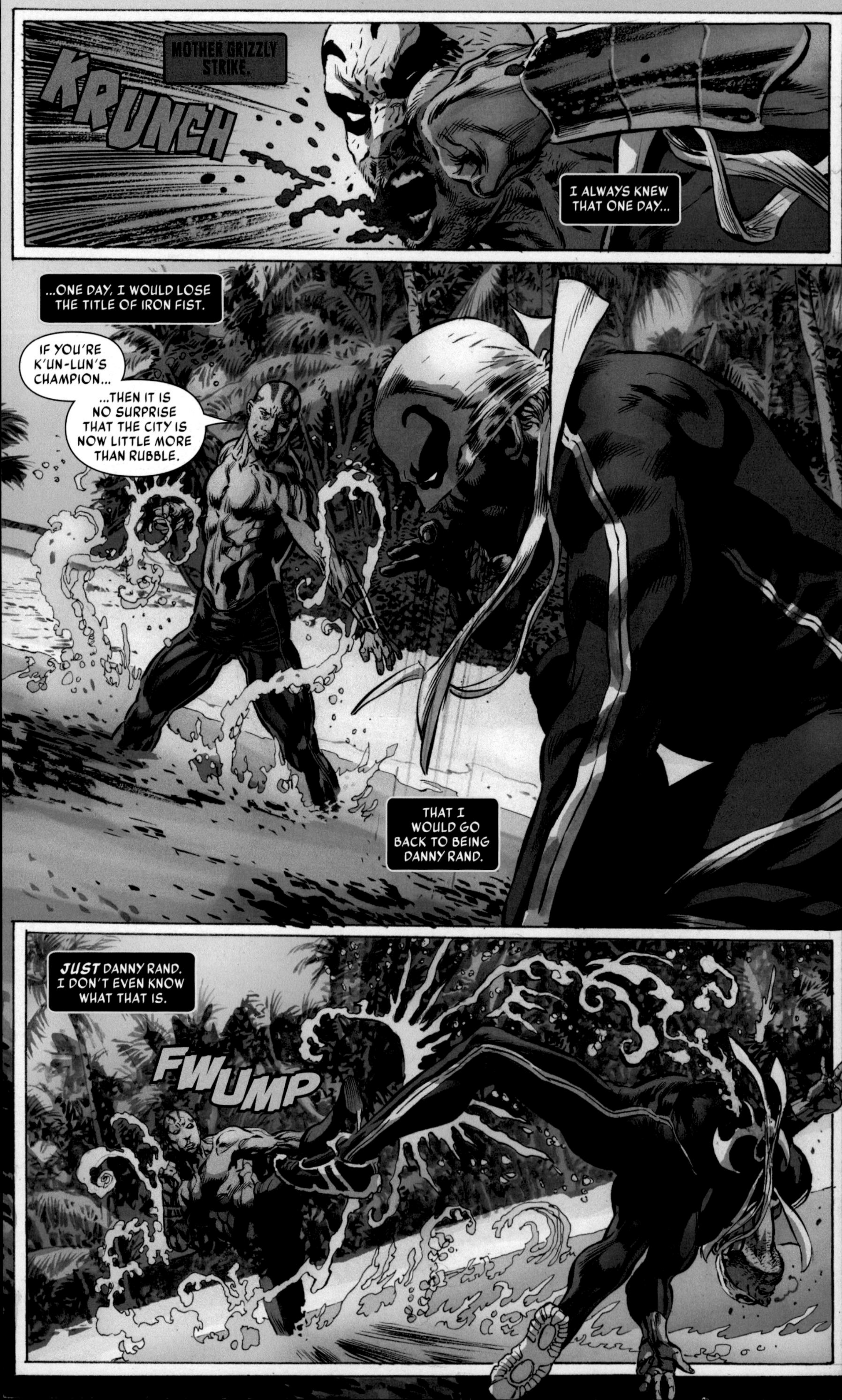
MOTHER GRIZZLY STRIKE.
KRUNCH
I ALWAYS KNEW THAT ONE DAY...
...ONE DAY, I WOULD LOSE THE TITLE OF IRON FIST.
IF YOU'RE K'UN-LUN'S CHAMPION...
...THEN IT IS NO SURPRISE THAT THE CITY IS NOW LITTLE MORE THAN RUBBLE.
THAT I WOULD GO BACK TO BEING DANNY RAND.
JUST DANNY RAND. I DON'T EVEN KNOW WHAT THAT IS.
FWUMP

"THE TRIAL OF THE SEVEN MASTERS"
PART TWO

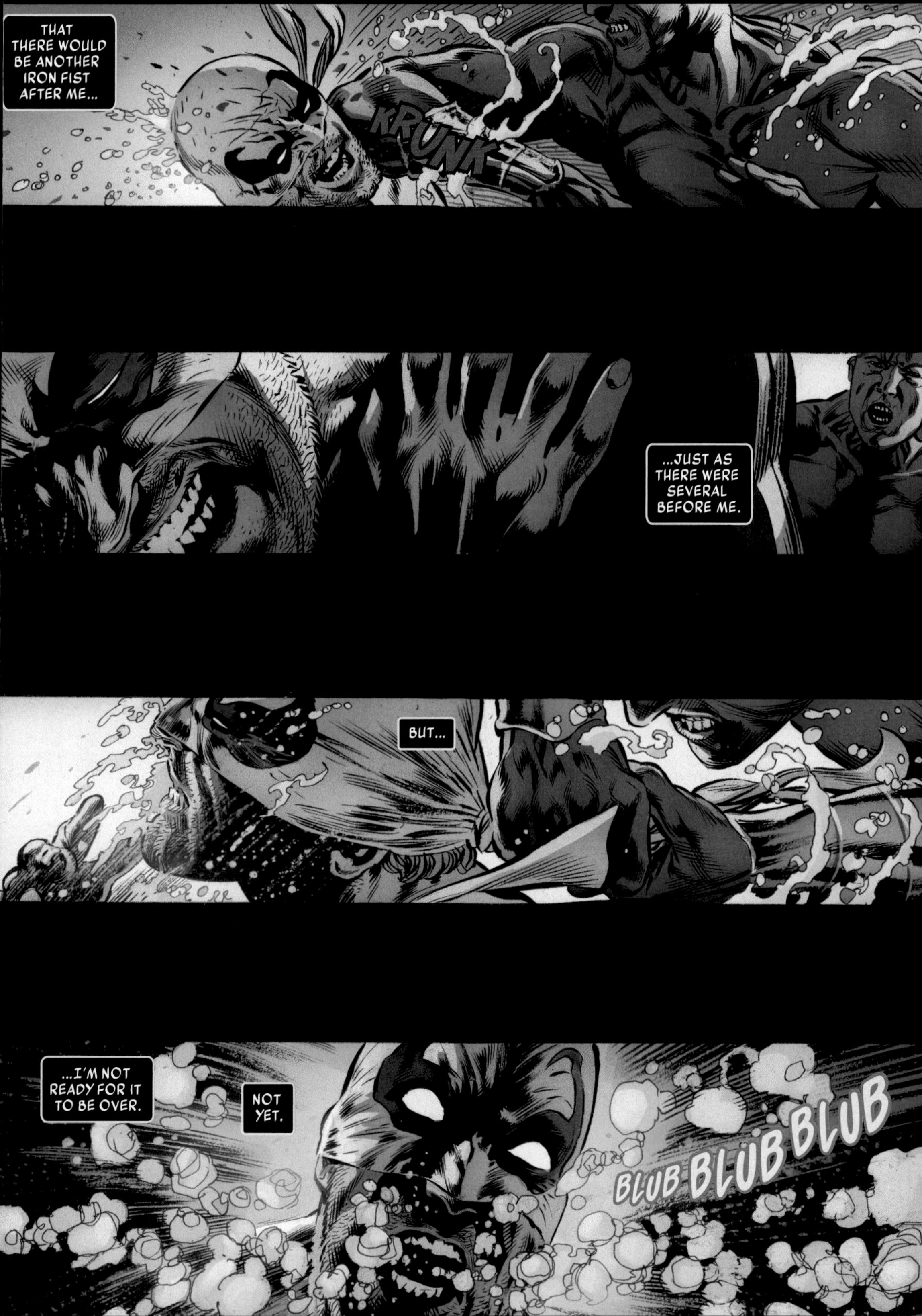
THAT THERE WOULD BE ANOTHER IRON FIST AFTER ME...
KRUNK
...JUST AS THERE WERE SEVERAL BEFORE ME.
BUT...
...I'M NOT READY FOR IT TO BE OVER.
NOT YET.
BLUB BLUB BLUB

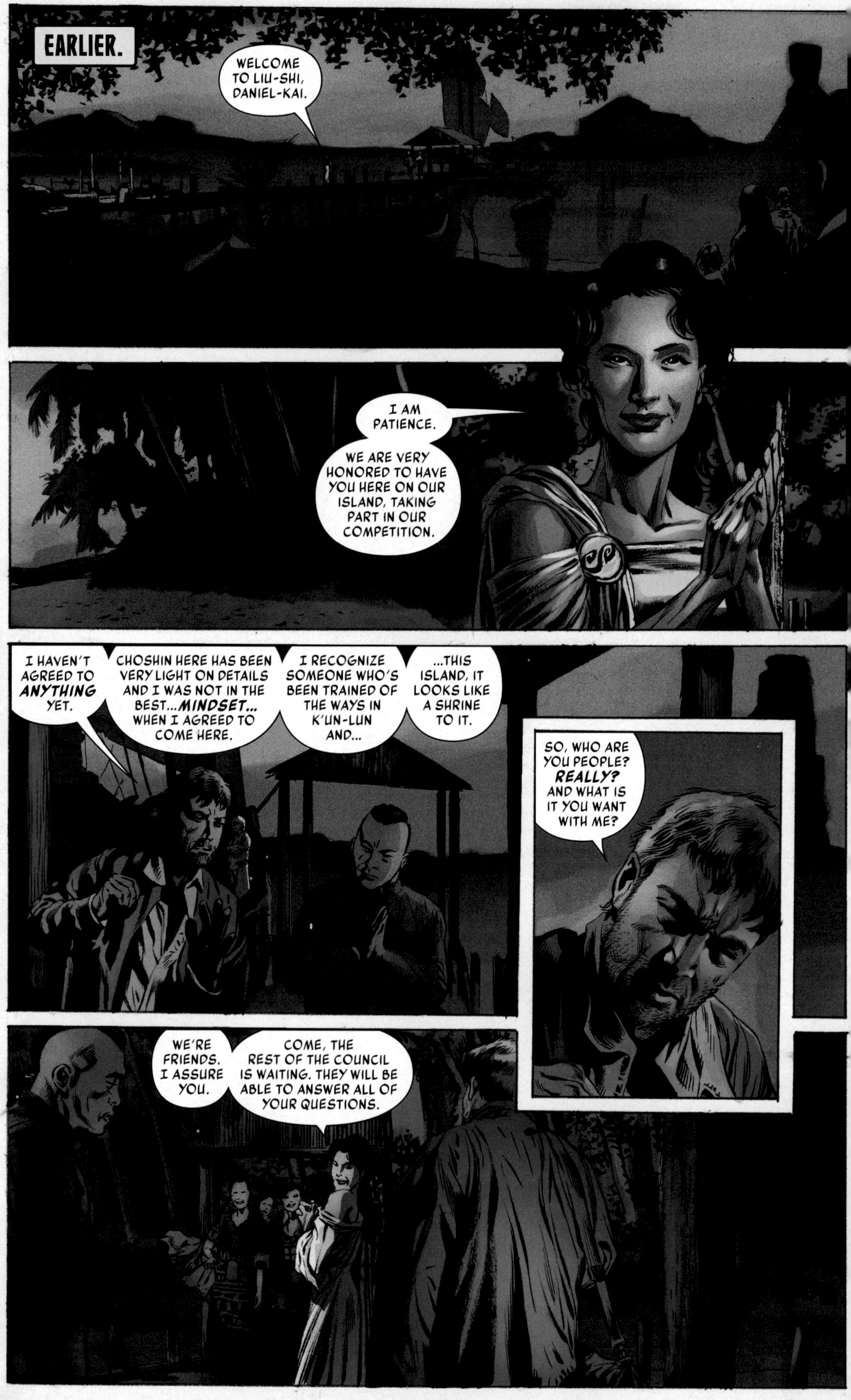
EARLIER.
WELCOME TO LIU-SHI, DANIEL-KAI.
I AM PATIENCE.
WE ARE VERY HONORED TO HAVE YOU HERE ON OUR ISLAND, TAKING PART IN OUR COMPETITION.
I HAVEN'T AGREED TO ***ANYTHING*** YET.
CHOSHIN HERE HAS BEEN VERY LIGHT ON DETAILS AND I WAS NOT IN THE BEST...***MINDSET...*** WHEN I AGREED TO COME HERE.
I RECOGNIZE SOMEONE WHO'S BEEN TRAINED OF THE WAYS IN K'UN-LUN AND...
...THIS ISLAND, IT LOOKS LIKE A SHRINE TO IT.
SO, WHO ARE YOU PEOPLE? ***REALLY?*** AND WHAT IS IT YOU WANT WITH ME?
WE'RE FRIENDS. I ASSURE YOU.
COME, THE REST OF THE COUNCIL IS WAITING. THEY WILL BE ABLE TO ANSWER ALL OF YOUR QUESTIONS.

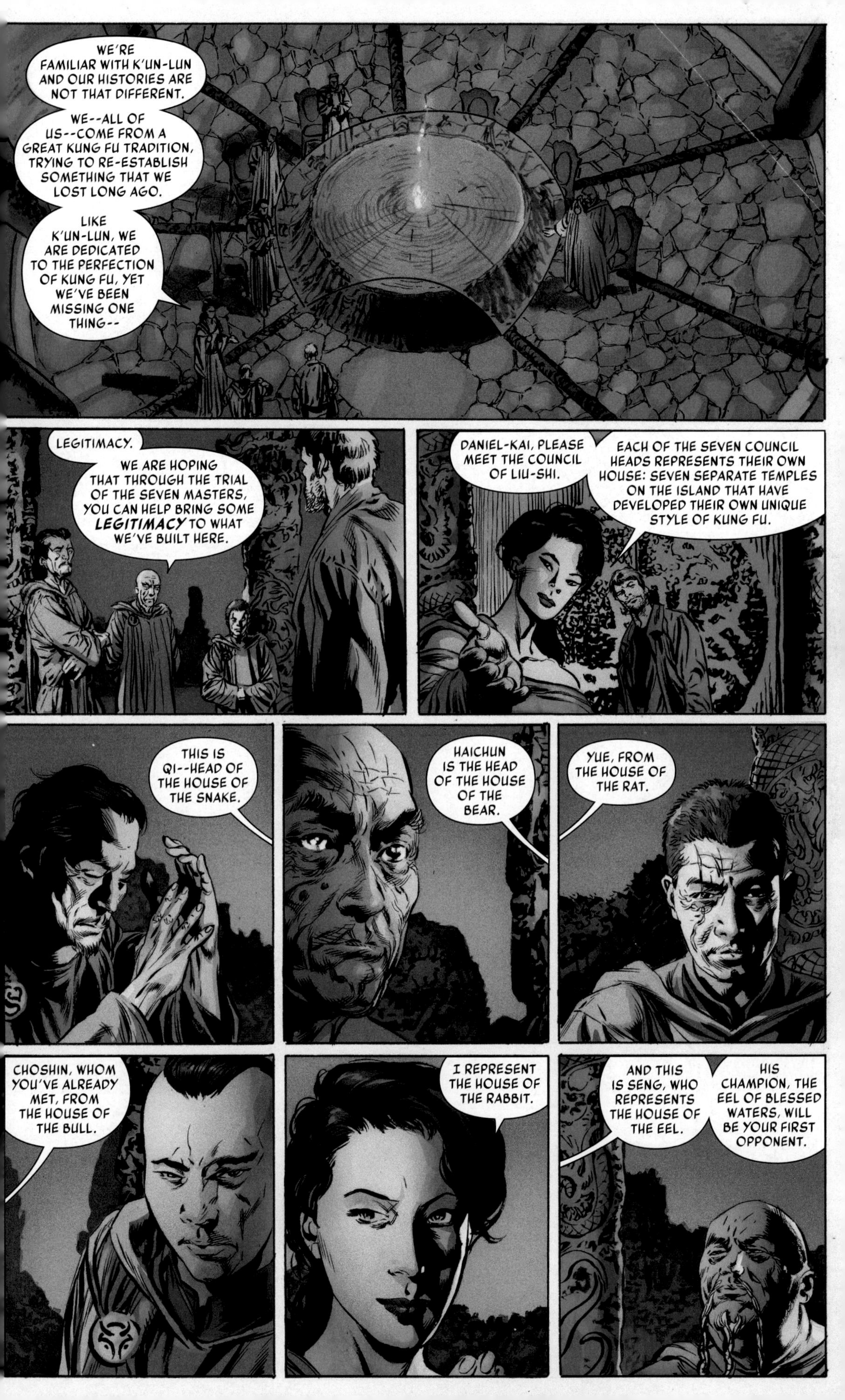

WE'RE FAMILIAR WITH K'UN-LUN AND OUR HISTORIES ARE NOT THAT DIFFERENT.
WE--ALL OF US--COME FROM A GREAT KUNG FU TRADITION, TRYING TO RE-ESTABLISH SOMETHING THAT WE LOST LONG AGO.
LIKE K'UN-LUN, WE ARE DEDICATED TO THE PERFECTION OF KUNG FU, YET WE'VE BEEN MISSING ONE THING--
LEGITIMACY.
WE ARE HOPING THAT THROUGH THE TRIAL OF THE SEVEN MASTERS, YOU CAN HELP BRING SOME LEGITIMACY TO WHAT WE'VE BUILT HERE.
DANIEL-KAI, PLEASE MEET THE COUNCIL OF LIU-SHI.
EACH OF THE SEVEN COUNCIL HEADS REPRESENTS THEIR OWN HOUSE: SEVEN SEPARATE TEMPLES ON THE ISLAND THAT HAVE DEVELOPED THEIR OWN UNIQUE STYLE OF KUNG FU.
THIS IS QI--HEAD OF THE HOUSE OF THE SNAKE.
HAICHUN IS THE HEAD OF THE HOUSE OF THE BEAR.
YUE, FROM THE HOUSE OF THE RAT.
CHOSHIN, WHOM YOU'VE ALREADY MET, FROM THE HOUSE OF THE BULL.
I REPRESENT THE HOUSE OF THE RABBIT.
AND THIS IS SENG, WHO REPRESENTS THE HOUSE OF THE EEL.
HIS CHAMPION, THE EEL OF BLESSED WATERS, WILL BE YOUR FIRST OPPONENT.

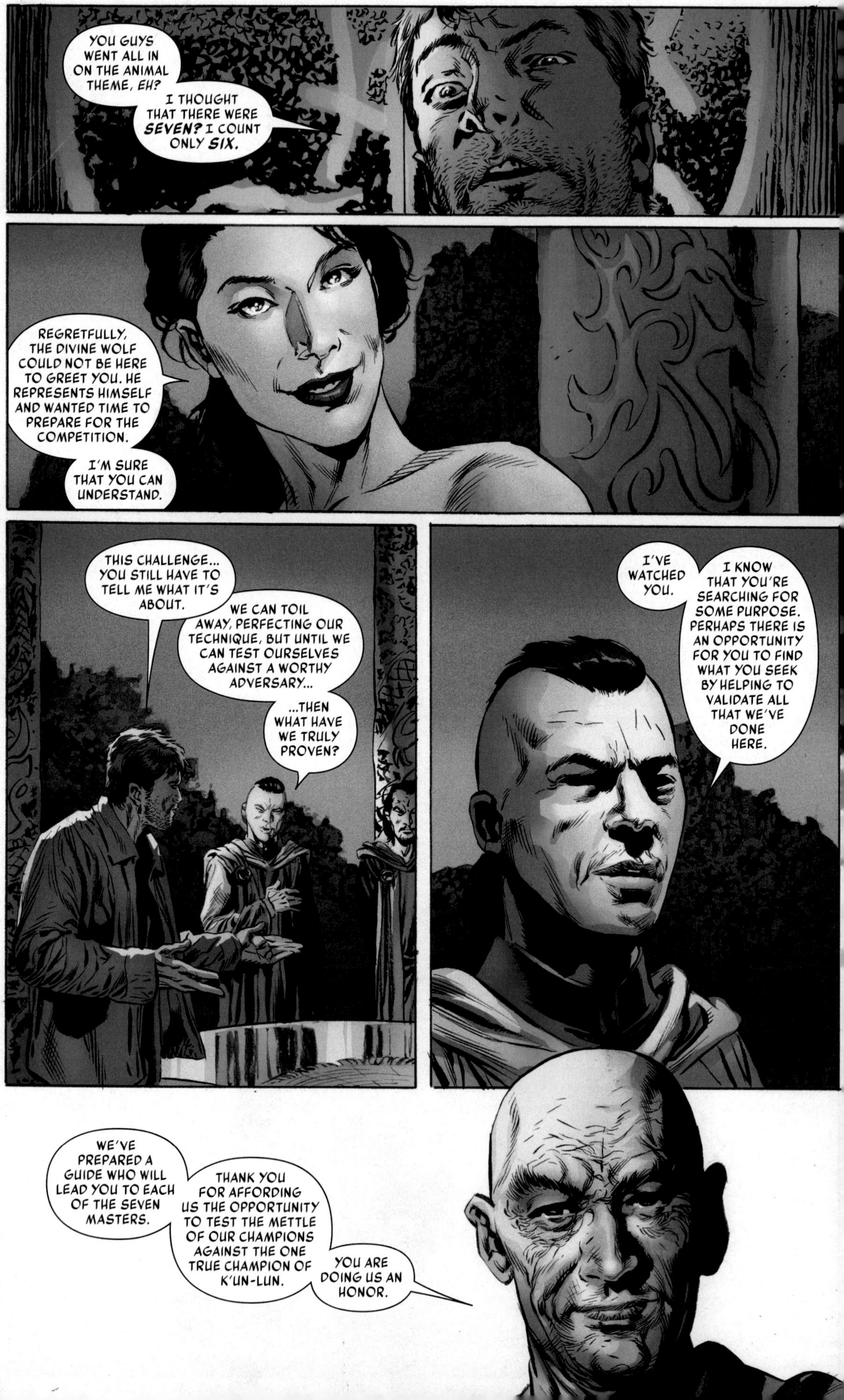
YOU GUYS WENT ALL IN ON THE ANIMAL THEME, *EH?*
I THOUGHT THAT THERE WERE ***SEVEN?*** I COUNT ONLY ***SIX.***
REGRETFULLY, THE DIVINE WOLF COULD NOT BE HERE TO GREET YOU. HE REPRESENTS HIMSELF AND WANTED TIME TO PREPARE FOR THE COMPETITION.
I'M SURE THAT YOU CAN UNDERSTAND.
THIS CHALLENGE... YOU STILL HAVE TO TELL ME WHAT IT'S ABOUT.
WE CAN TOIL AWAY, PERFECTING OUR TECHNIQUE, BUT UNTIL WE CAN TEST OURSELVES AGAINST A WORTHY ADVERSARY...
...THEN WHAT HAVE WE TRULY PROVEN?
I'VE WATCHED YOU.
I KNOW THAT YOU'RE SEARCHING FOR SOME PURPOSE. PERHAPS THERE IS AN OPPORTUNITY FOR YOU TO FIND WHAT YOU SEEK BY HELPING TO VALIDATE ALL THAT WE'VE DONE HERE.
WE'VE PREPARED A GUIDE WHO WILL LEAD YOU TO EACH OF THE SEVEN MASTERS.
THANK YOU FOR AFFORDING US THE OPPORTUNITY TO TEST THE METTLE OF OUR CHAMPIONS AGAINST THE ONE TRUE CHAMPION OF K'UN-LUN.
YOU ARE DOING US AN HONOR.

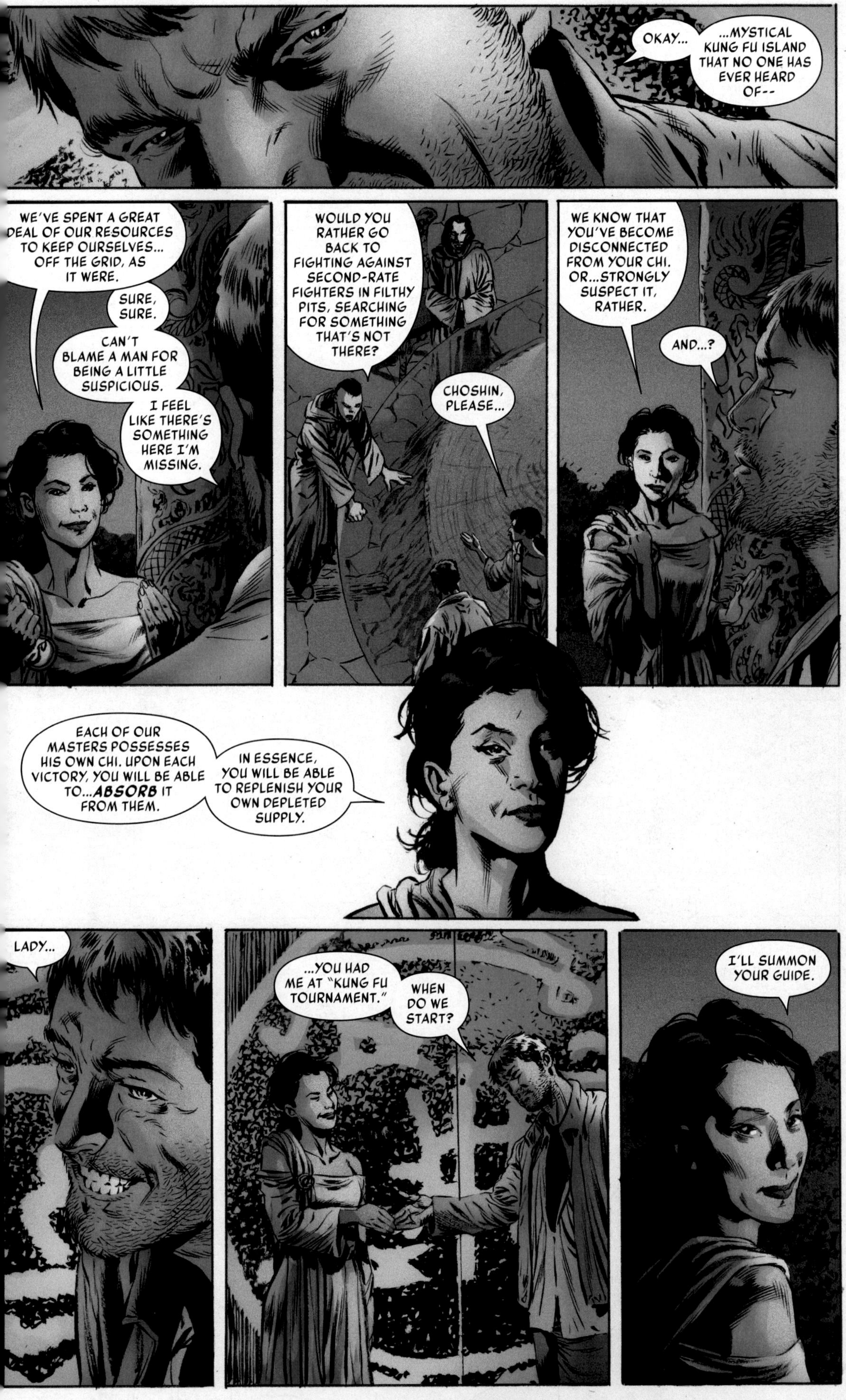
OKAY...
...MYSTICAL KUNG FU ISLAND THAT NO ONE HAS EVER HEARD OF--
WE'VE SPENT A GREAT DEAL OF OUR RESOURCES TO KEEP OURSELVES... OFF THE GRID, AS IT WERE.
SURE, SURE.
CAN'T BLAME A MAN FOR BEING A LITTLE SUSPICIOUS.
I FEEL LIKE THERE'S SOMETHING HERE I'M MISSING.
WOULD YOU RATHER GO BACK TO FIGHTING AGAINST SECOND-RATE FIGHTERS IN FILTHY PITS, SEARCHING FOR SOMETHING THAT'S NOT THERE?
CHOSHIN, PLEASE...
WE KNOW THAT YOU'VE BECOME DISCONNECTED FROM YOUR CHI. OR...STRONGLY SUSPECT IT, RATHER.
AND...?
EACH OF OUR MASTERS POSSESSES HIS OWN CHI. UPON EACH VICTORY, YOU WILL BE ABLE TO...ABSORB IT FROM THEM.
IN ESSENCE, YOU WILL BE ABLE TO REPLENISH YOUR OWN DEPLETED SUPPLY.
LADY...
...YOU HAD ME AT "KUNG FU TOURNAMENT."
WHEN DO WE START?
I'LL SUMMON YOUR GUIDE.

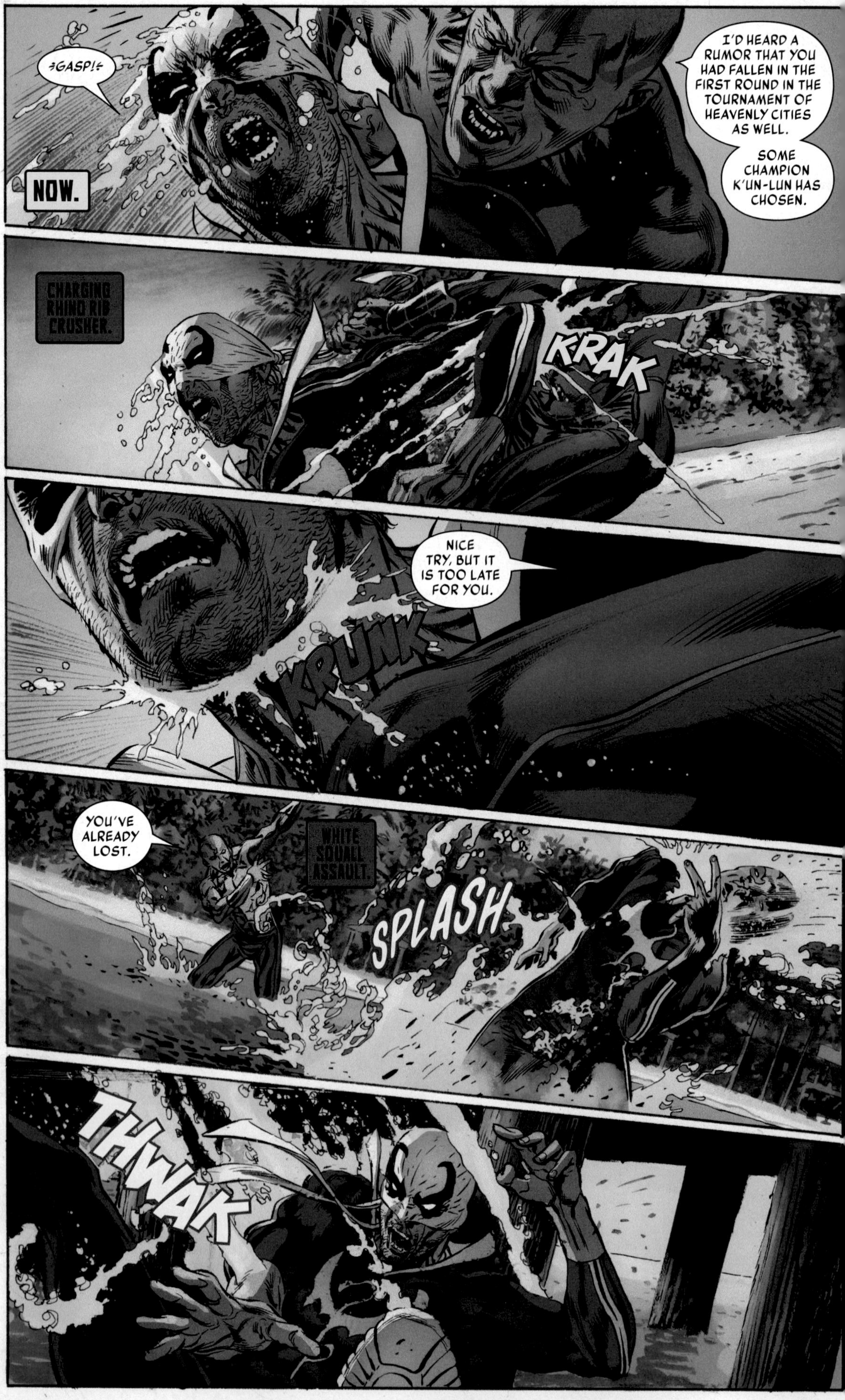

GASP!
NOW.
I'D HEARD A RUMOR THAT YOU HAD FALLEN IN THE FIRST ROUND IN THE TOURNAMENT OF HEAVENLY CITIES AS WELL.
SOME CHAMPION K'UN-LUN HAS CHOSEN.
CHARGING RHINO RIB CRUSHER.
KRAK
NICE TRY, BUT IT IS TOO LATE FOR YOU.
KRUNK
YOU'VE ALREADY LOST.
WHITE SQUALL ASSAULT.
SPLASH
THWAK

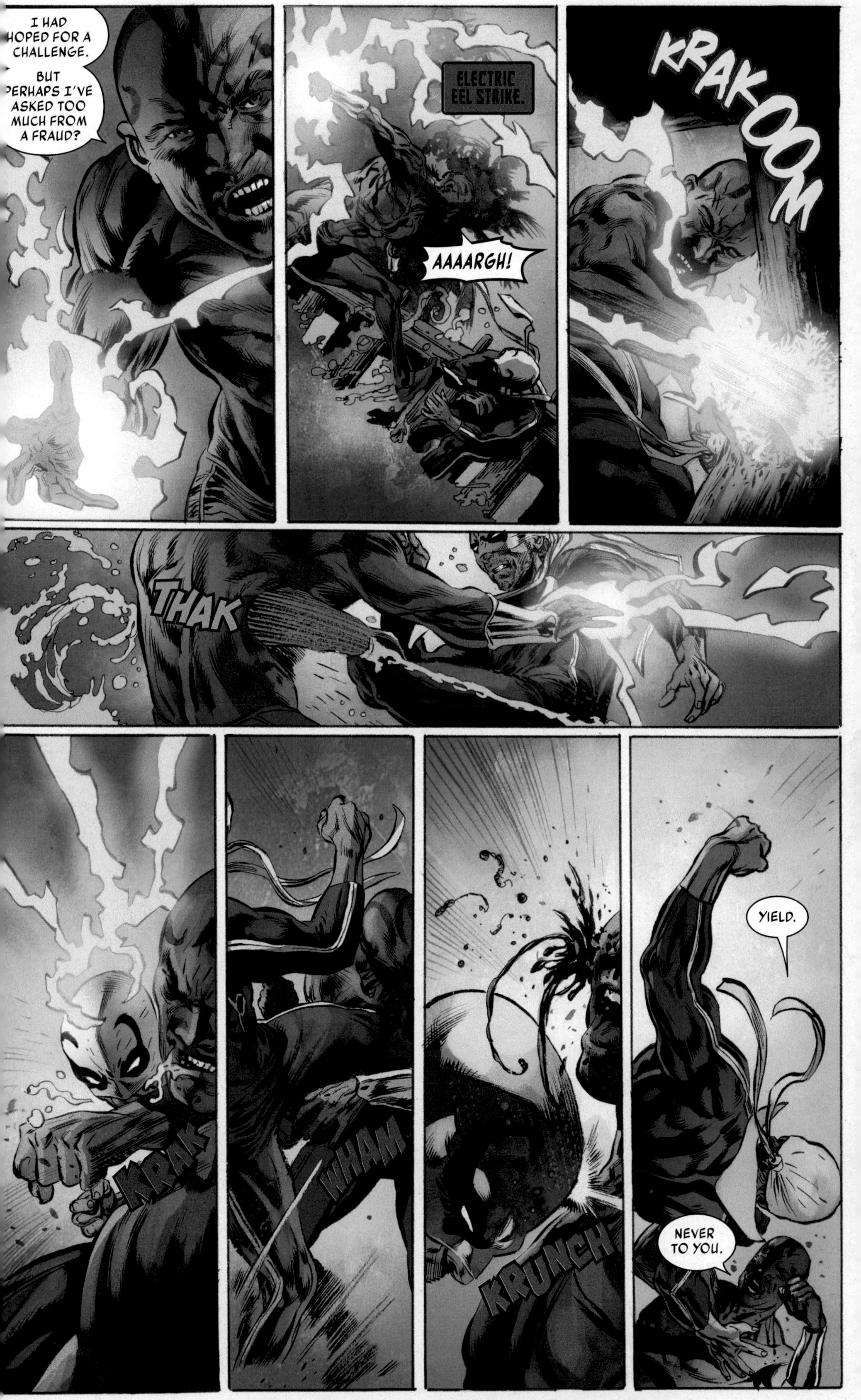
I HAD HOPED FOR A CHALLENGE.
BUT PERHAPS I'VE ASKED TOO MUCH FROM A FRAUD?
ELECTRIC EEL STRIKE.
AAAARGH!
KRAKOOOM
THAK
KRAK
WHAM
KRUNCH
YIELD.
NEVER TO YOU.

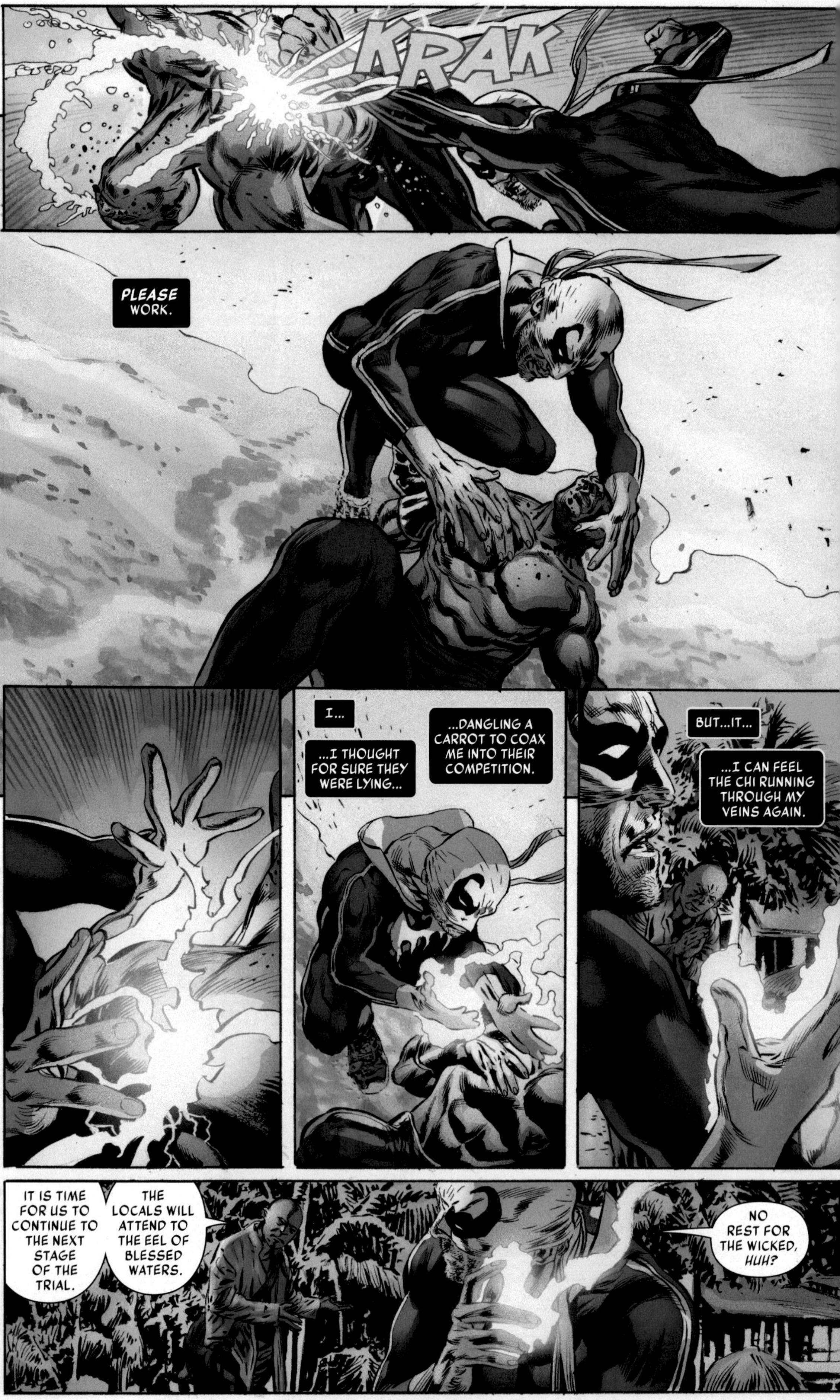
KRAK
PLEASE WORK.
I...
...I THOUGHT FOR SURE THEY WERE LYING...
...DANGLING A CARROT TO COAX ME INTO THEIR COMPETITION.
BUT...IT...
...I CAN FEEL THE CHI RUNNING THROUGH MY VEINS AGAIN.
IT IS TIME FOR US TO CONTINUE TO THE NEXT STAGE OF THE TRIAL.
THE LOCALS WILL ATTEND TO THE EEL OF BLESSED WATERS.
NO REST FOR THE WICKED, HUH?

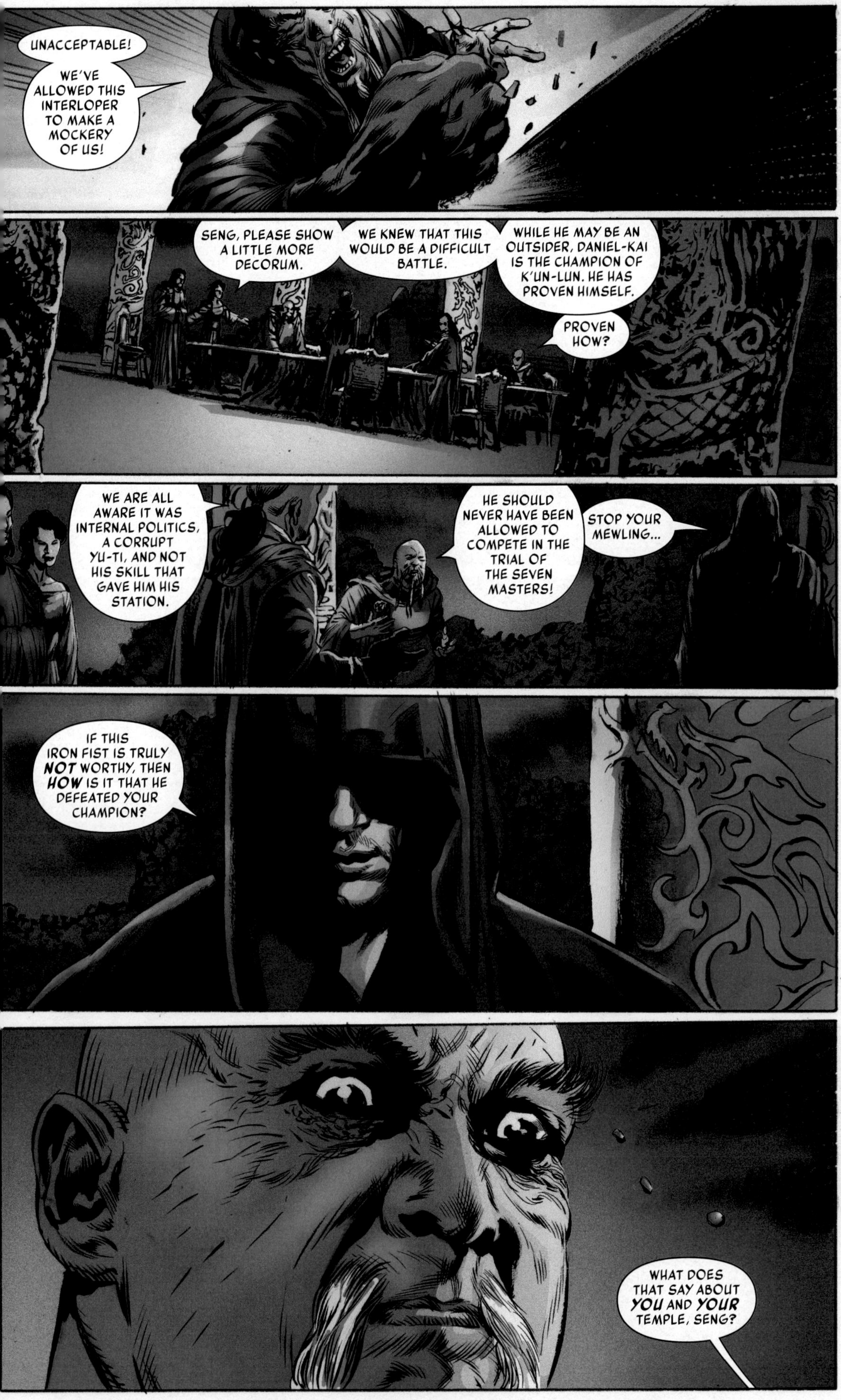
UNACCEPTABLE!
WE'VE ALLOWED THIS INTERLOPER TO MAKE A MOCKERY OF US!
SENG, PLEASE SHOW A LITTLE MORE DECORUM.
WE KNEW THAT THIS WOULD BE A DIFFICULT BATTLE.
WHILE HE MAY BE AN OUTSIDER, DANIEL-KAI IS THE CHAMPION OF K'UN-LUN. HE HAS PROVEN HIMSELF.
PROVEN HOW?
WE ARE ALL AWARE IT WAS INTERNAL POLITICS, A CORRUPT YU-TI, AND NOT HIS SKILL THAT GAVE HIM HIS STATION.
HE SHOULD NEVER HAVE BEEN ALLOWED TO COMPETE IN THE TRIAL OF THE SEVEN MASTERS!
STOP YOUR MEWLING...
IF THIS IRON FIST IS TRULY **NOT** WORTHY, THEN **HOW** IS IT THAT HE DEFEATED YOUR CHAMPION?
WHAT DOES THAT SAY ABOUT **YOU** AND **YOUR** TEMPLE, SENG?

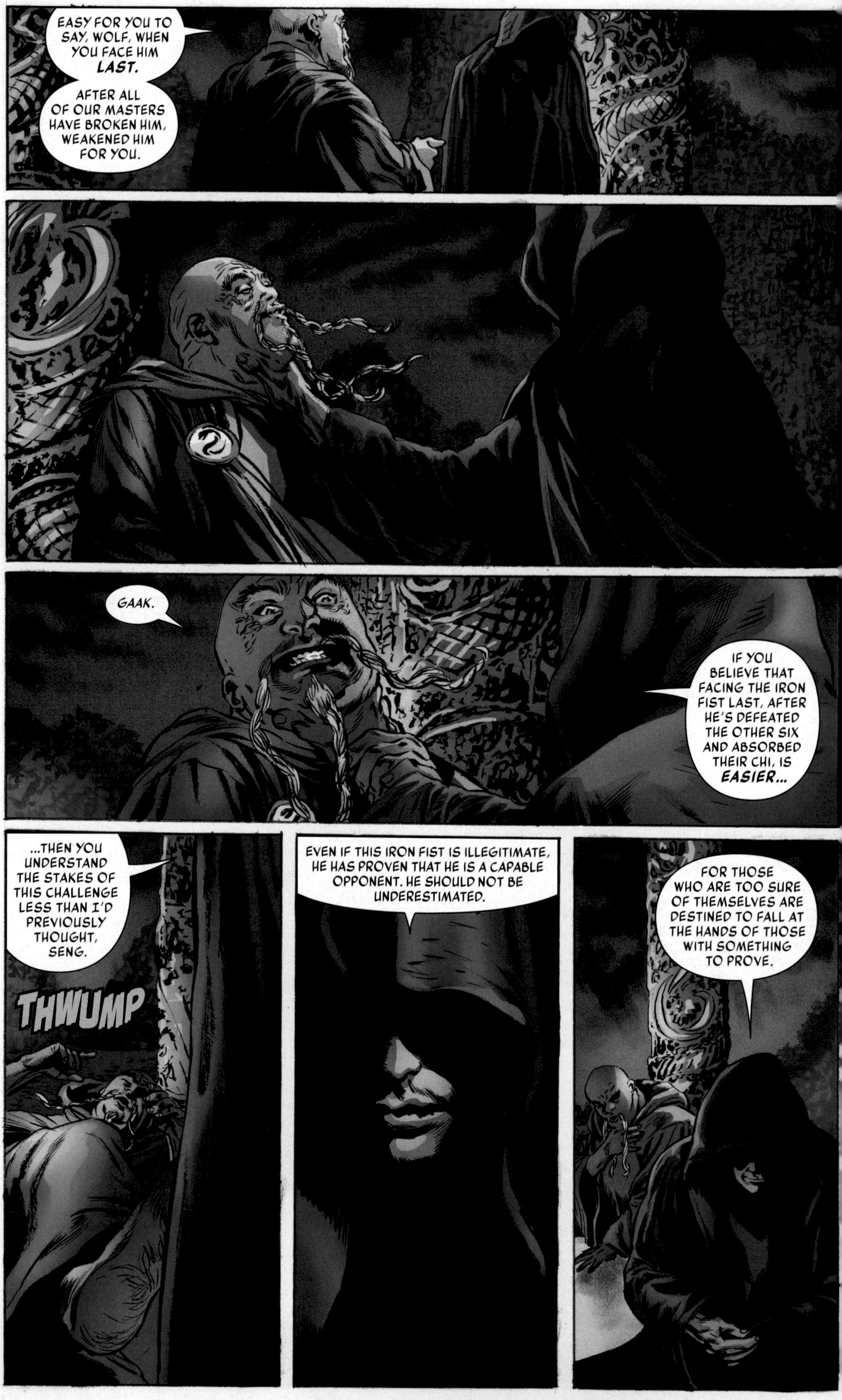
EASY FOR YOU TO SAY, WOLF, WHEN YOU FACE HIM **LAST.**
AFTER ALL OF OUR MASTERS HAVE BROKEN HIM, WEAKENED HIM FOR YOU.
GAAK.
IF YOU BELIEVE THAT FACING THE IRON FIST LAST, AFTER HE'S DEFEATED THE OTHER SIX AND ABSORBED THEIR CHI, IS **EASIER...**
...THEN YOU UNDERSTAND THE STAKES OF THIS CHALLENGE LESS THAN I'D PREVIOUSLY THOUGHT, SENG.
THWUMP
EVEN IF THIS IRON FIST IS ILLEGITIMATE, HE HAS PROVEN THAT HE IS A CAPABLE OPPONENT. HE SHOULD NOT BE UNDERESTIMATED.
FOR THOSE WHO ARE TOO SURE OF THEMSELVES ARE DESTINED TO FALL AT THE HANDS OF THOSE WITH SOMETHING TO PROVE.

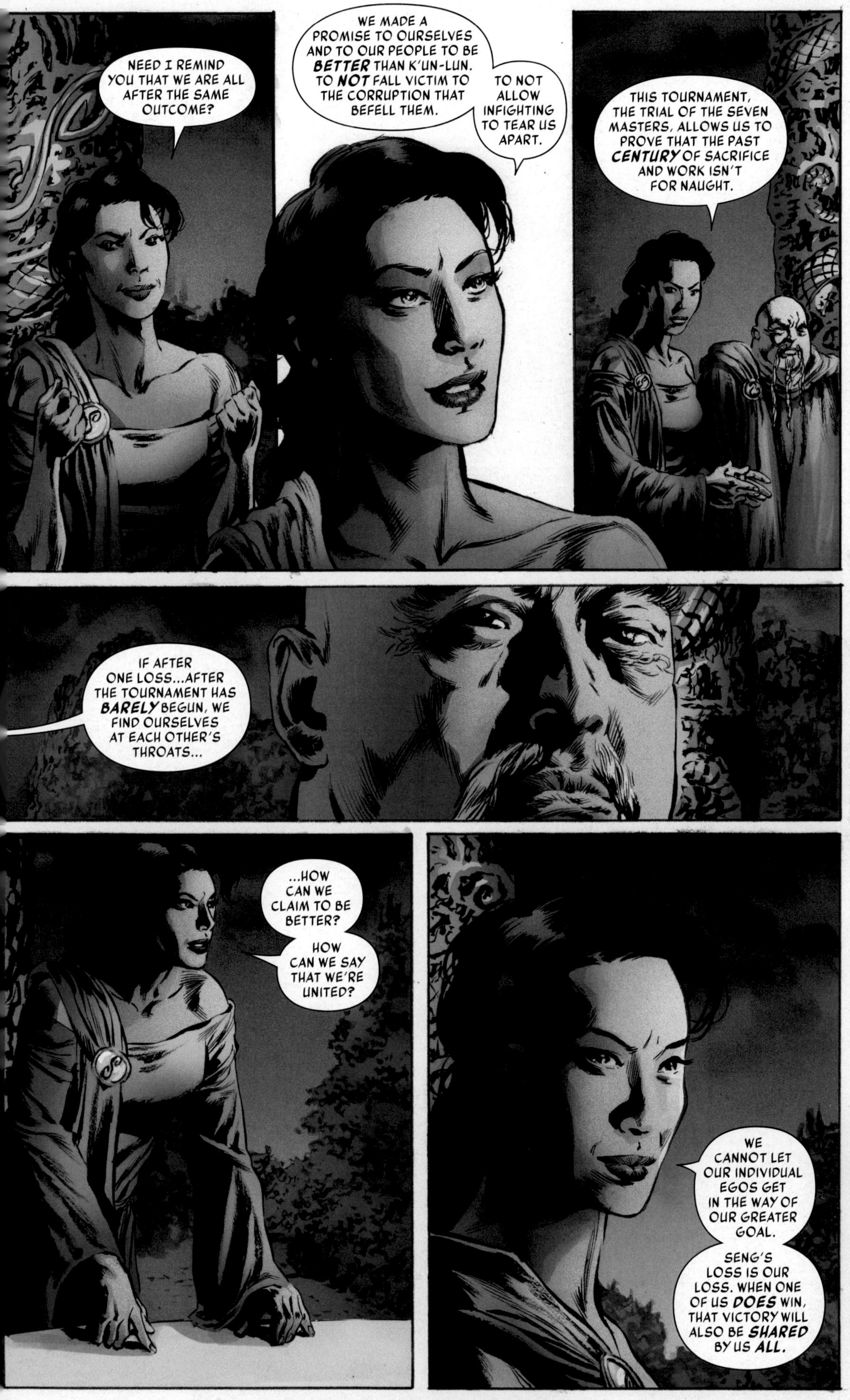
NEED I REMIND YOU THAT WE ARE ALL AFTER THE SAME OUTCOME?
WE MADE A PROMISE TO OURSELVES AND TO OUR PEOPLE TO BE BETTER THAN K'UN-LUN. TO NOT FALL VICTIM TO THE CORRUPTION THAT BEFELL THEM.
TO NOT ALLOW INFIGHTING TO TEAR US APART.
THIS TOURNAMENT, THE TRIAL OF THE SEVEN MASTERS, ALLOWS US TO PROVE THAT THE PAST CENTURY OF SACRIFICE AND WORK ISN'T FOR NAUGHT.
IF AFTER ONE LOSS...AFTER THE TOURNAMENT HAS BARELY BEGUN, WE FIND OURSELVES AT EACH OTHER'S THROATS...
...HOW CAN WE CLAIM TO BE BETTER?
HOW CAN WE SAY THAT WE'RE UNITED?
WE CANNOT LET OUR INDIVIDUAL EGOS GET IN THE WAY OF OUR GREATER GOAL.
SENG'S LOSS IS OUR LOSS. WHEN ONE OF US DOES WIN, THAT VICTORY WILL ALSO BE SHARED BY US ALL.

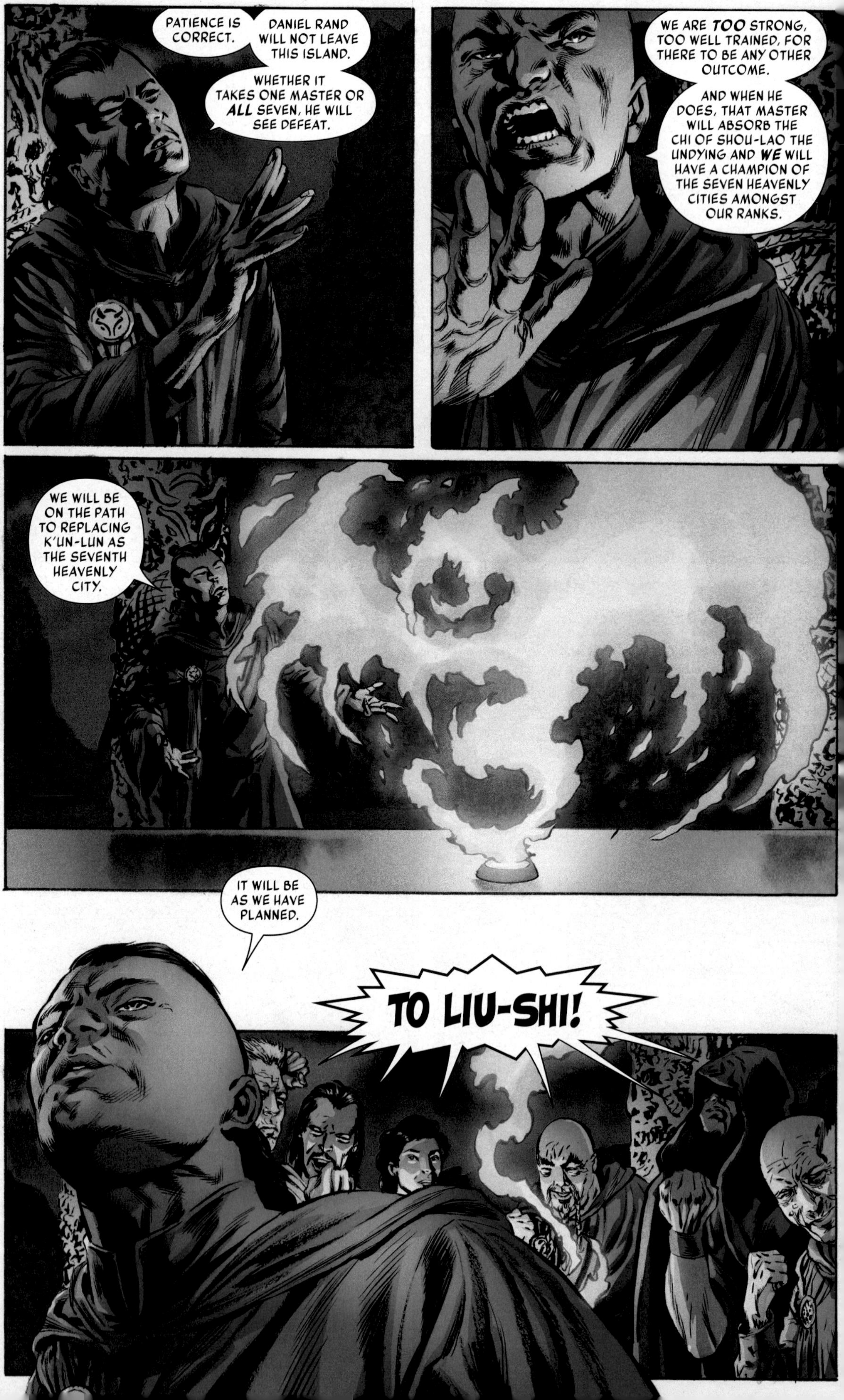
PATIENCE IS CORRECT.
DANIEL RAND WILL NOT LEAVE THIS ISLAND.
WHETHER IT TAKES ONE MASTER OR ALL SEVEN, HE WILL SEE DEFEAT.
WE ARE TOO STRONG, TOO WELL TRAINED, FOR THERE TO BE ANY OTHER OUTCOME.
AND WHEN HE DOES, THAT MASTER WILL ABSORB THE CHI OF SHOU-LAO THE UNDYING AND WE WILL HAVE A CHAMPION OF THE SEVEN HEAVENLY CITIES AMONGST OUR RANKS.
WE WILL BE ON THE PATH TO REPLACING K'UN-LUN AS THE SEVENTH HEAVENLY CITY.
IT WILL BE AS WE HAVE PLANNED.
TO LIU-SHI!

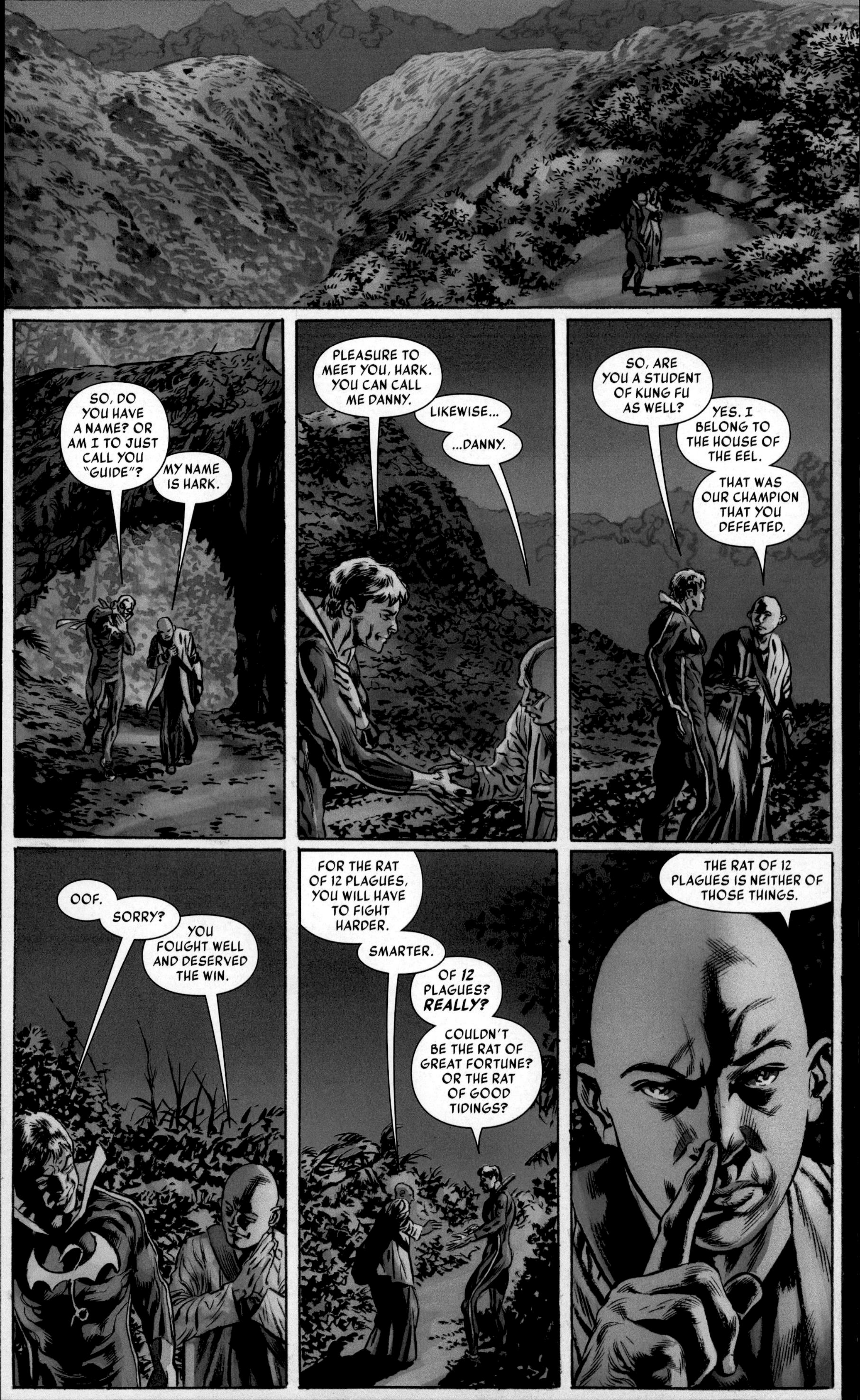
SO, DO YOU HAVE A NAME? OR AM I TO JUST CALL YOU "GUIDE"?
MY NAME IS HARK.
PLEASURE TO MEET YOU, HARK. YOU CAN CALL ME DANNY.
LIKEWISE...
...DANNY.
SO, ARE YOU A STUDENT OF KUNG FU AS WELL?
YES. I BELONG TO THE HOUSE OF THE EEL.
THAT WAS OUR CHAMPION THAT YOU DEFEATED.
OOF.
SORRY?
YOU FOUGHT WELL AND DESERVED THE WIN.
FOR THE RAT OF 12 PLAGUES, YOU WILL HAVE TO FIGHT HARDER.
SMARTER.
OF 12 PLAGUES? REALLY?
COULDN'T BE THE RAT OF GREAT FORTUNE? OR THE RAT OF GOOD TIDINGS?
THE RAT OF 12 PLAGUES IS NEITHER OF THOSE THINGS.

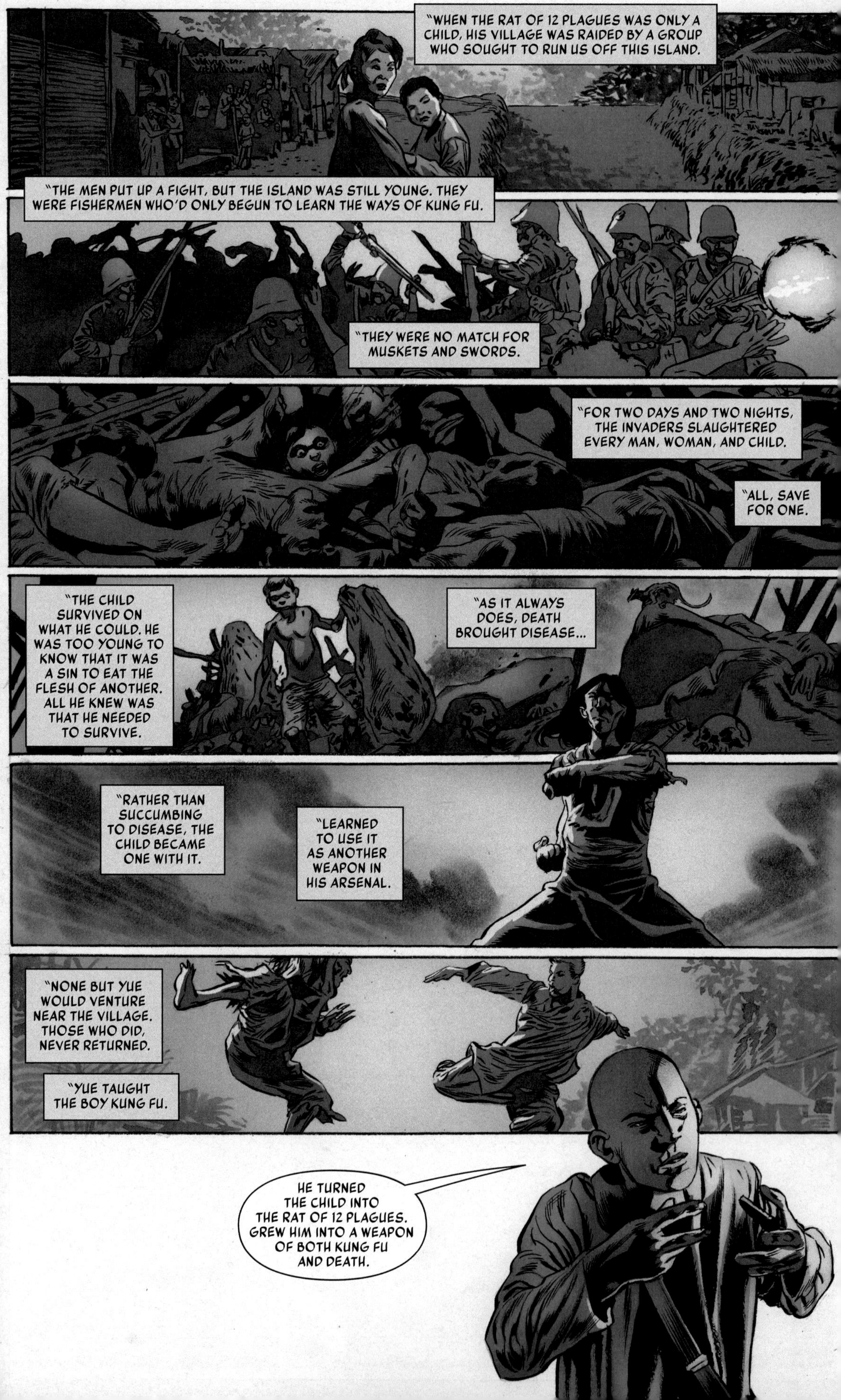
"WHEN THE RAT OF 12 PLAGUES WAS ONLY A CHILD, HIS VILLAGE WAS RAIDED BY A GROUP WHO SOUGHT TO RUN US OFF THIS ISLAND.
"THE MEN PUT UP A FIGHT, BUT THE ISLAND WAS STILL YOUNG. THEY WERE FISHERMEN WHO'D ONLY BEGUN TO LEARN THE WAYS OF KUNG FU.
"THEY WERE NO MATCH FOR MUSKETS AND SWORDS.
"FOR TWO DAYS AND TWO NIGHTS, THE INVADERS SLAUGHTERED EVERY MAN, WOMAN, AND CHILD.
"ALL, SAVE FOR ONE.
"THE CHILD SURVIVED ON WHAT HE COULD. HE WAS TOO YOUNG TO KNOW THAT IT WAS A SIN TO EAT THE FLESH OF ANOTHER. ALL HE KNEW WAS THAT HE NEEDED TO SURVIVE.
"AS IT ALWAYS DOES, DEATH BROUGHT DISEASE...
"RATHER THAN SUCCUMBING TO DISEASE, THE CHILD BECAME ONE WITH IT.
"LEARNED TO USE IT AS ANOTHER WEAPON IN HIS ARSENAL.
"NONE BUT YUE WOULD VENTURE NEAR THE VILLAGE. THOSE WHO DID, NEVER RETURNED.
"YUE TAUGHT THE BOY KUNG FU.
HE TURNED THE CHILD INTO THE RAT OF 12 PLAGUES. GREW HIM INTO A WEAPON OF BOTH KUNG FU AND DEATH.

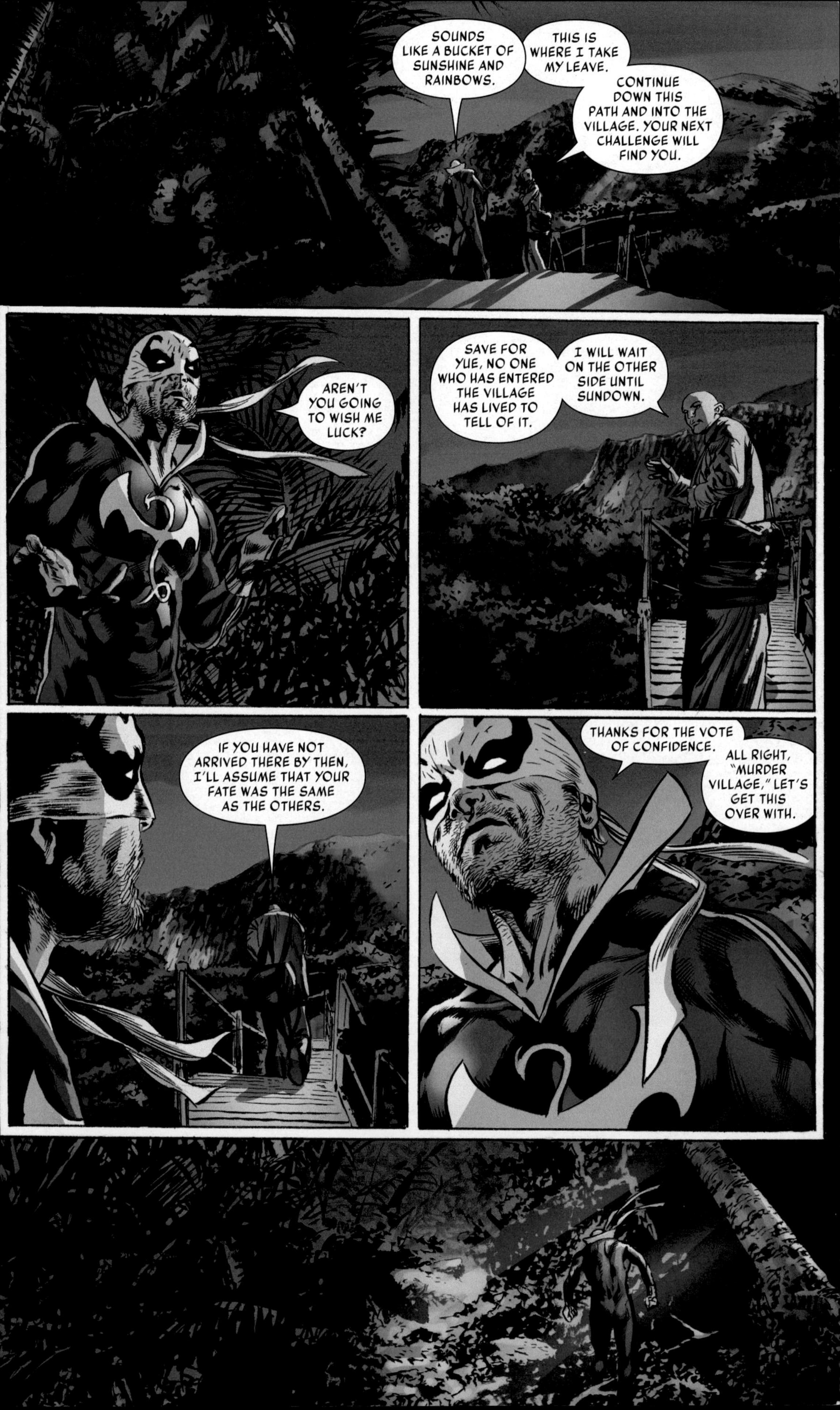
SOUNDS LIKE A BUCKET OF SUNSHINE AND RAINBOWS.
THIS IS WHERE I TAKE MY LEAVE.
CONTINUE DOWN THIS PATH AND INTO THE VILLAGE. YOUR NEXT CHALLENGE WILL FIND YOU.
AREN'T YOU GOING TO WISH ME LUCK?
SAVE FOR YUE, NO ONE WHO HAS ENTERED THE VILLAGE HAS LIVED TO TELL OF IT.
I WILL WAIT ON THE OTHER SIDE UNTIL SUNDOWN.
IF YOU HAVE NOT ARRIVED THERE BY THEN, I'LL ASSUME THAT YOUR FATE WAS THE SAME AS THE OTHERS.
THANKS FOR THE VOTE OF CONFIDENCE.
ALL RIGHT, "MURDER VILLAGE," LET'S GET THIS OVER WITH.

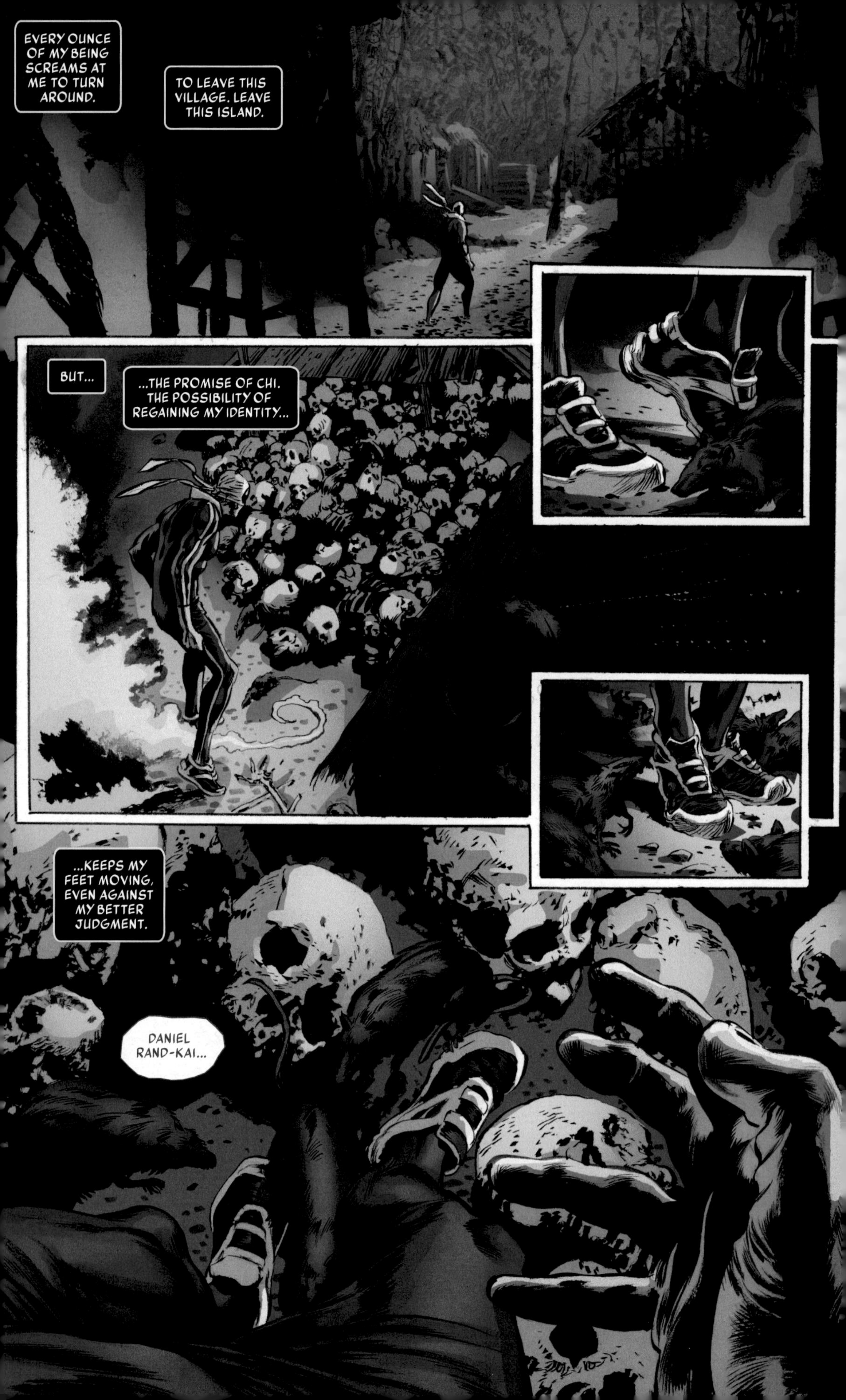
EVERY OUNCE OF MY BEING SCREAMS AT ME TO TURN AROUND.
TO LEAVE THIS VILLAGE. LEAVE THIS ISLAND.
BUT...
...THE PROMISE OF CHI. THE POSSIBILITY OF REGAINING MY IDENTITY...
...KEEPS MY FEET MOVING, EVEN AGAINST MY BETTER JUDGMENT.
DANIEL RAND-KAI...

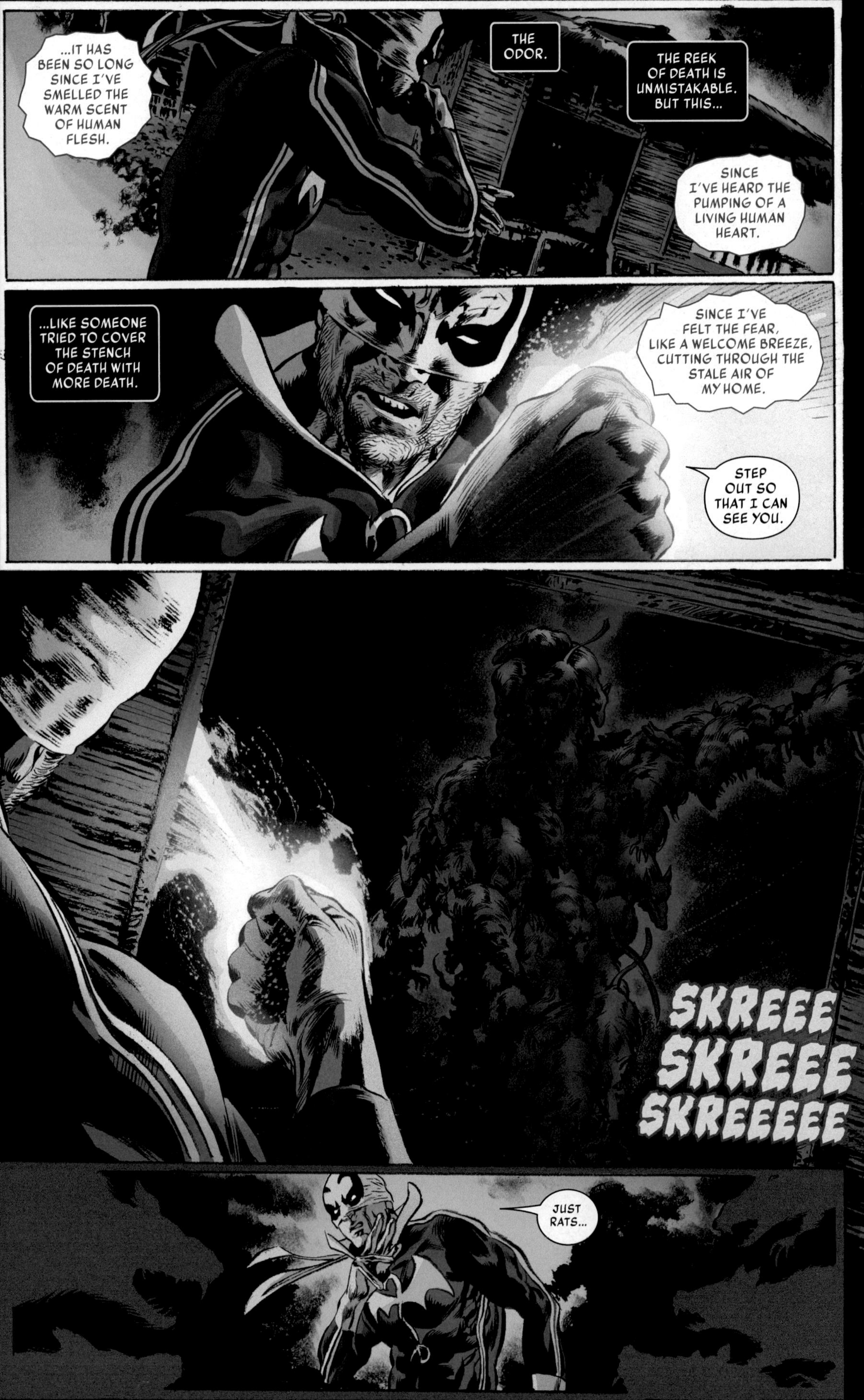
...IT HAS BEEN SO LONG SINCE I'VE SMELLED THE WARM SCENT OF HUMAN FLESH.
THE ODOR.
THE REEK OF DEATH IS UNMISTAKABLE. BUT THIS...
SINCE I'VE HEARD THE PUMPING OF A LIVING HUMAN HEART.
...LIKE SOMEONE TRIED TO COVER THE STENCH OF DEATH WITH MORE DEATH.
SINCE I'VE FELT THE FEAR, LIKE A WELCOME BREEZE, CUTTING THROUGH THE STALE AIR OF MY HOME.
STEP OUT SO THAT I CAN SEE YOU.
SKREEE
SKREEE
SKREEEEE
JUST RATS...

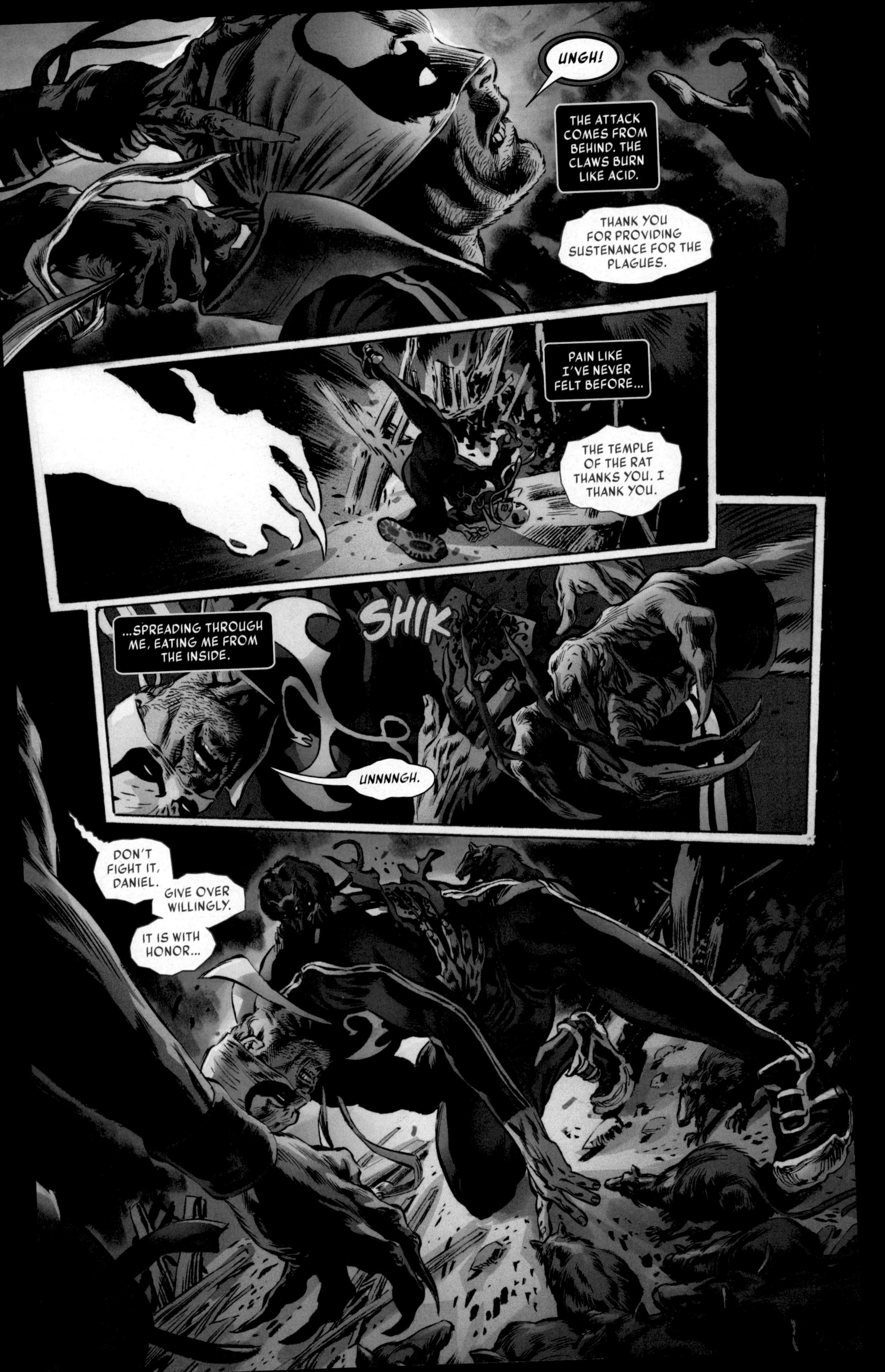
UNGH!
THE ATTACK COMES FROM BEHIND. THE CLAWS BURN LIKE ACID.
THANK YOU FOR PROVIDING SUSTENANCE FOR THE PLAGUES.
PAIN LIKE I'VE NEVER FELT BEFORE...
THE TEMPLE OF THE RAT THANKS YOU. I THANK YOU.
...SPREADING THROUGH ME, EATING ME FROM THE INSIDE.
SHIK
UNNNNGH.
DON'T FIGHT IT, DANIEL.
GIVE OVER WILLINGLY.
IT IS WITH HONOR...

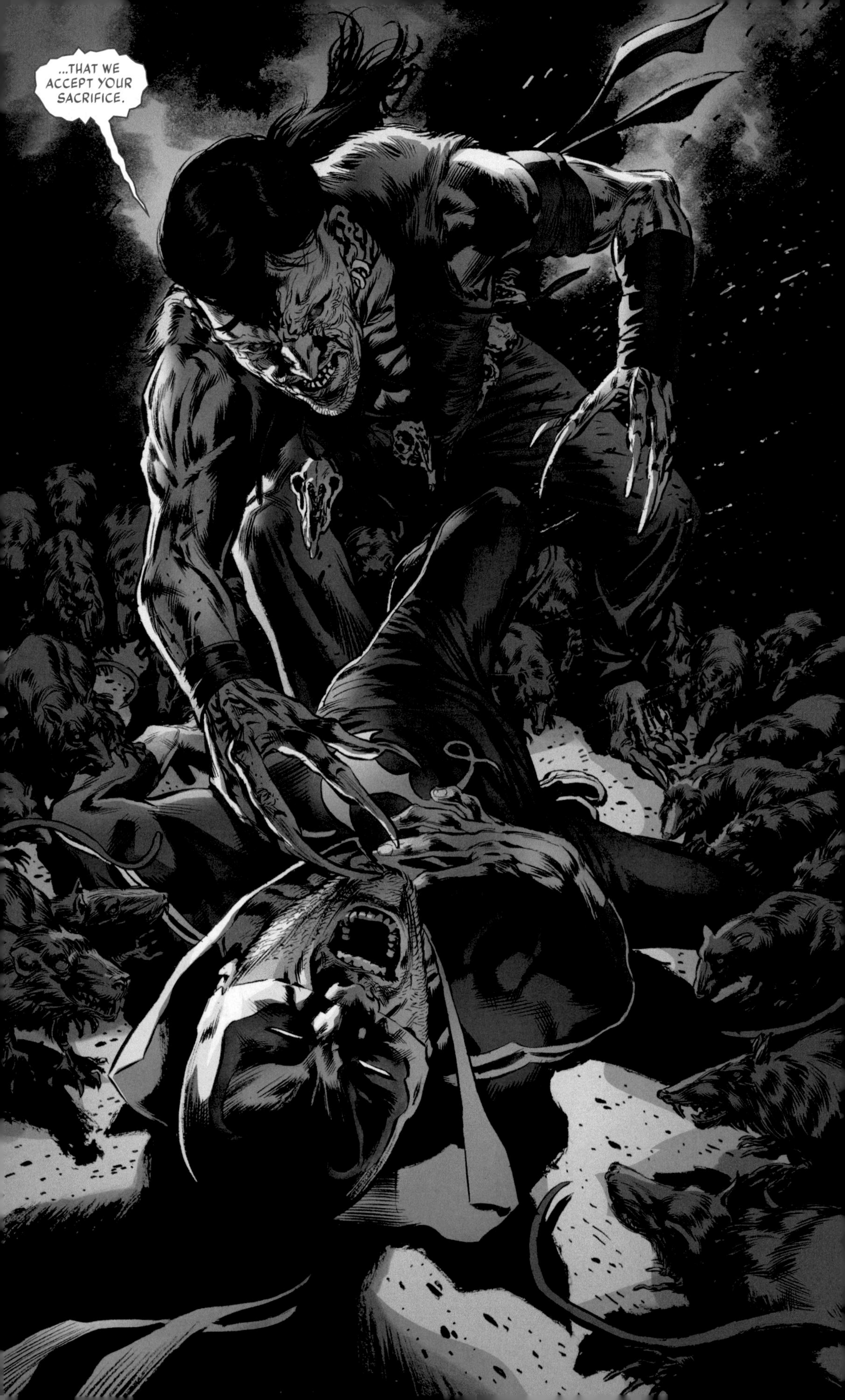
...THAT WE ACCEPT YOUR SACRIFICE.

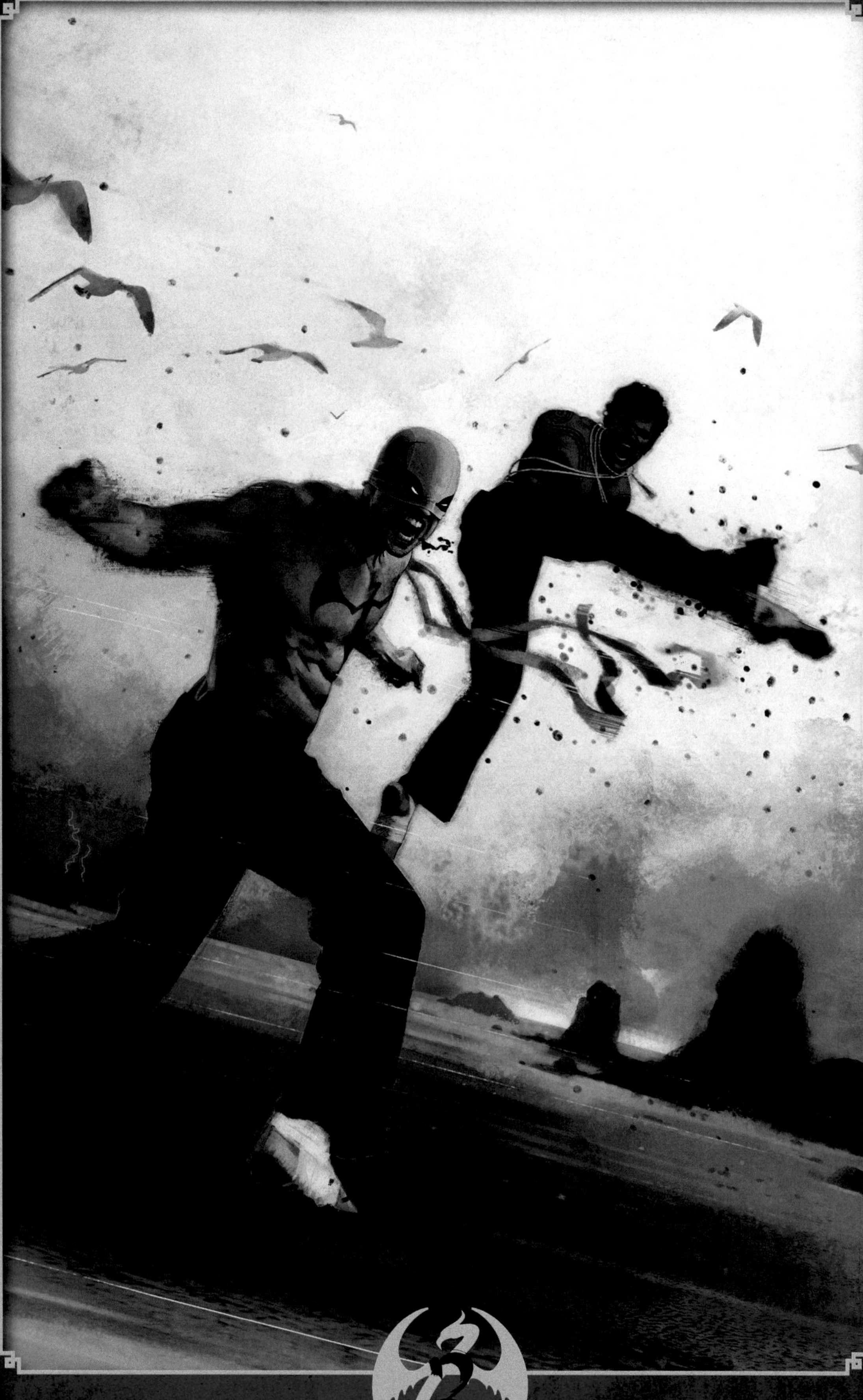

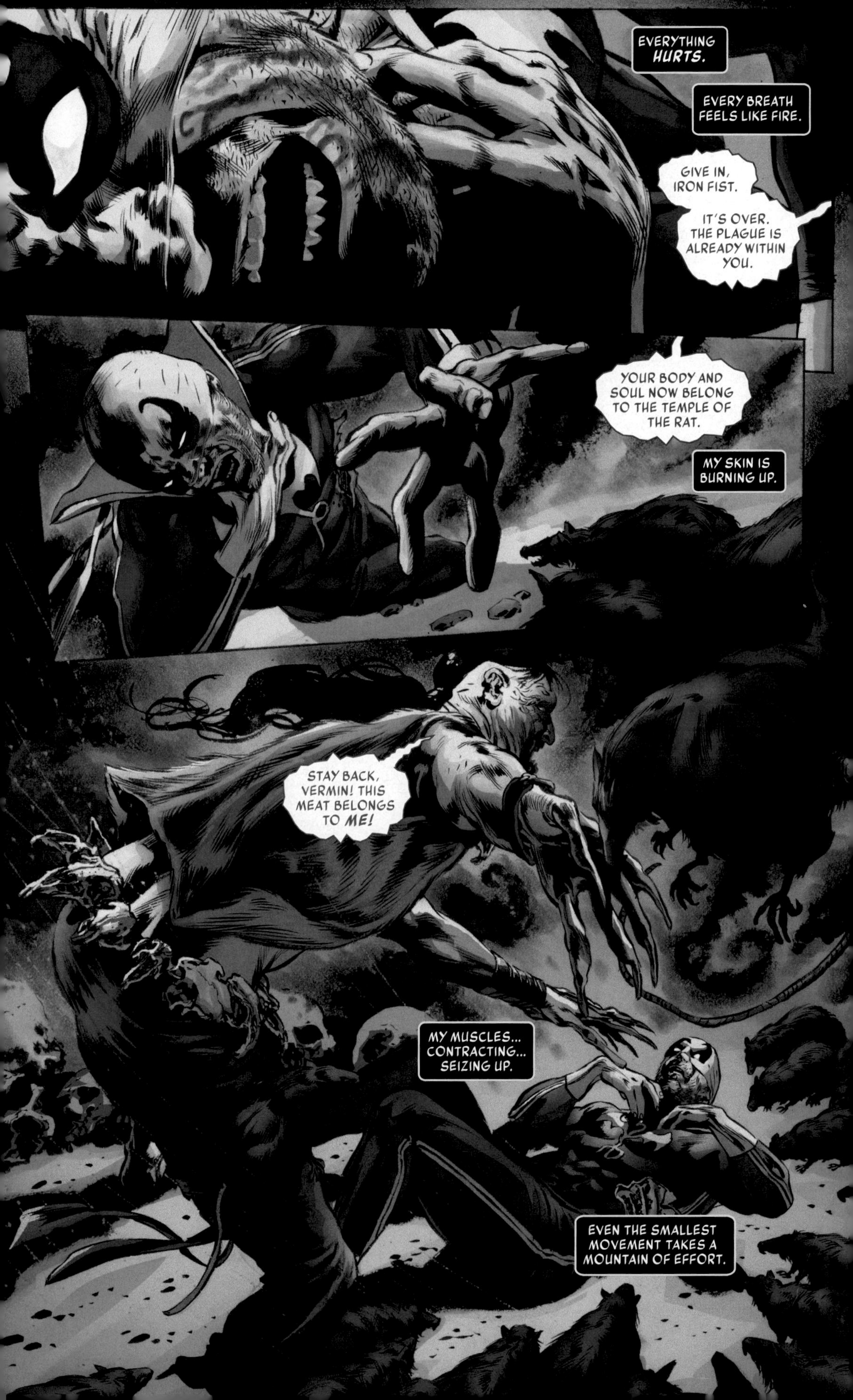
EVERYTHING HURTS.
EVERY BREATH FEELS LIKE FIRE.
GIVE IN, IRON FIST.
IT'S OVER. THE PLAGUE IS ALREADY WITHIN YOU.
YOUR BODY AND SOUL NOW BELONG TO THE TEMPLE OF THE RAT.
MY SKIN IS BURNING UP.
STAY BACK, VERMIN! THIS MEAT BELONGS TO ME!
MY MUSCLES... CONTRACTING... SEIZING UP.
EVEN THE SMALLEST MOVEMENT TAKES A MOUNTAIN OF EFFORT.

"THE TRIAL OF THE SEVEN MASTERS"
PART THREE

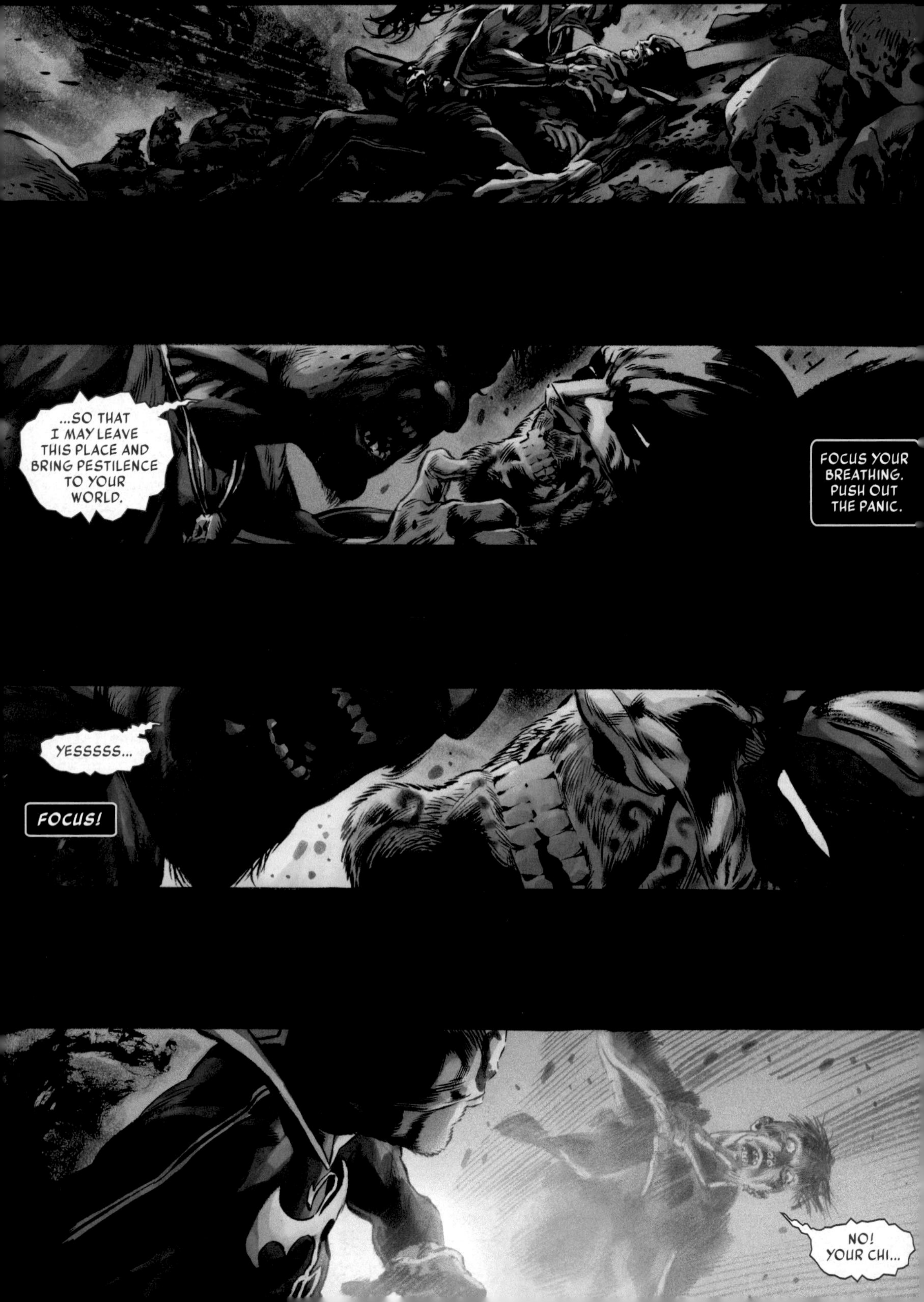
...SO THAT I MAY LEAVE THIS PLACE AND BRING PESTILENCE TO YOUR WORLD.
FOCUS YOUR BREATHING. PUSH OUT THE PANIC.
YESSSSS...
FOCUS!
NO! YOUR CHI...

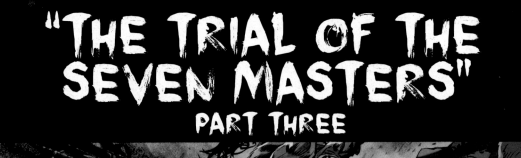

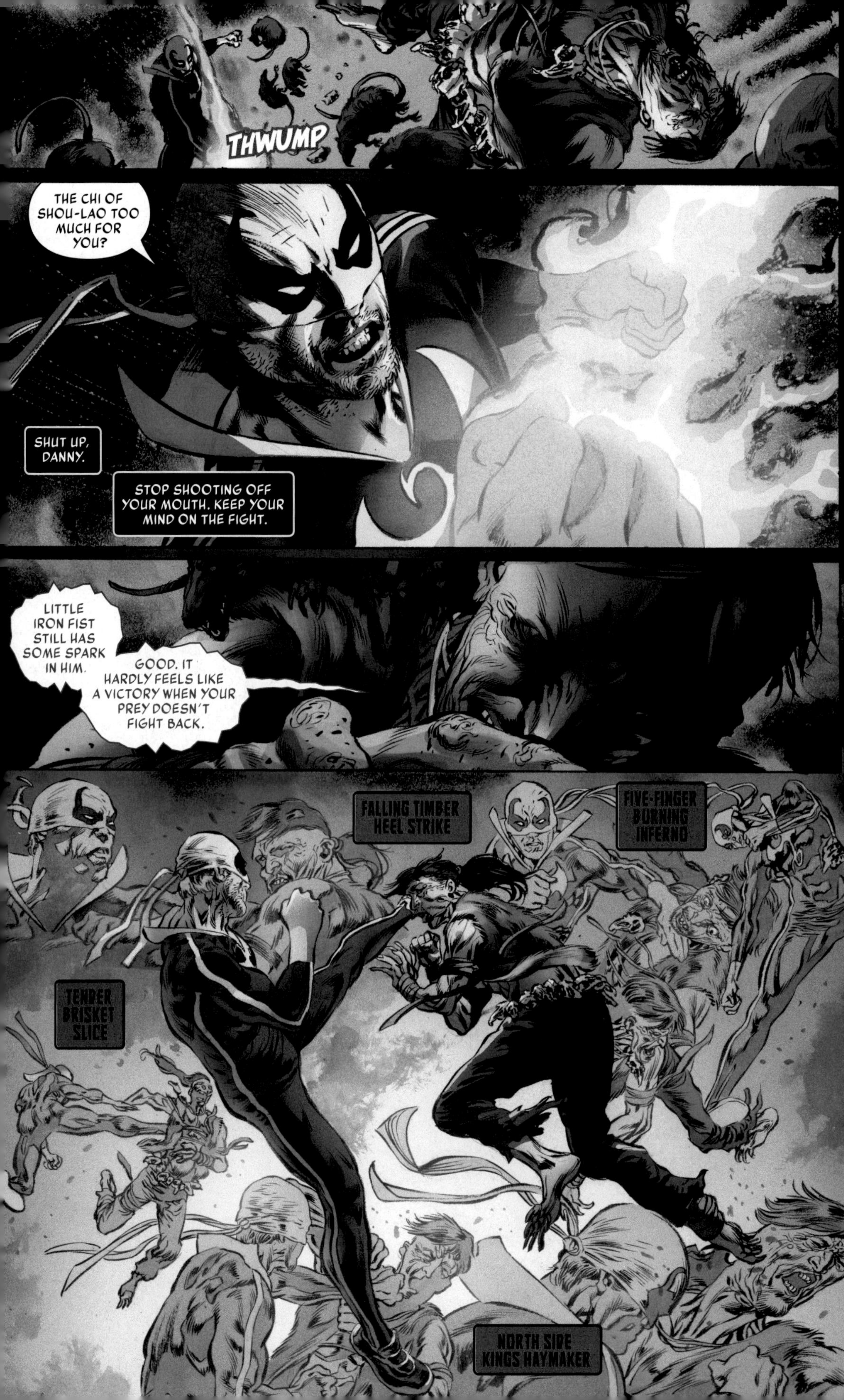
THWUMP
THE CHI OF SHOU-LAO TOO MUCH FOR YOU?
SHUT UP, DANNY.
STOP SHOOTING OFF YOUR MOUTH. KEEP YOUR MIND ON THE FIGHT.
LITTLE IRON FIST STILL HAS SOME SPARK IN HIM.
GOOD. IT HARDLY FEELS LIKE A VICTORY WHEN YOUR PREY DOESN'T FIGHT BACK.
FALLING TIMBER HEEL STRIKE
FIVE-FINGER BURNING INFERNO
TENDER BRISKET SLICE
NORTH SIDE KINGS HAYMAKER

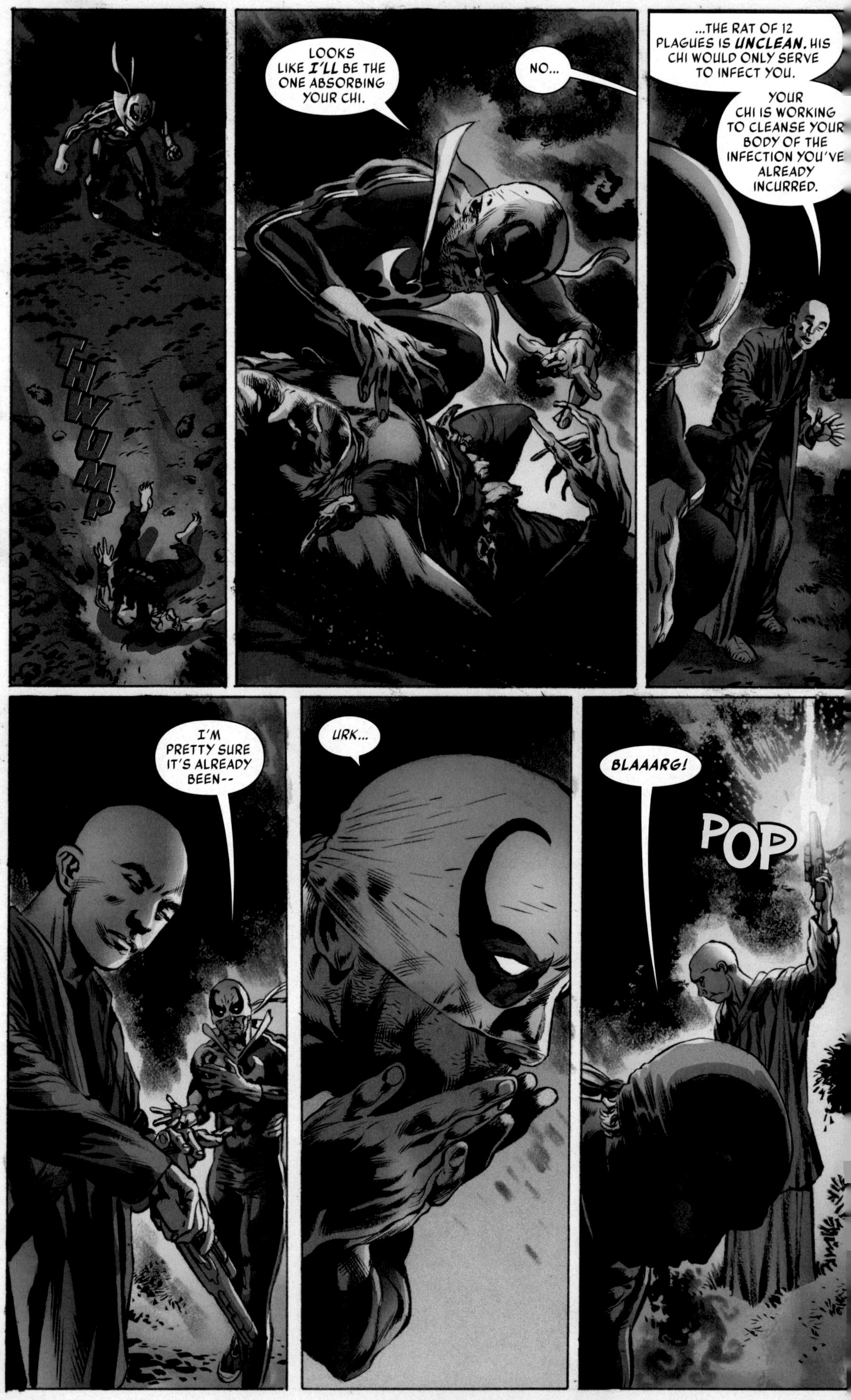
THWUMP
LOOKS LIKE I'LL BE THE ONE ABSORBING YOUR CHI.
NO...
...THE RAT OF 12 PLAGUES IS UNCLEAN. HIS CHI WOULD ONLY SERVE TO INFECT YOU.
YOUR CHI IS WORKING TO CLEANSE YOUR BODY OF THE INFECTION YOU'VE ALREADY INCURRED.
I'M PRETTY SURE IT'S ALREADY BEEN--
URK...
BLAAARG!
POP

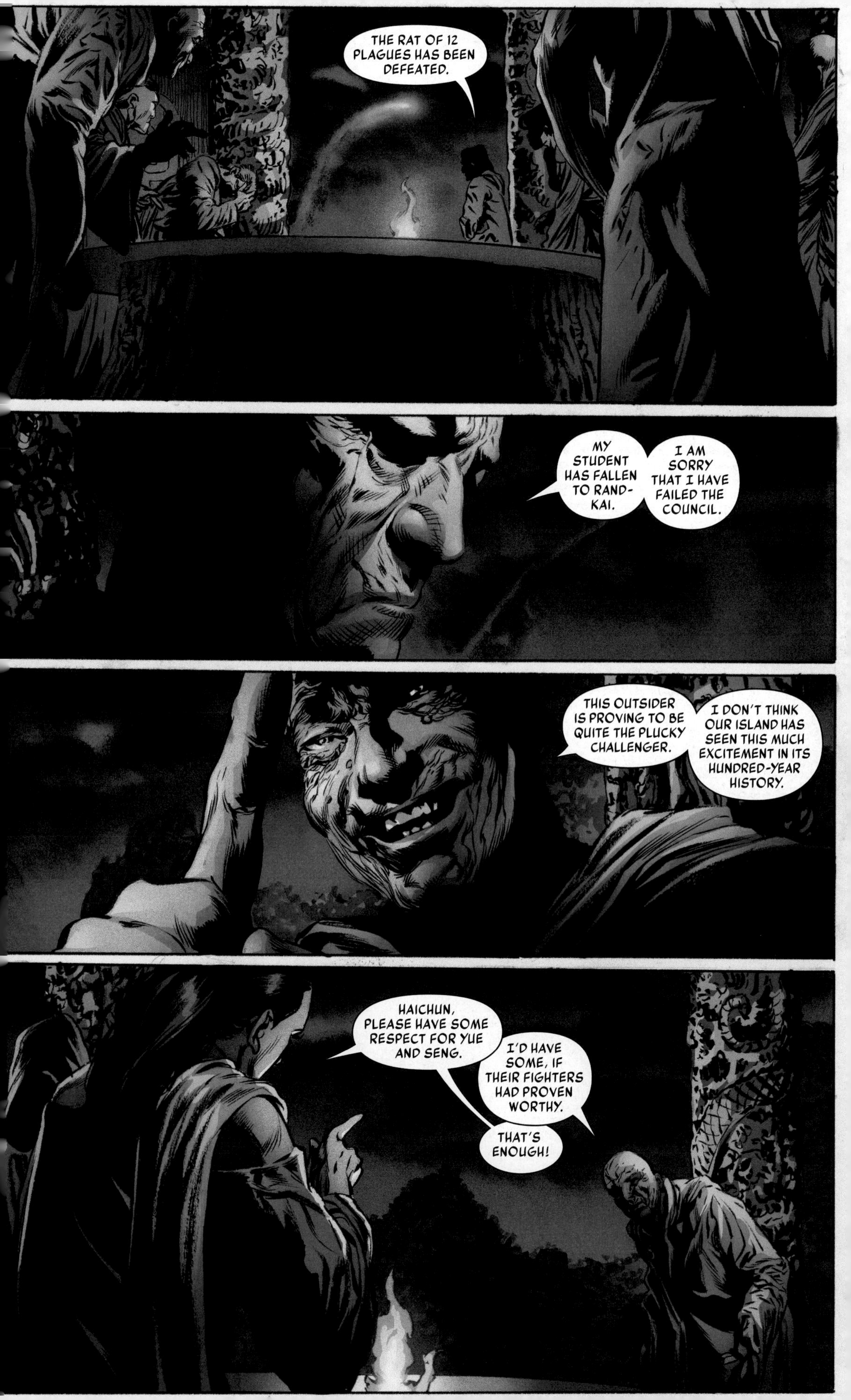
THE RAT OF 12 PLAGUES HAS BEEN DEFEATED.
MY STUDENT HAS FALLEN TO RAND-KAI.
I AM SORRY THAT I HAVE FAILED THE COUNCIL.
THIS OUTSIDER IS PROVING TO BE QUITE THE PLUCKY CHALLENGER.
I DON'T THINK OUR ISLAND HAS SEEN THIS MUCH EXCITEMENT IN ITS HUNDRED-YEAR HISTORY.
HAICHUN, PLEASE HAVE SOME RESPECT FOR YUE AND SENG.
I'D HAVE SOME, IF THEIR FIGHTERS HAD PROVEN WORTHY.
THAT'S ENOUGH!

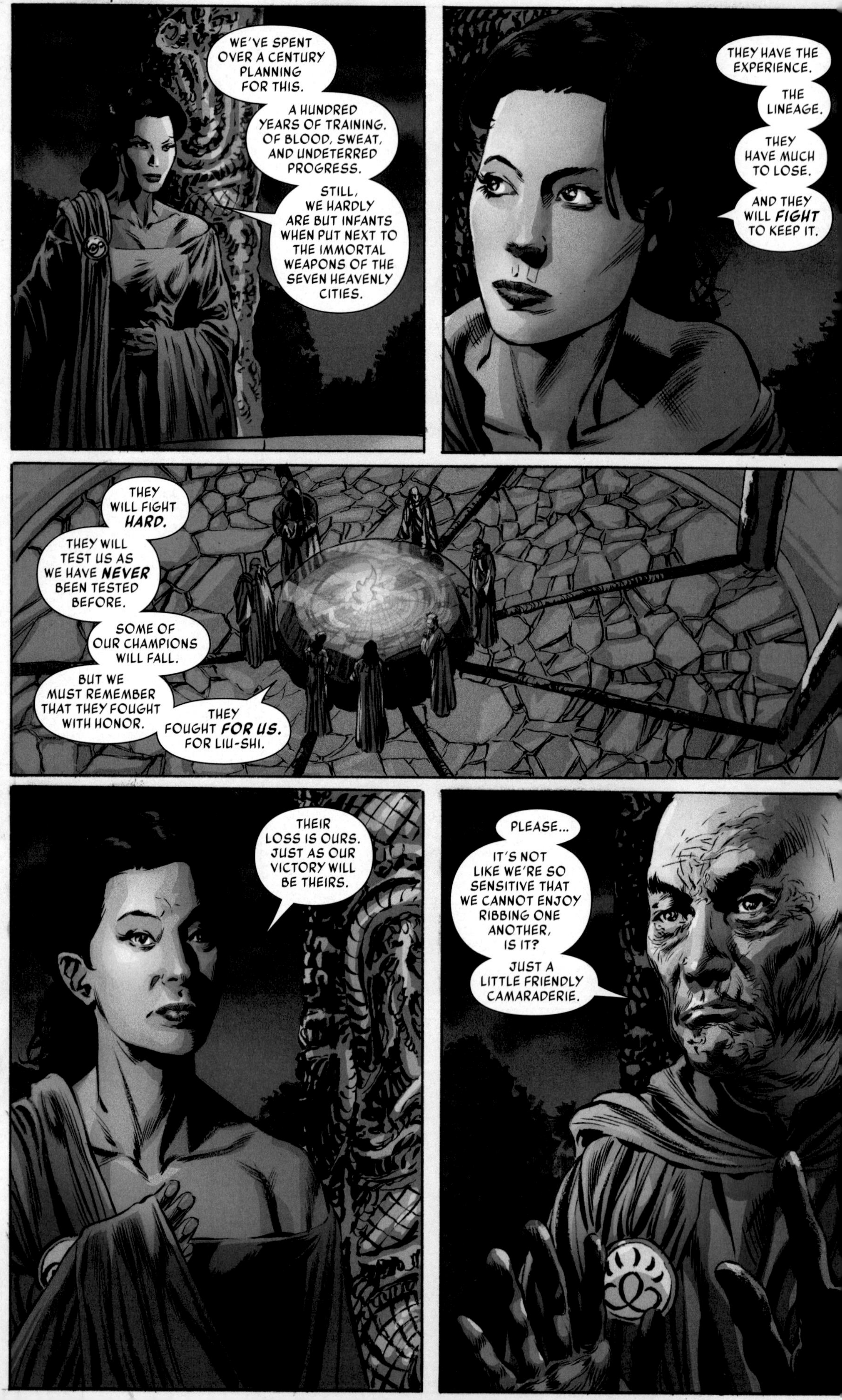
WE'VE SPENT OVER A CENTURY PLANNING FOR THIS.
A HUNDRED YEARS OF TRAINING. OF BLOOD, SWEAT, AND UNDETERRED PROGRESS.
STILL, WE HARDLY ARE BUT INFANTS WHEN PUT NEXT TO THE IMMORTAL WEAPONS OF THE SEVEN HEAVENLY CITIES.
THEY HAVE THE EXPERIENCE.
THE LINEAGE.
THEY HAVE MUCH TO LOSE.
AND THEY WILL FIGHT TO KEEP IT.
THEY WILL FIGHT HARD.
THEY WILL TEST US AS WE HAVE NEVER BEEN TESTED BEFORE.
SOME OF OUR CHAMPIONS WILL FALL.
BUT WE MUST REMEMBER THAT THEY FOUGHT WITH HONOR.
THEY FOUGHT FOR US. FOR LIU-SHI.
THEIR LOSS IS OURS. JUST AS OUR VICTORY WILL BE THEIRS.
PLEASE...
IT'S NOT LIKE WE'RE SO SENSITIVE THAT WE CANNOT ENJOY RIBBING ONE ANOTHER, IS IT?
JUST A LITTLE FRIENDLY CAMARADERIE.

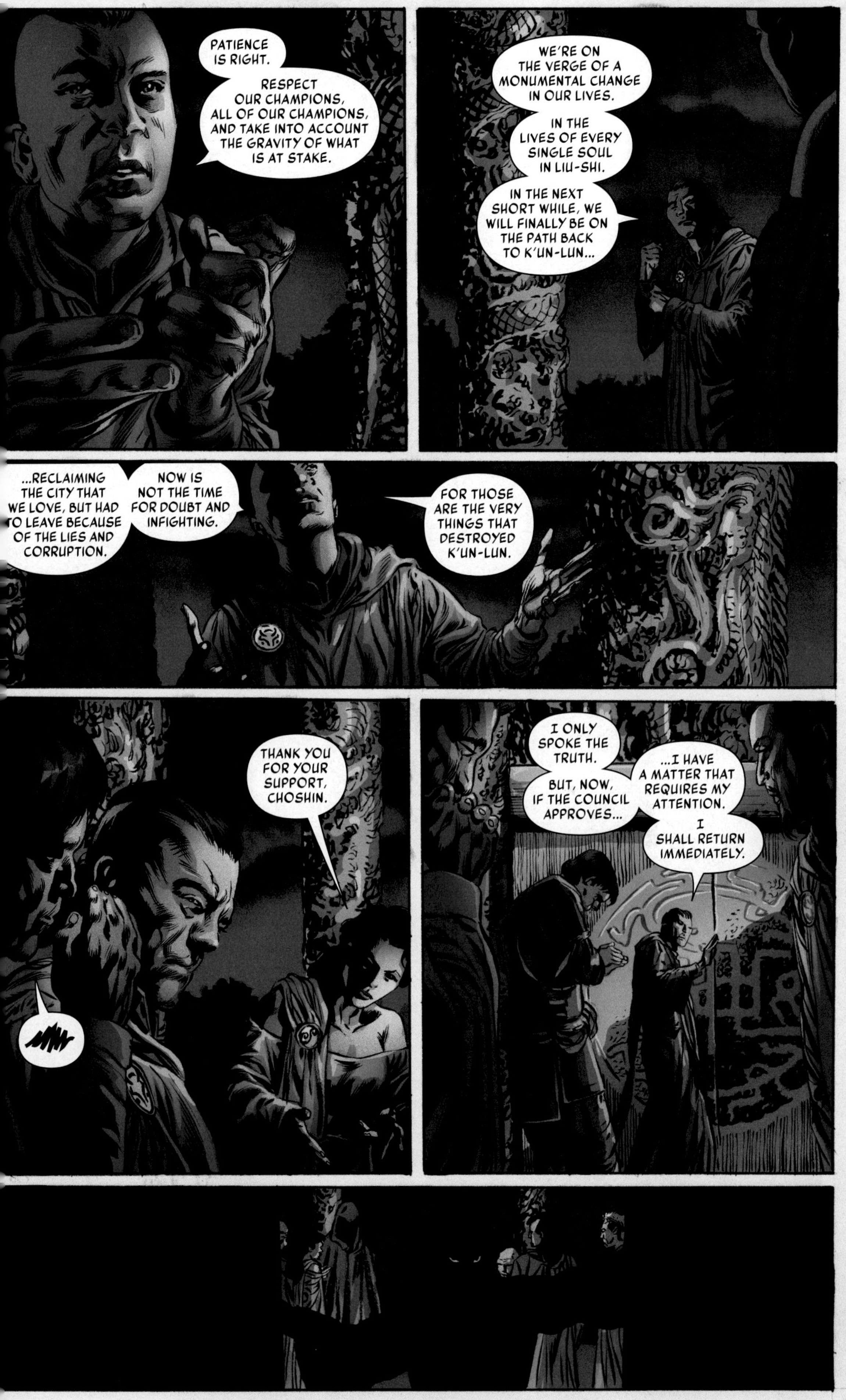
PATIENCE IS RIGHT.
RESPECT OUR CHAMPIONS, ALL OF OUR CHAMPIONS, AND TAKE INTO ACCOUNT THE GRAVITY OF WHAT IS AT STAKE.
WE'RE ON THE VERGE OF A MONUMENTAL CHANGE IN OUR LIVES.
IN THE LIVES OF EVERY SINGLE SOUL IN LIU-SHI.
IN THE NEXT SHORT WHILE, WE WILL FINALLY BE ON THE PATH BACK TO K'UN-LUN...
...RECLAIMING THE CITY THAT WE LOVE, BUT HAD TO LEAVE BECAUSE OF THE LIES AND CORRUPTION.
NOW IS NOT THE TIME FOR DOUBT AND INFIGHTING.
FOR THOSE ARE THE VERY THINGS THAT DESTROYED K'UN-LUN.
THANK YOU FOR YOUR SUPPORT, CHOSHIN.
I ONLY SPOKE THE TRUTH.
BUT, NOW, IF THE COUNCIL APPROVES...
...I HAVE A MATTER THAT REQUIRES MY ATTENTION.
I SHALL RETURN IMMEDIATELY.

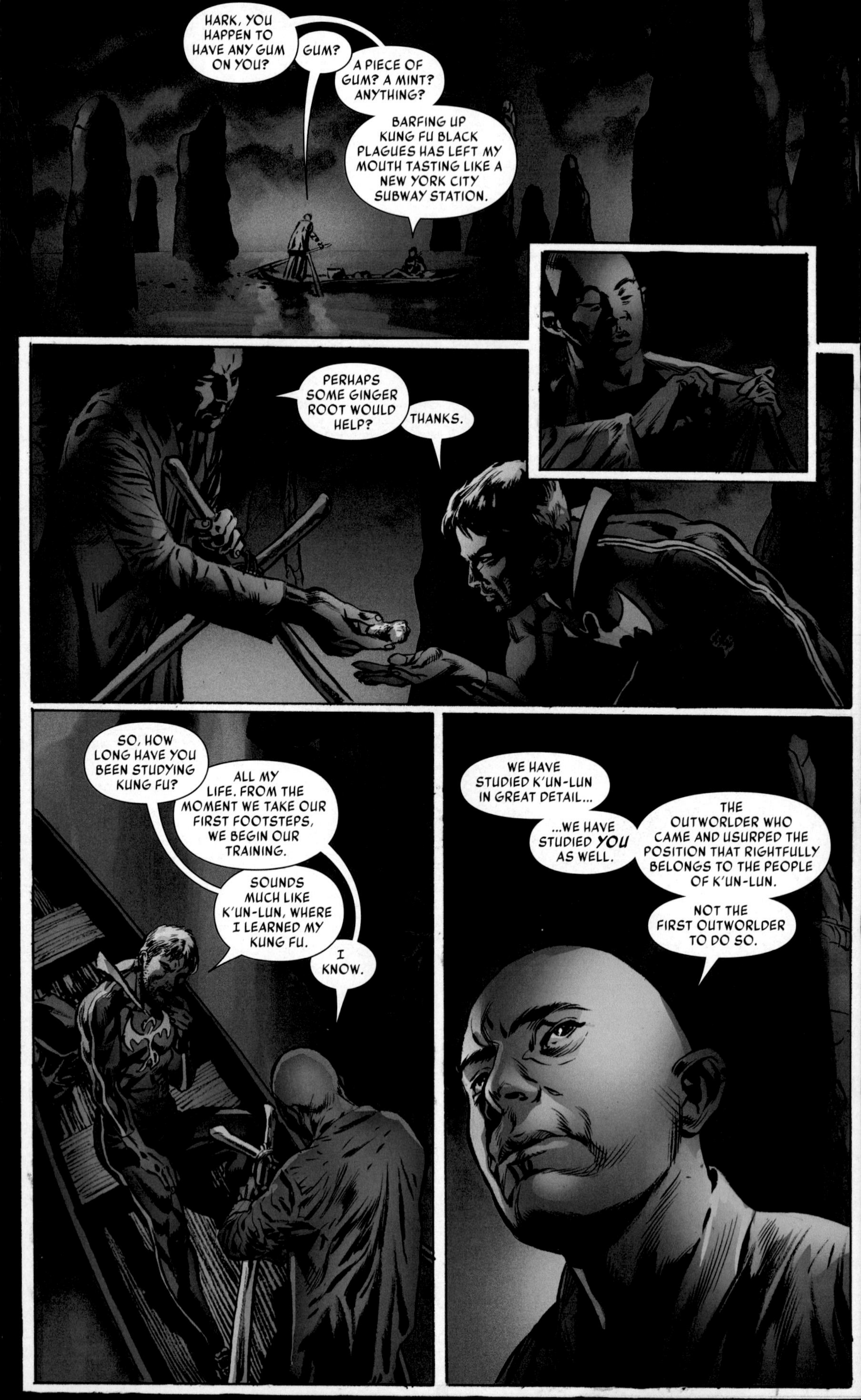
HARK, YOU HAPPEN TO HAVE ANY GUM ON YOU?
GUM?
A PIECE OF GUM? A MINT? ANYTHING?
BARFING UP KUNG FU BLACK PLAGUES HAS LEFT MY MOUTH TASTING LIKE A NEW YORK CITY SUBWAY STATION.
PERHAPS SOME GINGER ROOT WOULD HELP?
THANKS.
SO, HOW LONG HAVE YOU BEEN STUDYING KUNG FU?
ALL MY LIFE. FROM THE MOMENT WE TAKE OUR FIRST FOOTSTEPS, WE BEGIN OUR TRAINING.
SOUNDS MUCH LIKE K'UN-LUN, WHERE I LEARNED MY KUNG FU.
I KNOW.
WE HAVE STUDIED K'UN-LUN IN GREAT DETAIL...
...WE HAVE STUDIED YOU AS WELL.
THE OUTWORLDER WHO CAME AND USURPED THE POSITION THAT RIGHTFULLY BELONGS TO THE PEOPLE OF K'UN-LUN.
NOT THE FIRST OUTWORLDER TO DO SO.

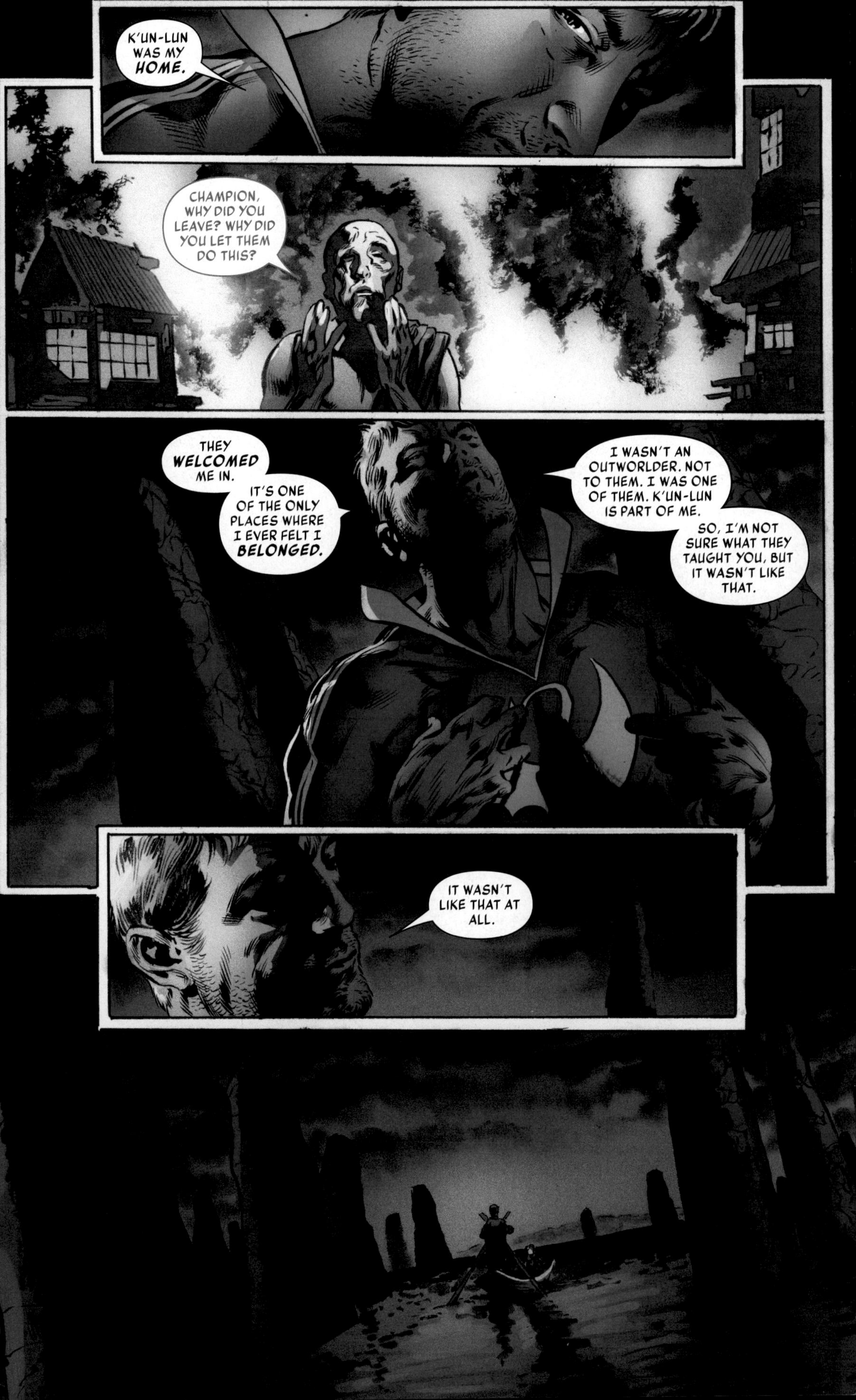
K'UN-LUN WAS MY HOME.
CHAMPION, WHY DID YOU LEAVE? WHY DID YOU LET THEM DO THIS?
THEY WELCOMED ME IN.
IT'S ONE OF THE ONLY PLACES WHERE I EVER FELT I BELONGED.
I WASN'T AN OUTWORLDER. NOT TO THEM. I WAS ONE OF THEM. K'UN-LUN IS PART OF ME.
SO, I'M NOT SURE WHAT THEY TAUGHT YOU, BUT IT WASN'T LIKE THAT.
IT WASN'T LIKE THAT AT ALL.

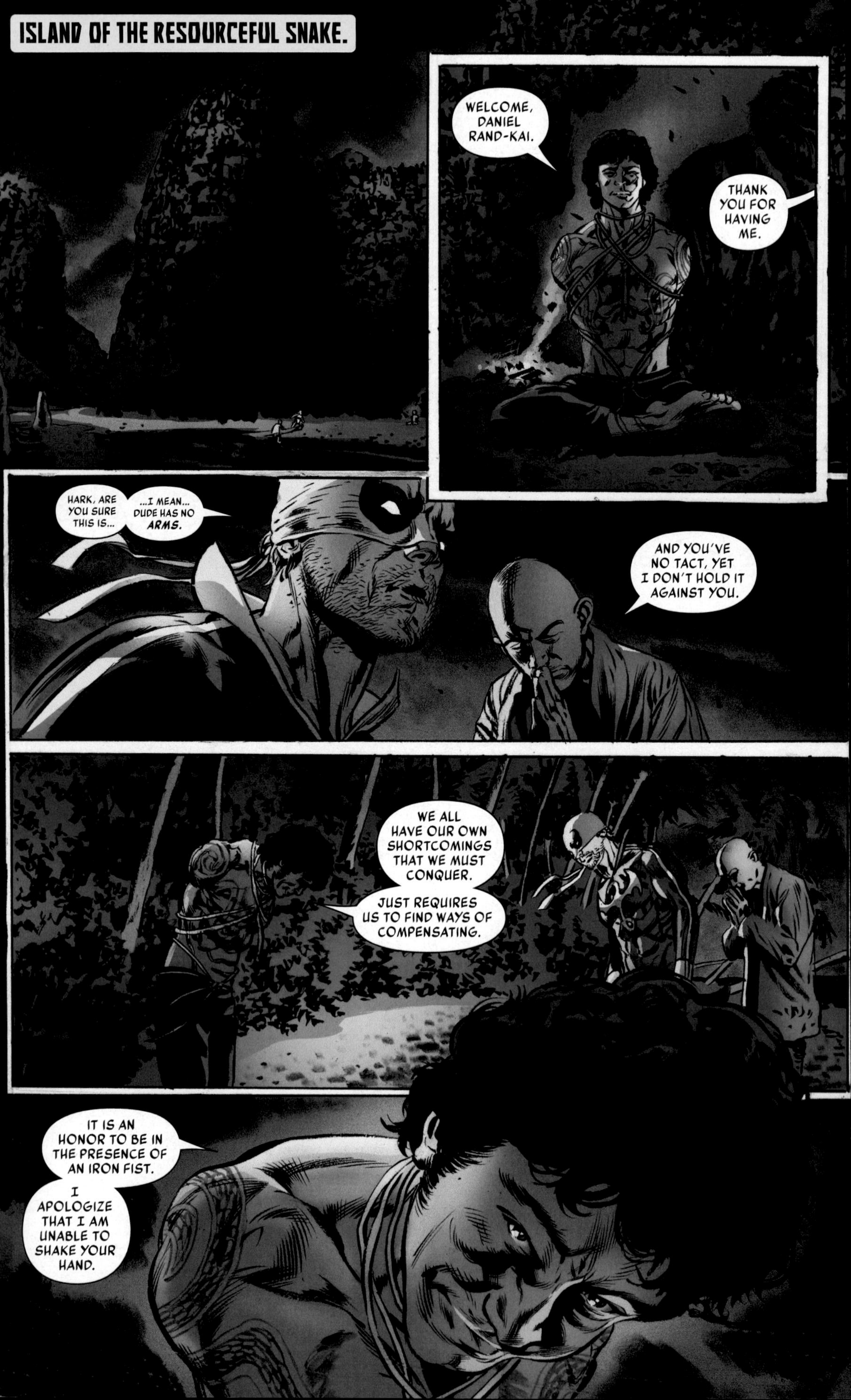
ISLAND OF THE RESOURCEFUL SNAKE.
WELCOME, DANIEL RAND-KAI.
THANK YOU FOR HAVING ME.
HARK, ARE YOU SURE THIS IS...
...I MEAN... DUDE HAS NO ARMS.
AND YOU'VE NO TACT, YET I DON'T HOLD IT AGAINST YOU.
WE ALL HAVE OUR OWN SHORTCOMINGS THAT WE MUST CONQUER.
JUST REQUIRES US TO FIND WAYS OF COMPENSATING.
IT IS AN HONOR TO BE IN THE PRESENCE OF AN IRON FIST.
I APOLOGIZE THAT I AM UNABLE TO SHAKE YOUR HAND.

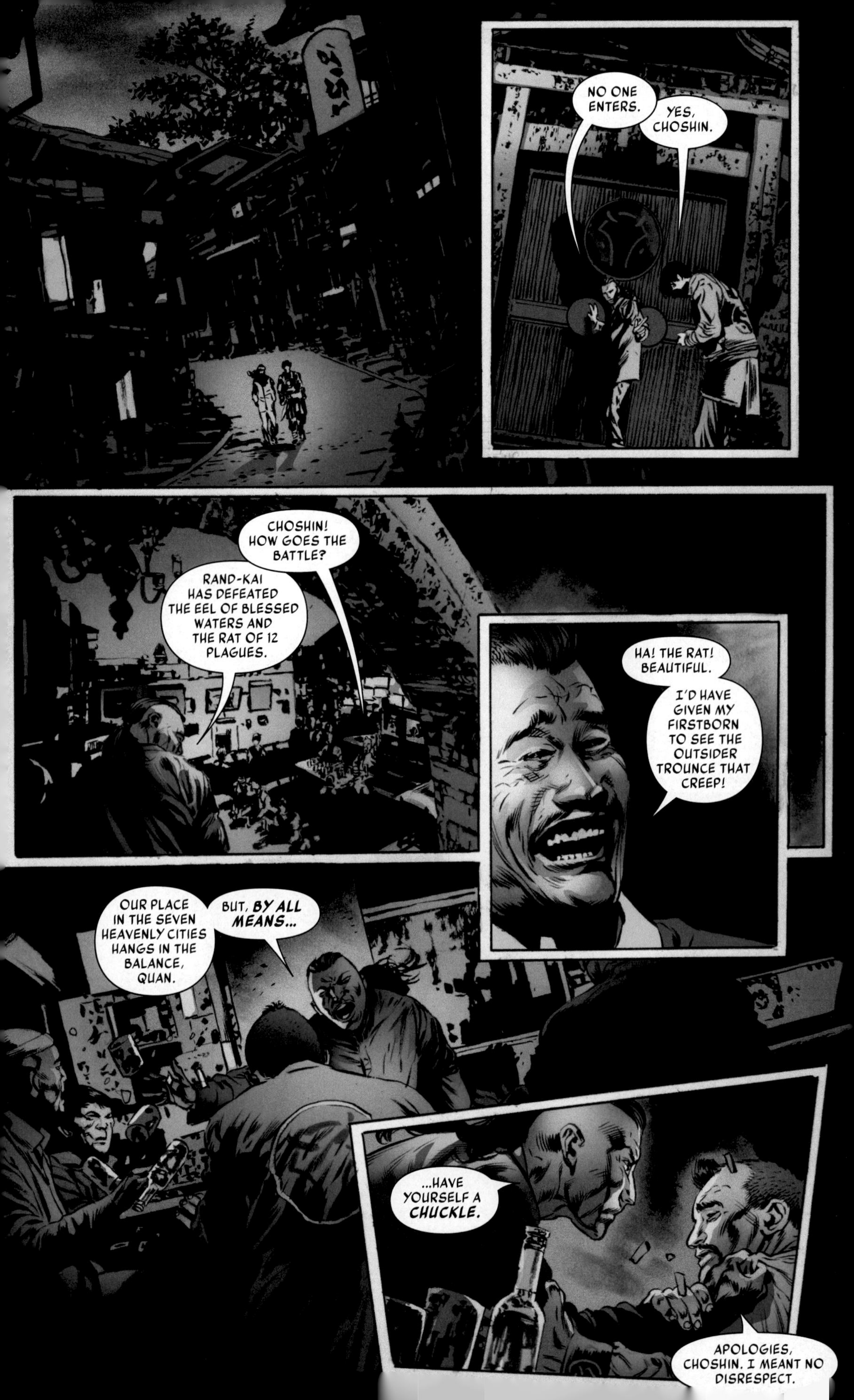
NO ONE ENTERS.
YES, CHOSHIN.
CHOSHIN! HOW GOES THE BATTLE?
RAND-KAI HAS DEFEATED THE EEL OF BLESSED WATERS AND THE RAT OF 12 PLAGUES.
HA! THE RAT! BEAUTIFUL.
I'D HAVE GIVEN MY FIRSTBORN TO SEE THE OUTSIDER TROUNCE THAT CREEP!
OUR PLACE IN THE SEVEN HEAVENLY CITIES HANGS IN THE BALANCE, QUAN.
BUT, BY ALL MEANS...
...HAVE YOURSELF A CHUCKLE.
APOLOGIES, CHOSHIN. I MEANT NO DISRESPECT.

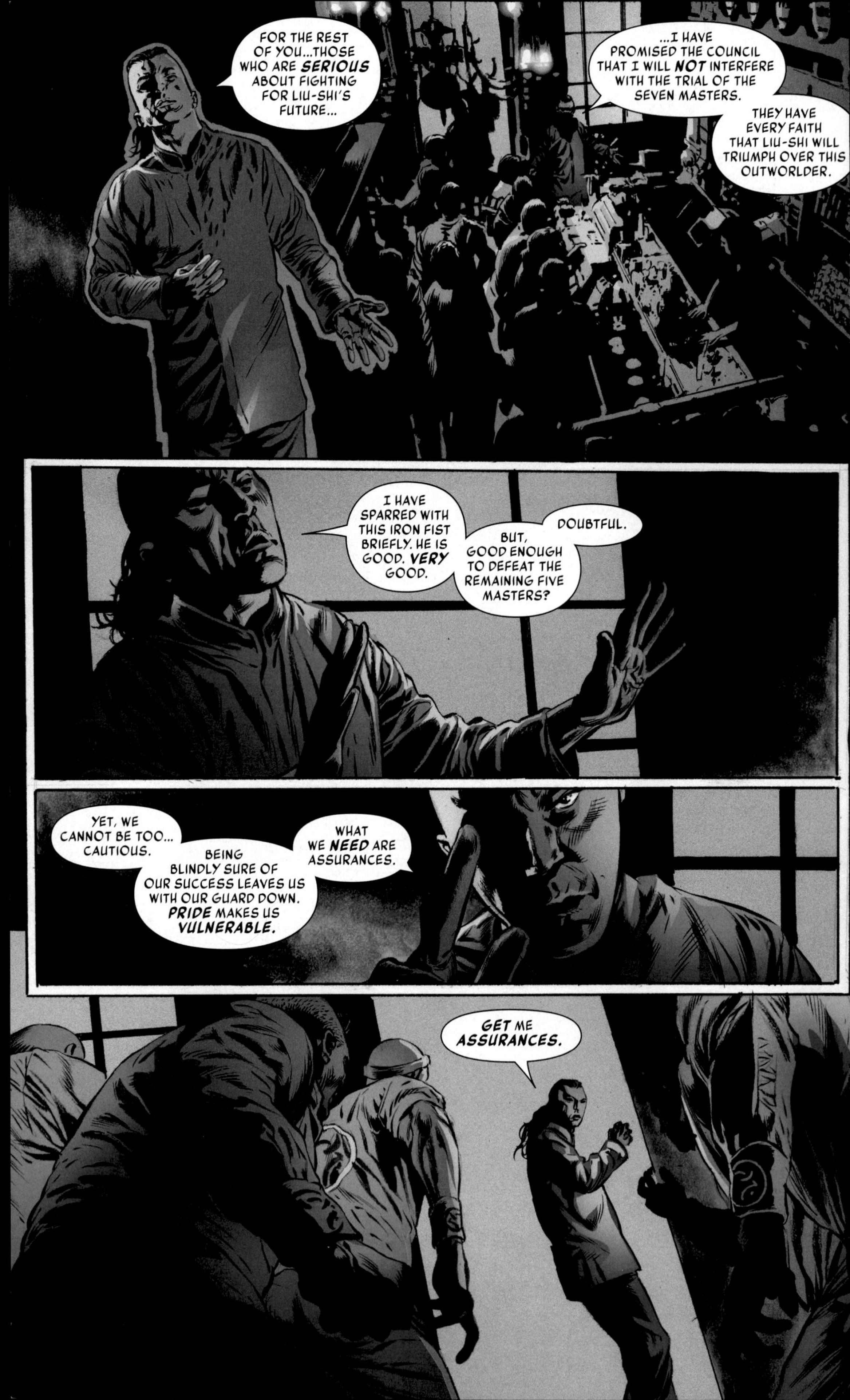
FOR THE REST OF YOU...THOSE WHO ARE SERIOUS ABOUT FIGHTING FOR LIU-SHI'S FUTURE...
...I HAVE PROMISED THE COUNCIL THAT I WILL NOT INTERFERE WITH THE TRIAL OF THE SEVEN MASTERS.
THEY HAVE EVERY FAITH THAT LIU-SHI WILL TRIUMPH OVER THIS OUTWORLDER.
I HAVE SPARRED WITH THIS IRON FIST BRIEFLY. HE IS GOOD. VERY GOOD.
BUT, GOOD ENOUGH TO DEFEAT THE REMAINING FIVE MASTERS?
DOUBTFUL.
YET, WE CANNOT BE TOO... CAUTIOUS.
BEING BLINDLY SURE OF OUR SUCCESS LEAVES US WITH OUR GUARD DOWN. PRIDE MAKES US VULNERABLE.
WHAT WE NEED ARE ASSURANCES.
GET ME ASSURANCES.

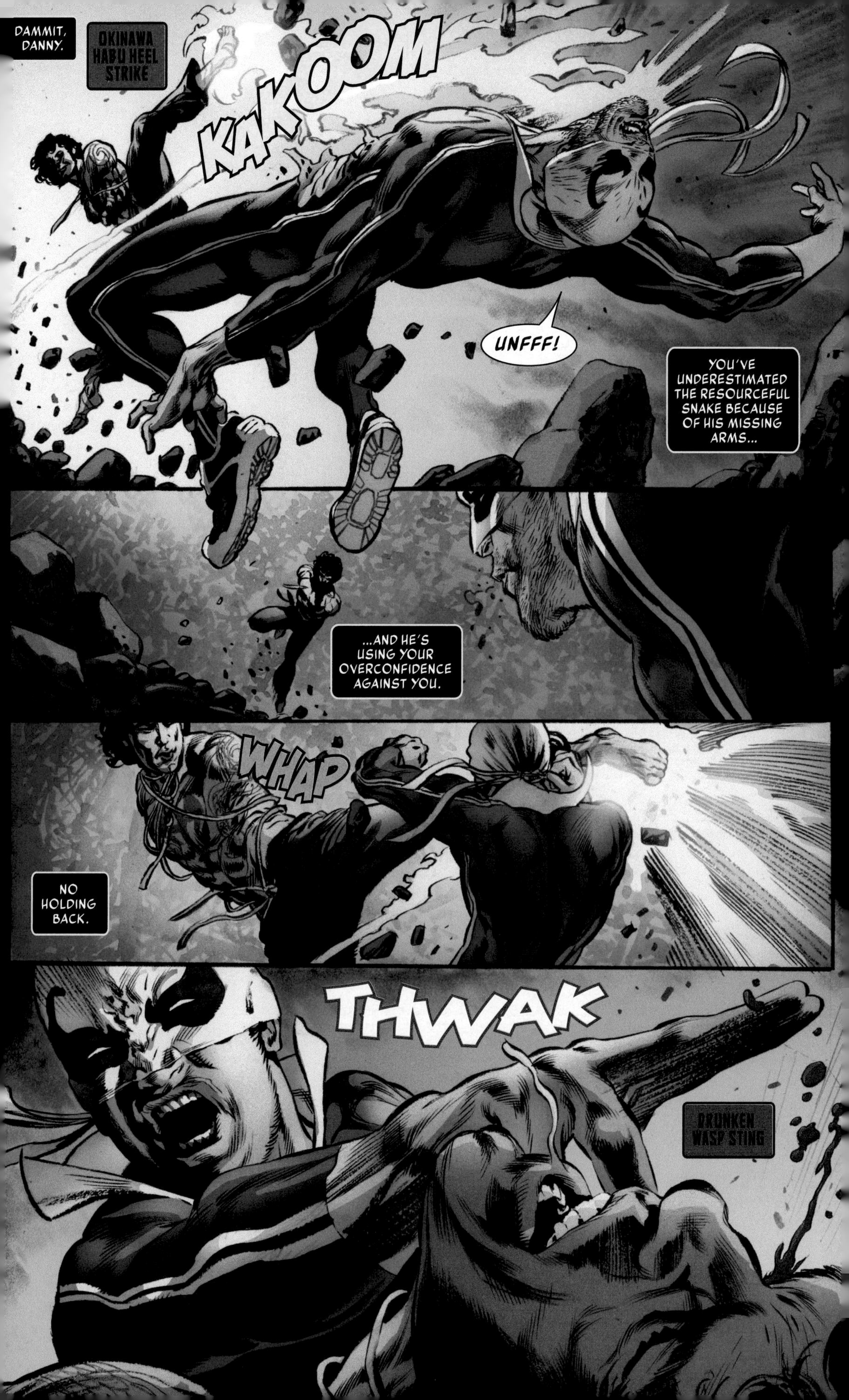
DAMMIT, DANNY.
OKINAWA HABU HEEL STRIKE
KAKOOM
UNFFF!
YOU'VE UNDERESTIMATED THE RESOURCEFUL SNAKE BECAUSE OF HIS MISSING ARMS...
...AND HE'S USING YOUR OVERCONFIDENCE AGAINST YOU.
WHAP
NO HOLDING BACK.
THWAK
DRUNKEN WASP STING

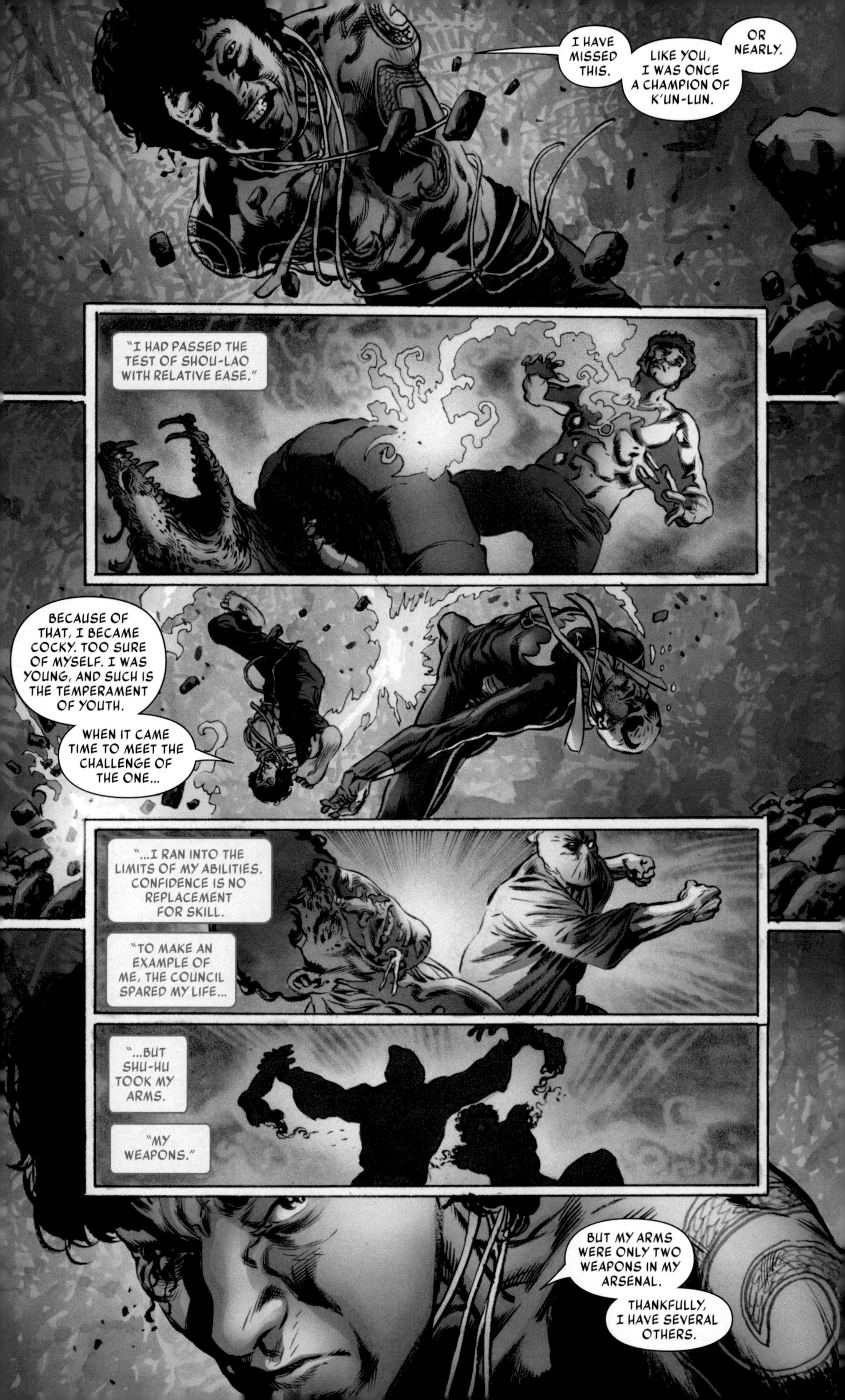
I HAVE MISSED THIS.
LIKE YOU, I WAS ONCE A CHAMPION OF K'UN-LUN.
OR NEARLY.
"I HAD PASSED THE TEST OF SHOU-LAO WITH RELATIVE EASE."
BECAUSE OF THAT, I BECAME COCKY. TOO SURE OF MYSELF. I WAS YOUNG, AND SUCH IS THE TEMPERAMENT OF YOUTH.
WHEN IT CAME TIME TO MEET THE CHALLENGE OF THE ONE...
"...I RAN INTO THE LIMITS OF MY ABILITIES. CONFIDENCE IS NO REPLACEMENT FOR SKILL.
"TO MAKE AN EXAMPLE OF ME, THE COUNCIL SPARED MY LIFE...
"...BUT SHU-HU TOOK MY ARMS.
"MY WEAPONS."
BUT MY ARMS WERE ONLY TWO WEAPONS IN MY ARSENAL.
THANKFULLY, I HAVE SEVERAL OTHERS.

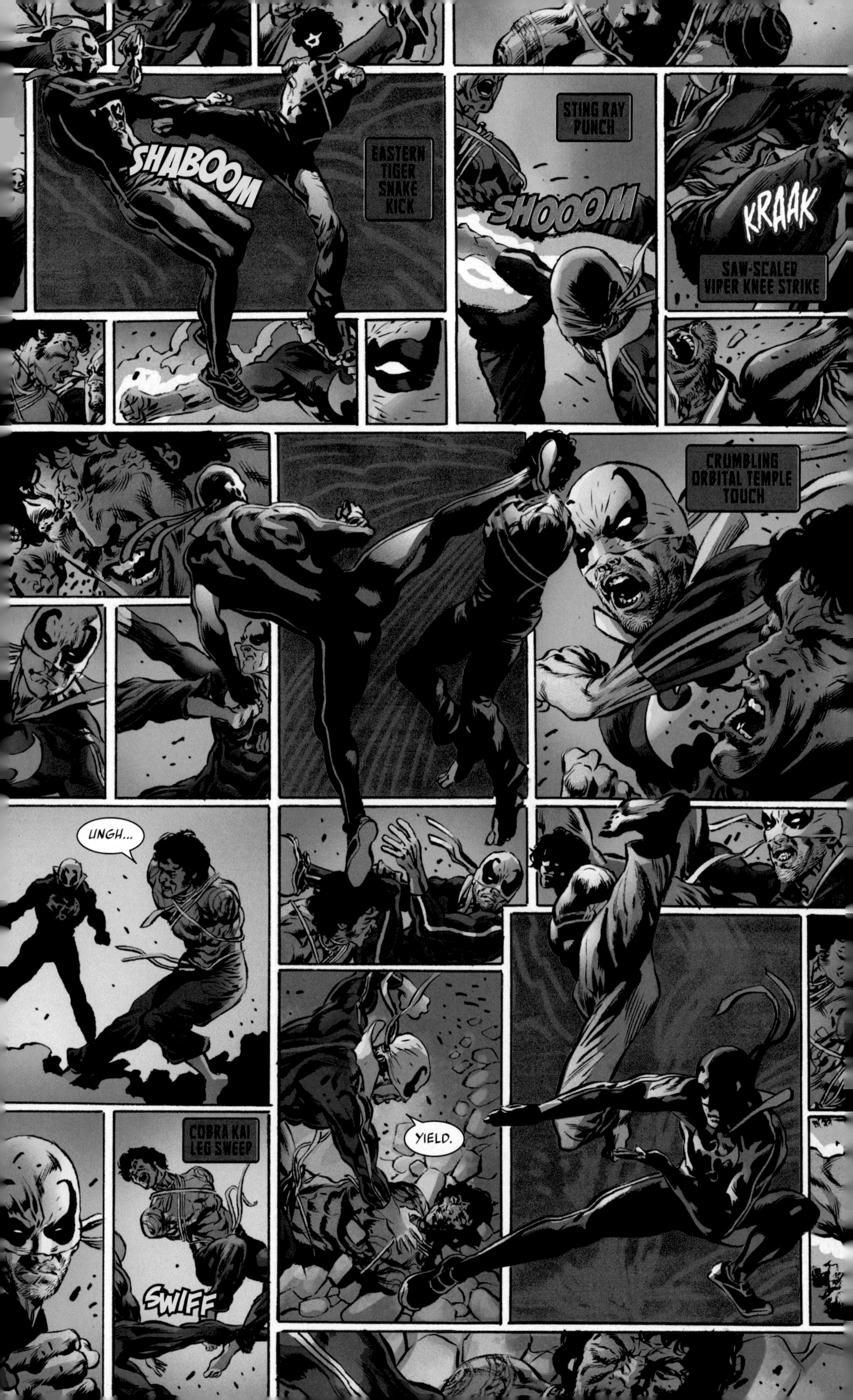
SHABOOM
EASTERN TIGER SNAKE KICK
STING RAY PUNCH
SHOOOM
KRAAK
SAW-SCALED VIPER KNEE STRIKE
CRUMBLING ORBITAL TEMPLE TOUCH
UNGH...
COBRA KAI LEG SWEEP
YIELD.
SWIFF

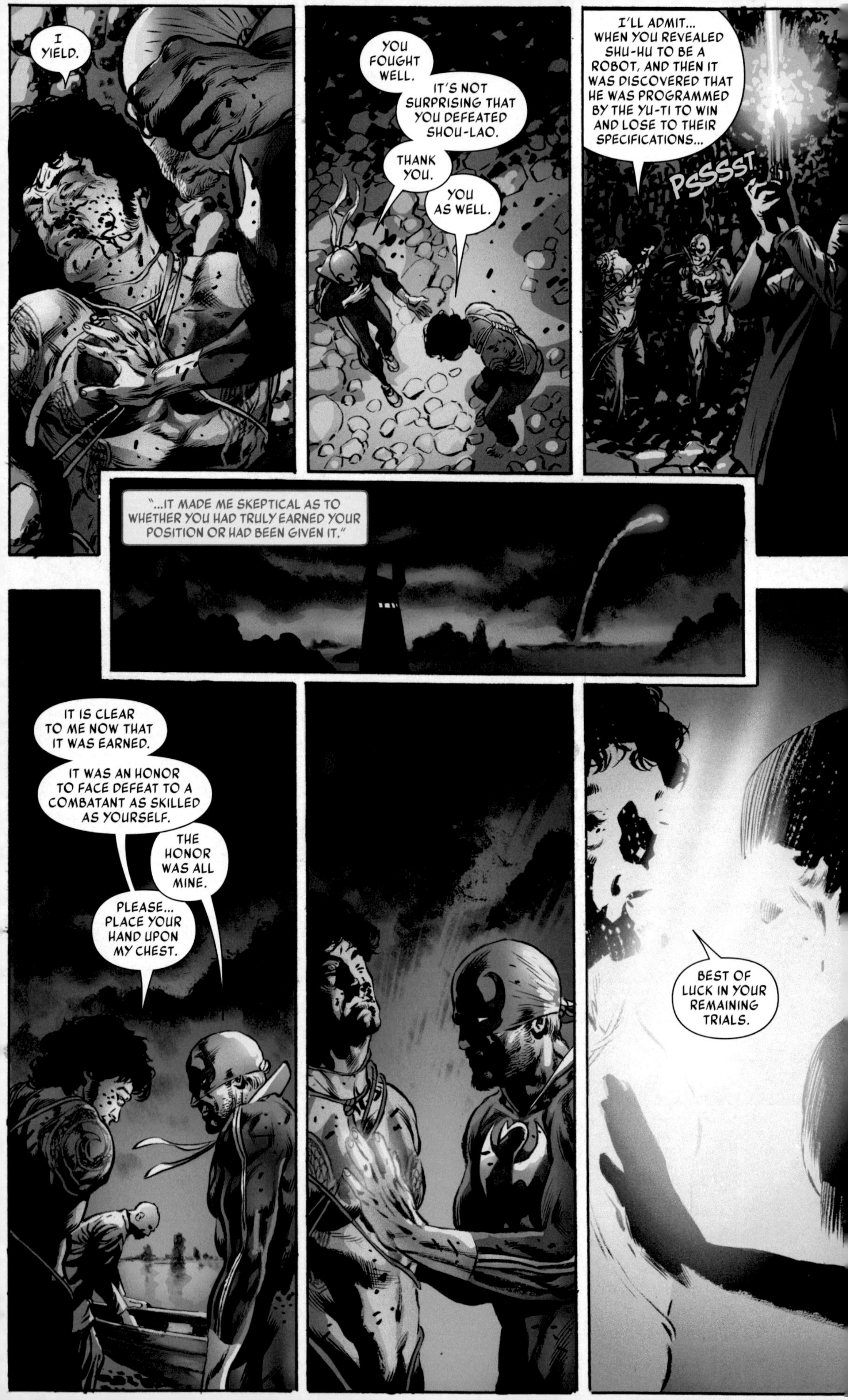
I YIELD.
YOU FOUGHT WELL.
IT'S NOT SURPRISING THAT YOU DEFEATED SHOU-LAO.
THANK YOU.
YOU AS WELL.
I'LL ADMIT... WHEN YOU REVEALED SHU-HU TO BE A ROBOT, AND THEN IT WAS DISCOVERED THAT HE WAS PROGRAMMED BY THE YU-TI TO WIN AND LOSE TO THEIR SPECIFICATIONS...
PSSSST
"...IT MADE ME SKEPTICAL AS TO WHETHER YOU HAD TRULY EARNED YOUR POSITION OR HAD BEEN GIVEN IT."
IT IS CLEAR TO ME NOW THAT IT WAS EARNED.
IT WAS AN HONOR TO FACE DEFEAT TO A COMBATANT AS SKILLED AS YOURSELF.
THE HONOR WAS ALL MINE.
PLEASE... PLACE YOUR HAND UPON MY CHEST.
BEST OF LUCK IN YOUR REMAINING TRIALS.

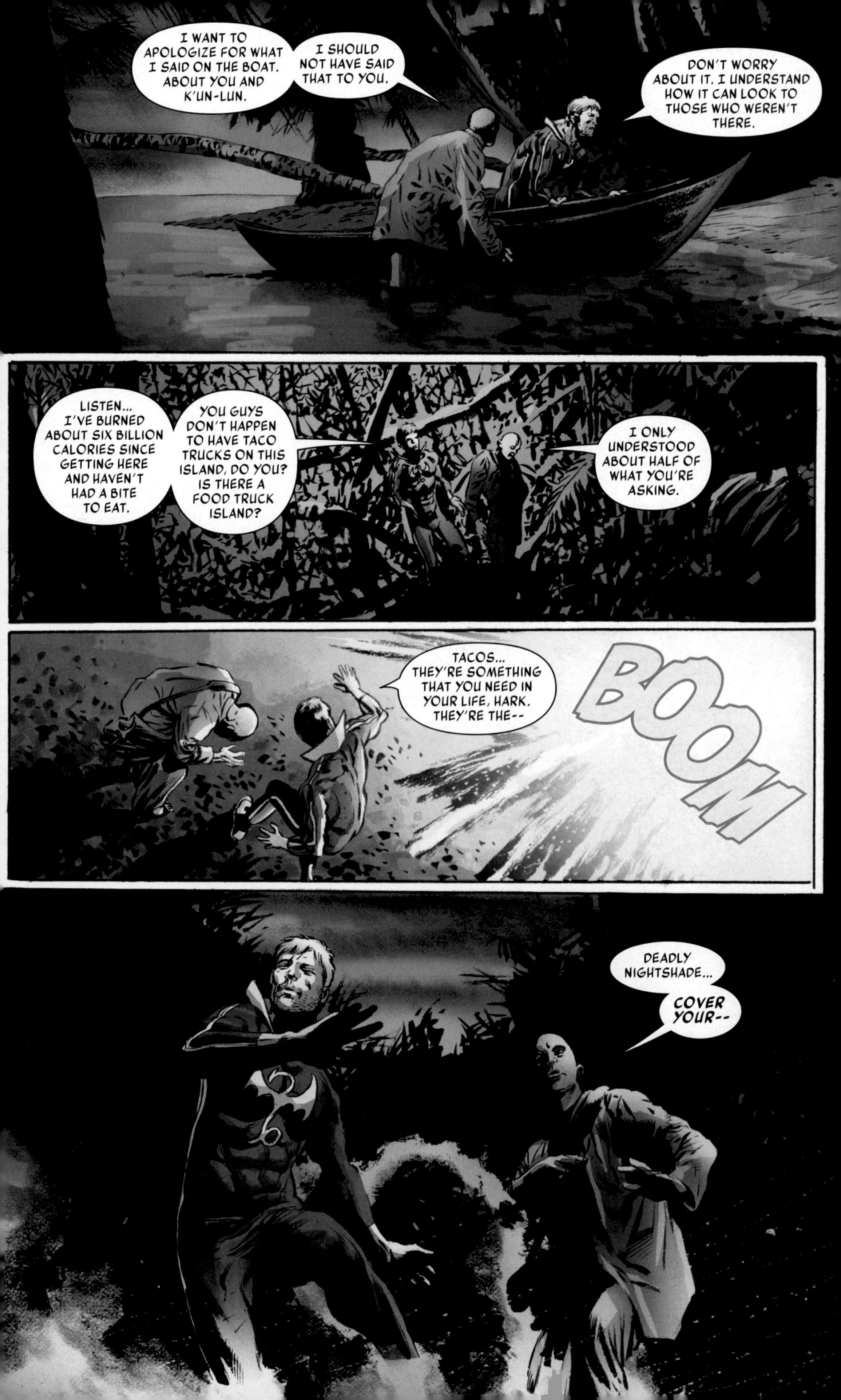
I WANT TO APOLOGIZE FOR WHAT I SAID ON THE BOAT. ABOUT YOU AND K'UN-LUN.
I SHOULD NOT HAVE SAID THAT TO YOU.
DON'T WORRY ABOUT IT. I UNDERSTAND HOW IT CAN LOOK TO THOSE WHO WEREN'T THERE.
LISTEN... I'VE BURNED ABOUT SIX BILLION CALORIES SINCE GETTING HERE AND HAVEN'T HAD A BITE TO EAT.
YOU GUYS DON'T HAPPEN TO HAVE TACO TRUCKS ON THIS ISLAND, DO YOU? IS THERE A FOOD TRUCK ISLAND?
I ONLY UNDERSTOOD ABOUT HALF OF WHAT YOU'RE ASKING.
TACOS... THEY'RE SOMETHING THAT YOU NEED IN YOUR LIFE, HARK. THEY'RE THE--
BOOM
DEADLY NIGHTSHADE...
COVER YOUR--

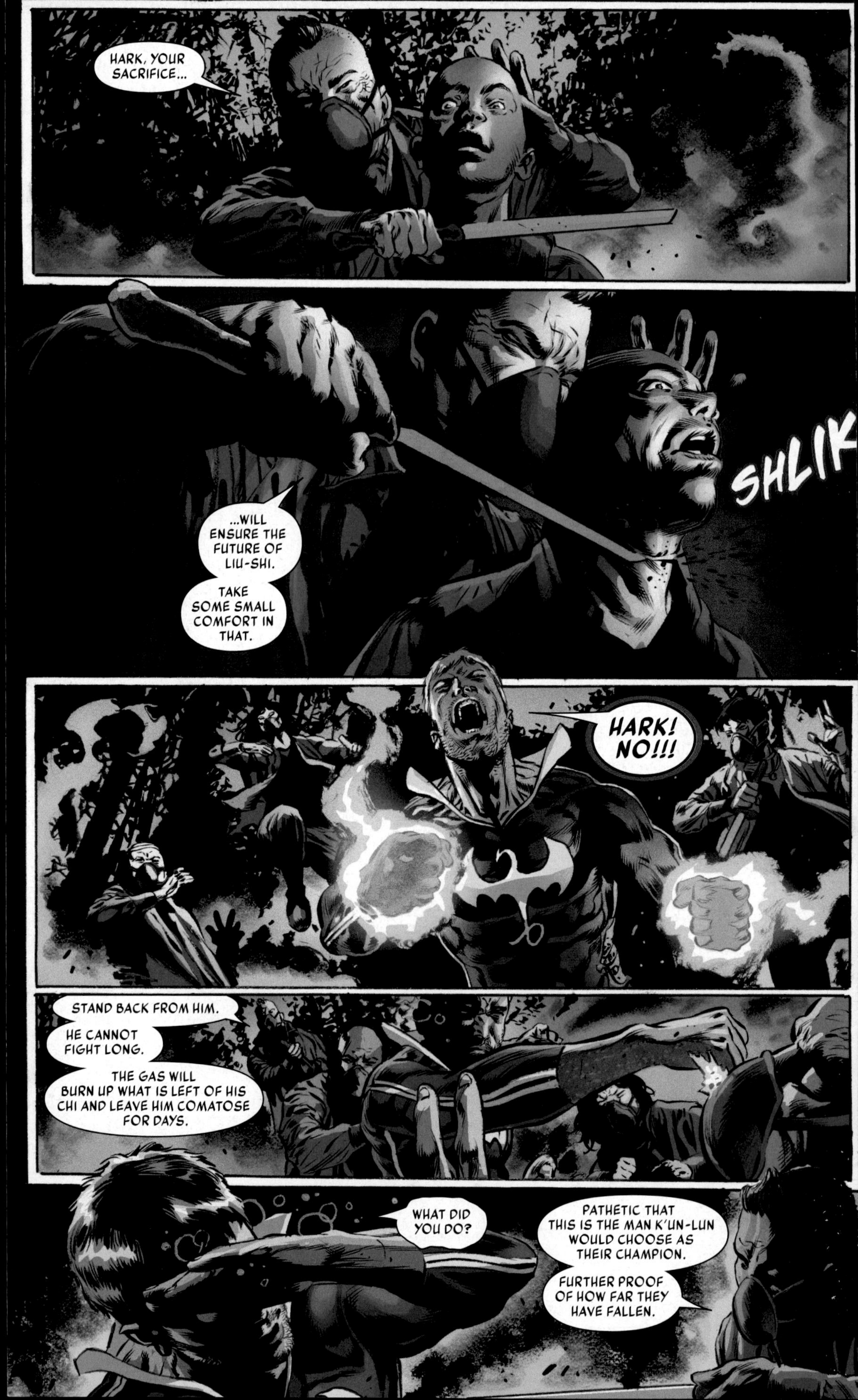
HARK, YOUR SACRIFICE...
...WILL ENSURE THE FUTURE OF LIU-SHI.
TAKE SOME SMALL COMFORT IN THAT.
SHLIK
HARK! NO!!!
STAND BACK FROM HIM.
HE CANNOT FIGHT LONG.
THE GAS WILL BURN UP WHAT IS LEFT OF HIS CHI AND LEAVE HIM COMATOSE FOR DAYS.
WHAT DID YOU DO?
PATHETIC THAT THIS IS THE MAN K'UN-LUN WOULD CHOOSE AS THEIR CHAMPION.
FURTHER PROOF OF HOW FAR THEY HAVE FALLEN.

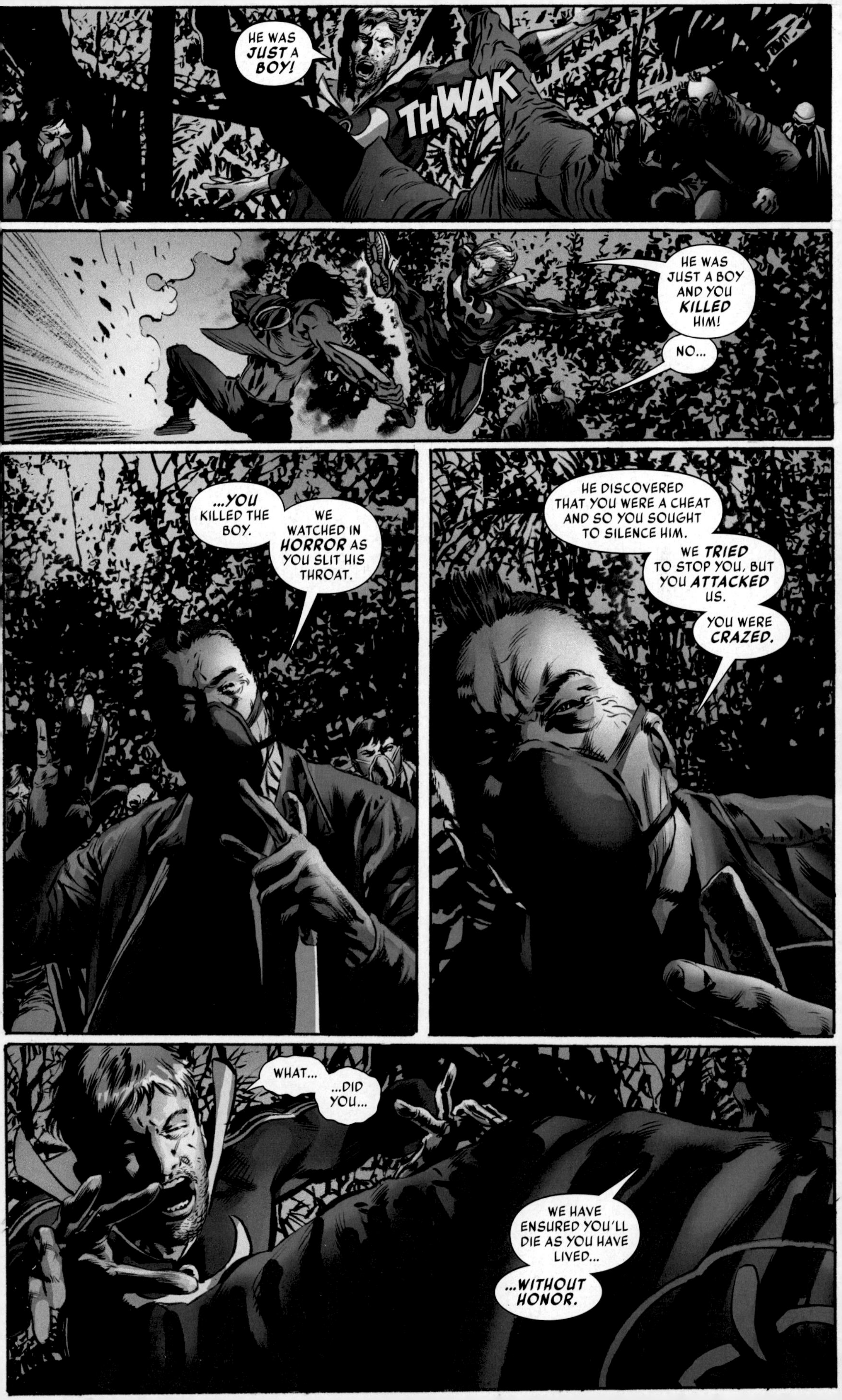

HE WAS JUST A BOY!
THWAK
HE WAS JUST A BOY AND YOU KILLED HIM!
NO...
...YOU KILLED THE BOY.
WE WATCHED IN HORROR AS YOU SLIT HIS THROAT.
HE DISCOVERED THAT YOU WERE A CHEAT AND SO YOU SOUGHT TO SILENCE HIM.
WE TRIED TO STOP YOU, BUT YOU ATTACKED US.
YOU WERE CRAZED.
WHAT...
...DID YOU...
WE HAVE ENSURED YOU'LL DIE AS YOU HAVE LIVED...
...WITHOUT HONOR.

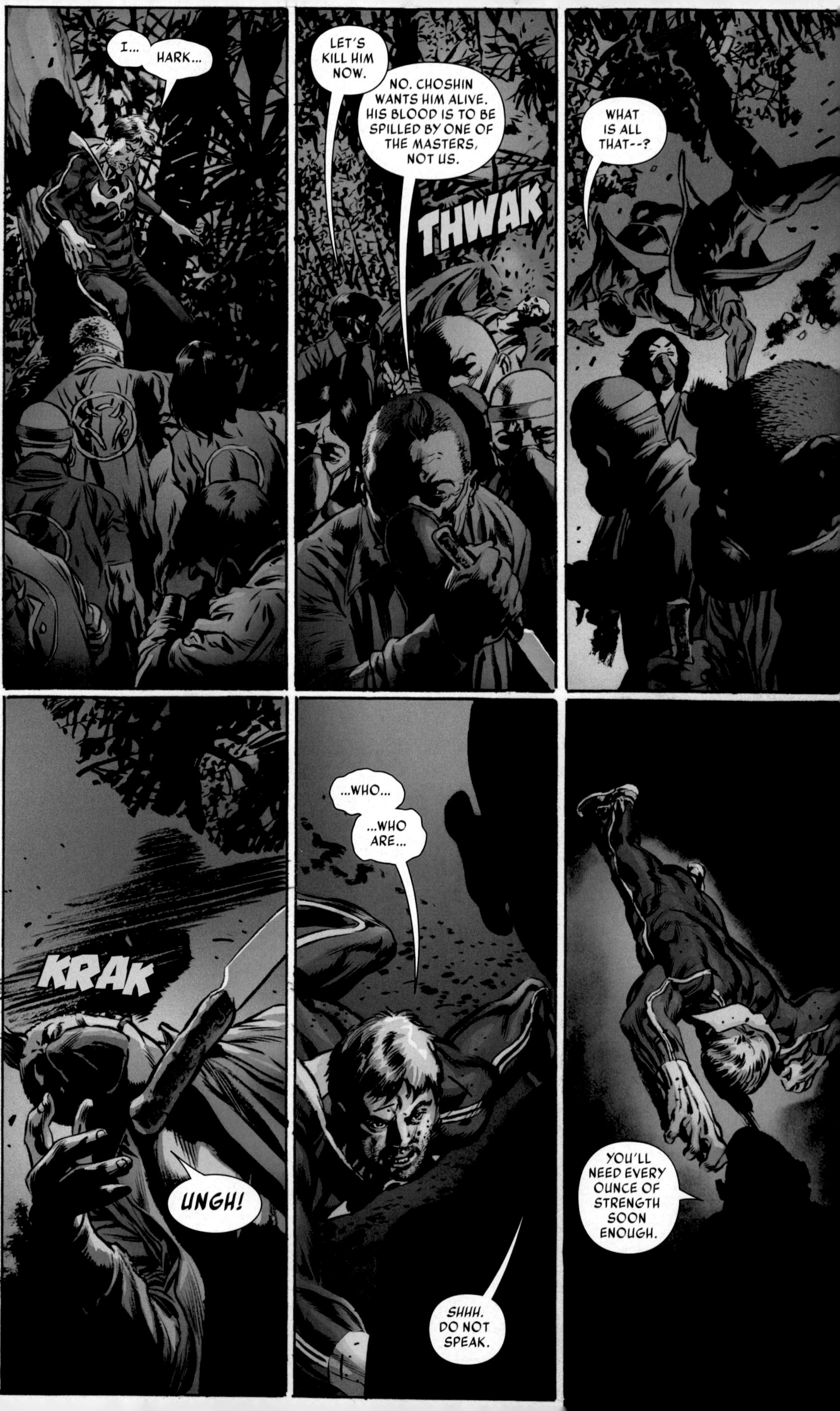
I...
HARK...
LET'S KILL HIM NOW.
NO. CHOSHIN WANTS HIM ALIVE. HIS BLOOD IS TO BE SPILLED BY ONE OF THE MASTERS, NOT US.
THWAK
WHAT IS ALL THAT--?
KRAK
UNGH!
...WHO...
...WHO ARE...
SHHH. DO NOT SPEAK.
YOU'LL NEED EVERY OUNCE OF STRENGTH SOON ENOUGH.

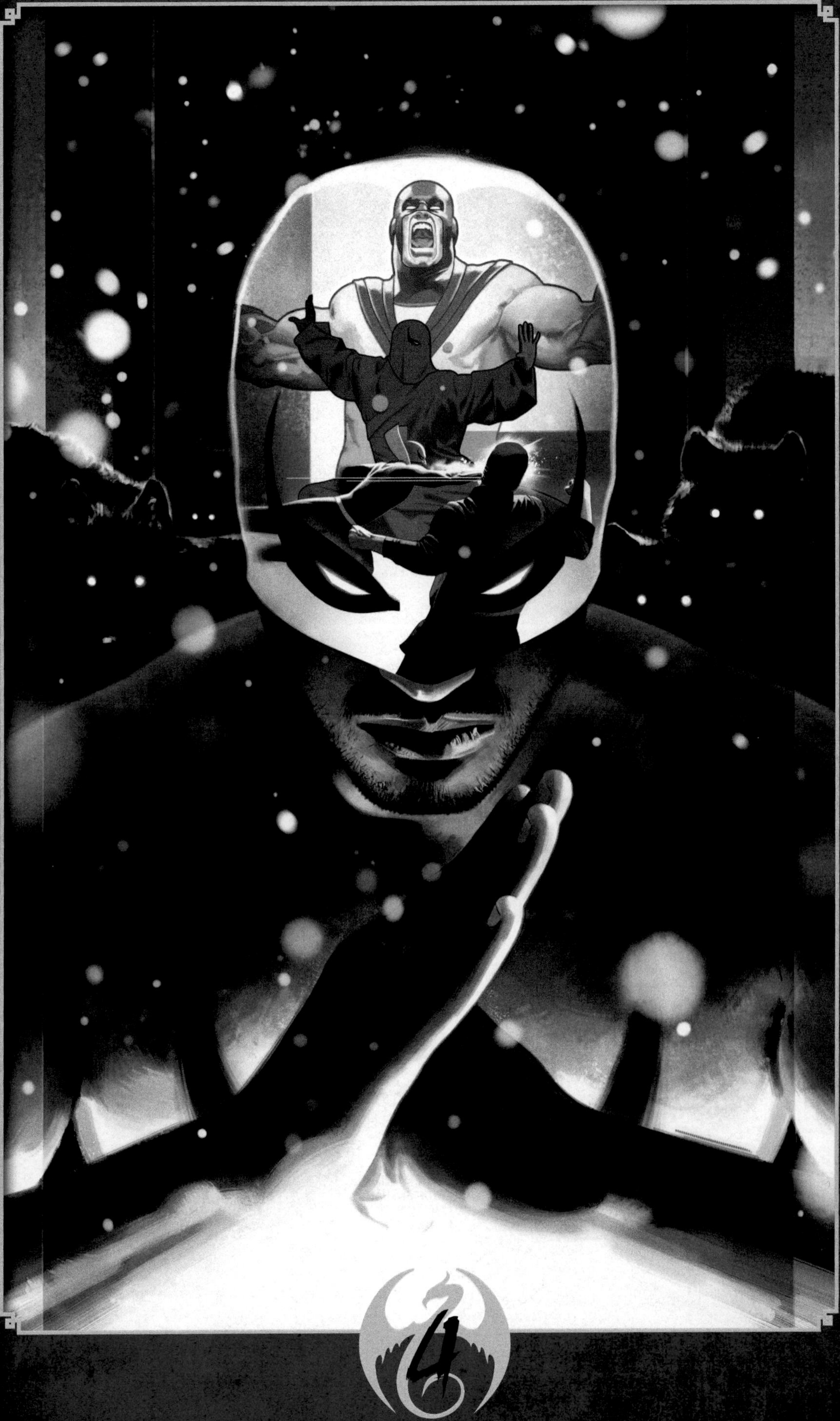

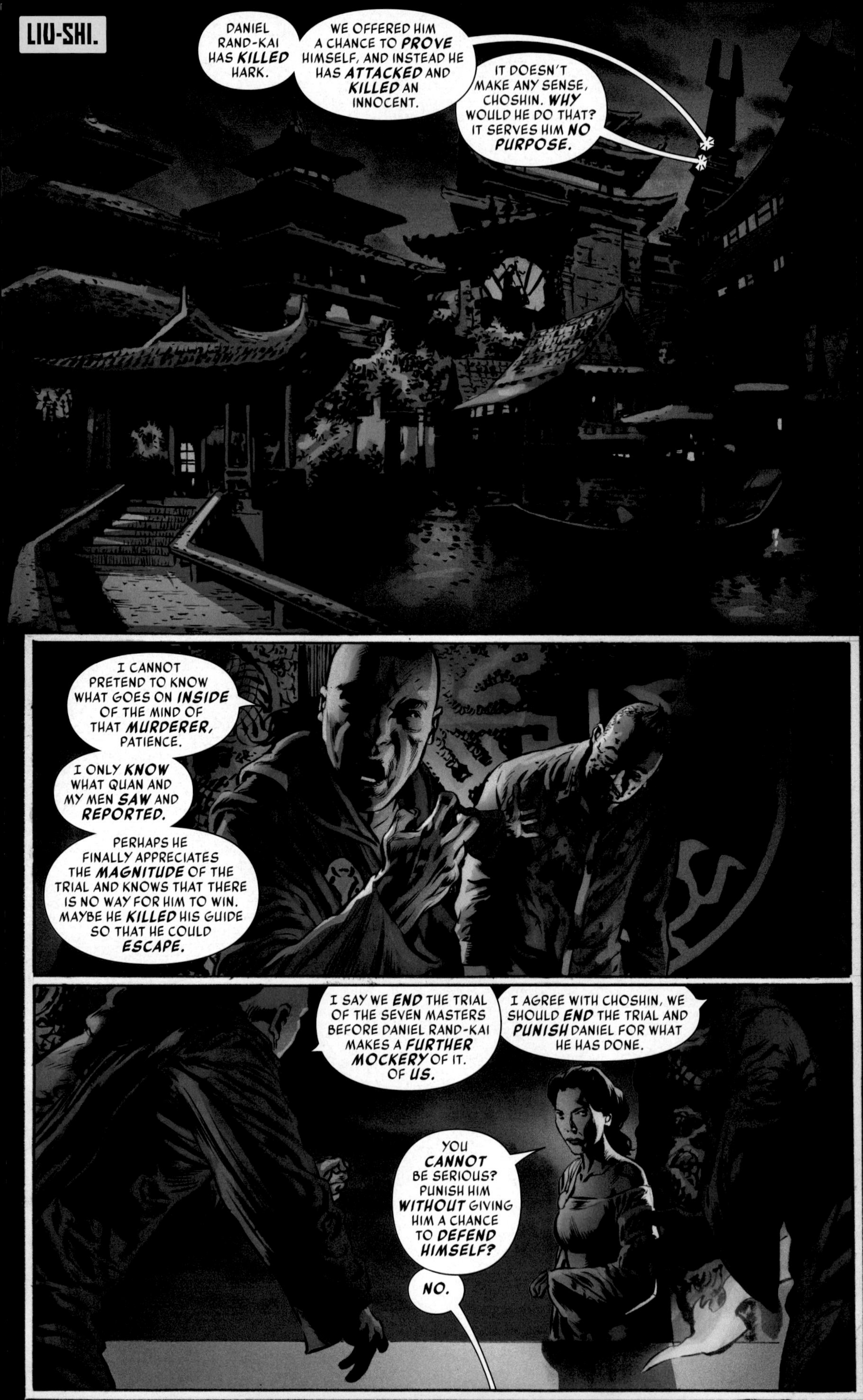
LIU-SHI.
DANIEL RAND-KAI HAS KILLED HARK.
WE OFFERED HIM A CHANCE TO PROVE HIMSELF, AND INSTEAD HE HAS ATTACKED AND KILLED AN INNOCENT.
IT DOESN'T MAKE ANY SENSE, CHOSHIN. WHY WOULD HE DO THAT? IT SERVES HIM NO PURPOSE.
I CANNOT PRETEND TO KNOW WHAT GOES ON INSIDE OF THE MIND OF THAT MURDERER, PATIENCE.
I ONLY KNOW WHAT QUAN AND MY MEN SAW AND REPORTED.
PERHAPS HE FINALLY APPRECIATES THE MAGNITUDE OF THE TRIAL AND KNOWS THAT THERE IS NO WAY FOR HIM TO WIN. MAYBE HE KILLED HIS GUIDE SO THAT HE COULD ESCAPE.
I SAY WE END THE TRIAL OF THE SEVEN MASTERS BEFORE DANIEL RAND-KAI MAKES A FURTHER MOCKERY OF IT. OF US.
I AGREE WITH CHOSHIN, WE SHOULD END THE TRIAL AND PUNISH DANIEL FOR WHAT HE HAS DONE.
YOU CANNOT BE SERIOUS? PUNISH HIM WITHOUT GIVING HIM A CHANCE TO DEFEND HIMSELF?
NO.

"THE TRIAL OF THE SEVEN MASTERS"
PART FOUR

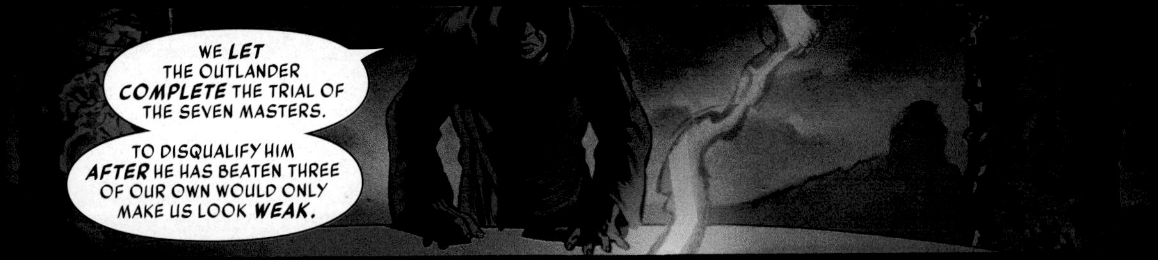
WE LET THE OUTLANDER COMPLETE THE TRIAL OF THE SEVEN MASTERS.
TO DISQUALIFY HIM AFTER HE HAS BEATEN THREE OF OUR OWN WOULD ONLY MAKE US LOOK WEAK.

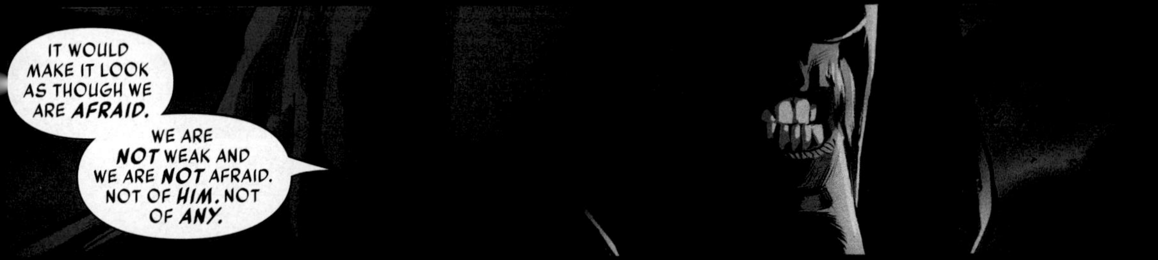
IT WOULD MAKE IT LOOK AS THOUGH WE ARE AFRAID.
WE ARE NOT WEAK AND WE ARE NOT AFRAID. NOT OF HIM. NOT OF ANY.

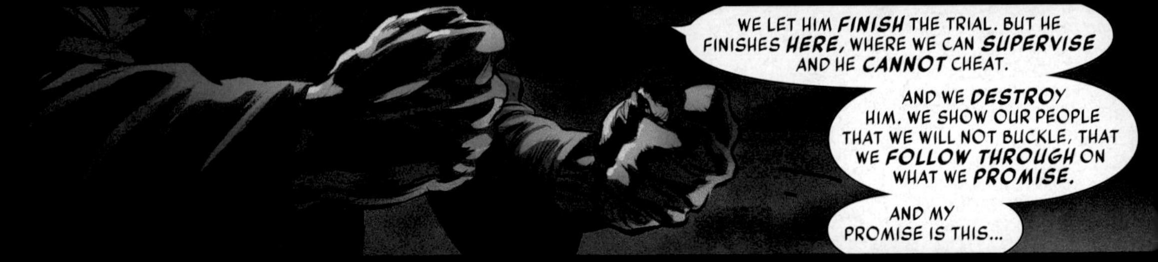
WE LET HIM FINISH THE TRIAL. BUT HE FINISHES HERE, WHERE WE CAN SUPERVISE AND HE CANNOT CHEAT.
AND WE DESTROY HIM. WE SHOW OUR PEOPLE THAT WE WILL NOT BUCKLE, THAT WE FOLLOW THROUGH ON WHAT WE PROMISE.
AND MY PROMISE IS THIS...

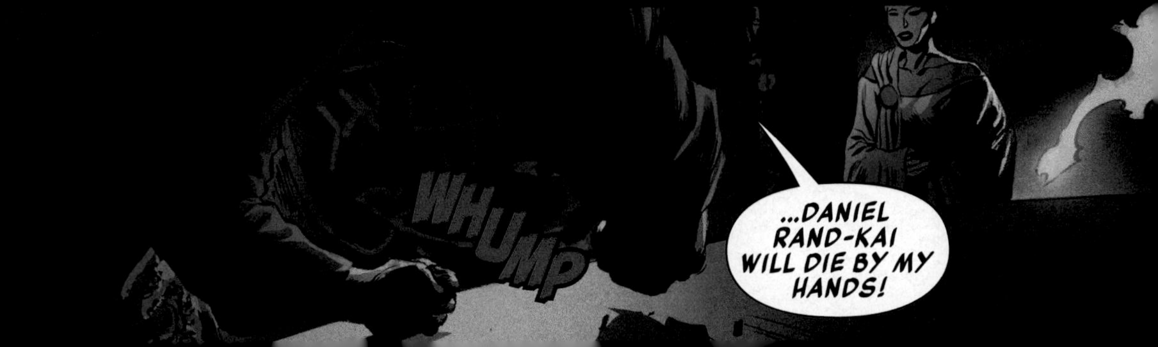
WHUMP
...DANIEL RAND-KAI WILL DIE BY MY HANDS!

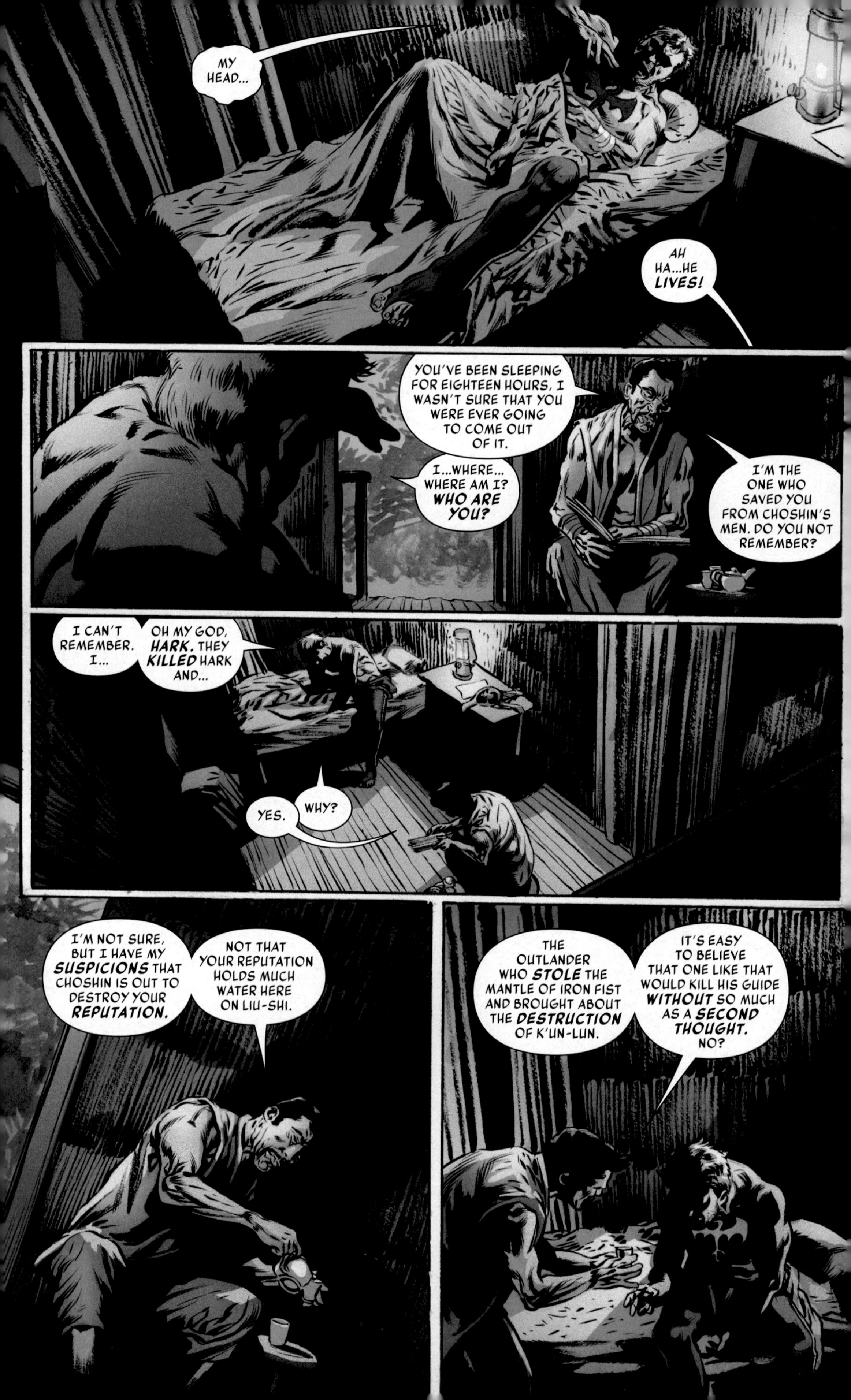
MY HEAD...
AH HA...HE LIVES!
YOU'VE BEEN SLEEPING FOR EIGHTEEN HOURS, I WASN'T SURE THAT YOU WERE EVER GOING TO COME OUT OF IT.
I...WHERE... WHERE AM I? WHO ARE YOU?
I'M THE ONE WHO SAVED YOU FROM CHOSHIN'S MEN. DO YOU NOT REMEMBER?
I CAN'T REMEMBER. I...
OH MY GOD, HARK. THEY KILLED HARK AND...
YES.
WHY?
I'M NOT SURE, BUT I HAVE MY SUSPICIONS THAT CHOSHIN IS OUT TO DESTROY YOUR REPUTATION.
NOT THAT YOUR REPUTATION HOLDS MUCH WATER HERE ON LIU-SHI.
THE OUTLANDER WHO STOLE THE MANTLE OF IRON FIST AND BROUGHT ABOUT THE DESTRUCTION OF K'UN-LUN.
IT'S EASY TO BELIEVE THAT ONE LIKE THAT WOULD KILL HIS GUIDE WITHOUT SO MUCH AS A SECOND THOUGHT. NO?

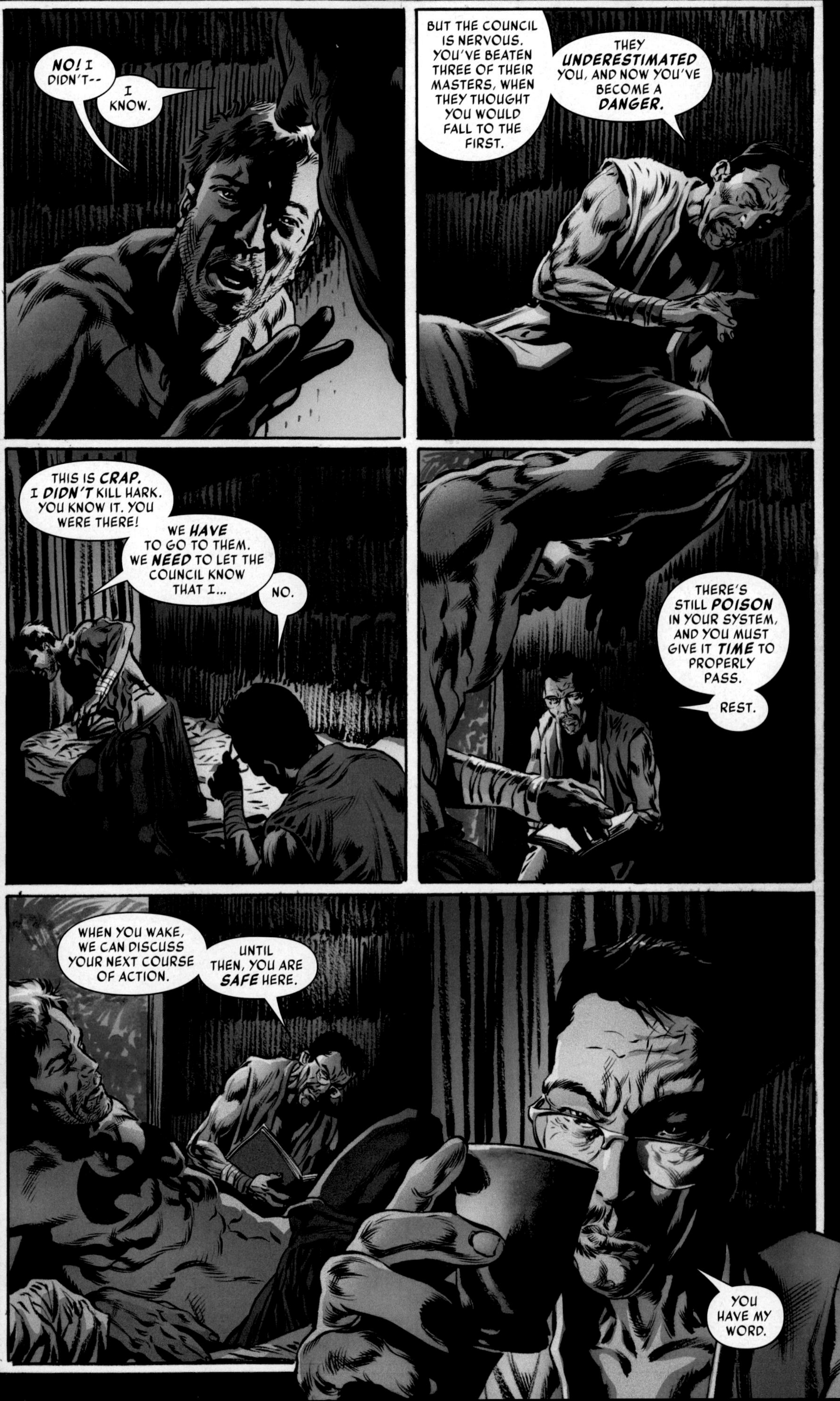
NO! I DIDN'T--
I KNOW.
BUT THE COUNCIL IS NERVOUS. YOU'VE BEATEN THREE OF THEIR MASTERS, WHEN THEY THOUGHT YOU WOULD FALL TO THE FIRST.
THEY UNDERESTIMATED YOU, AND NOW YOU'VE BECOME A DANGER.
THIS IS CRAP. I DIDN'T KILL HARK. YOU KNOW IT. YOU WERE THERE!
WE HAVE TO GO TO THEM. WE NEED TO LET THE COUNCIL KNOW THAT I...
NO.
THERE'S STILL POISON IN YOUR SYSTEM, AND YOU MUST GIVE IT TIME TO PROPERLY PASS.
REST.
WHEN YOU WAKE, WE CAN DISCUSS YOUR NEXT COURSE OF ACTION.
UNTIL THEN, YOU ARE SAFE HERE.
YOU HAVE MY WORD.

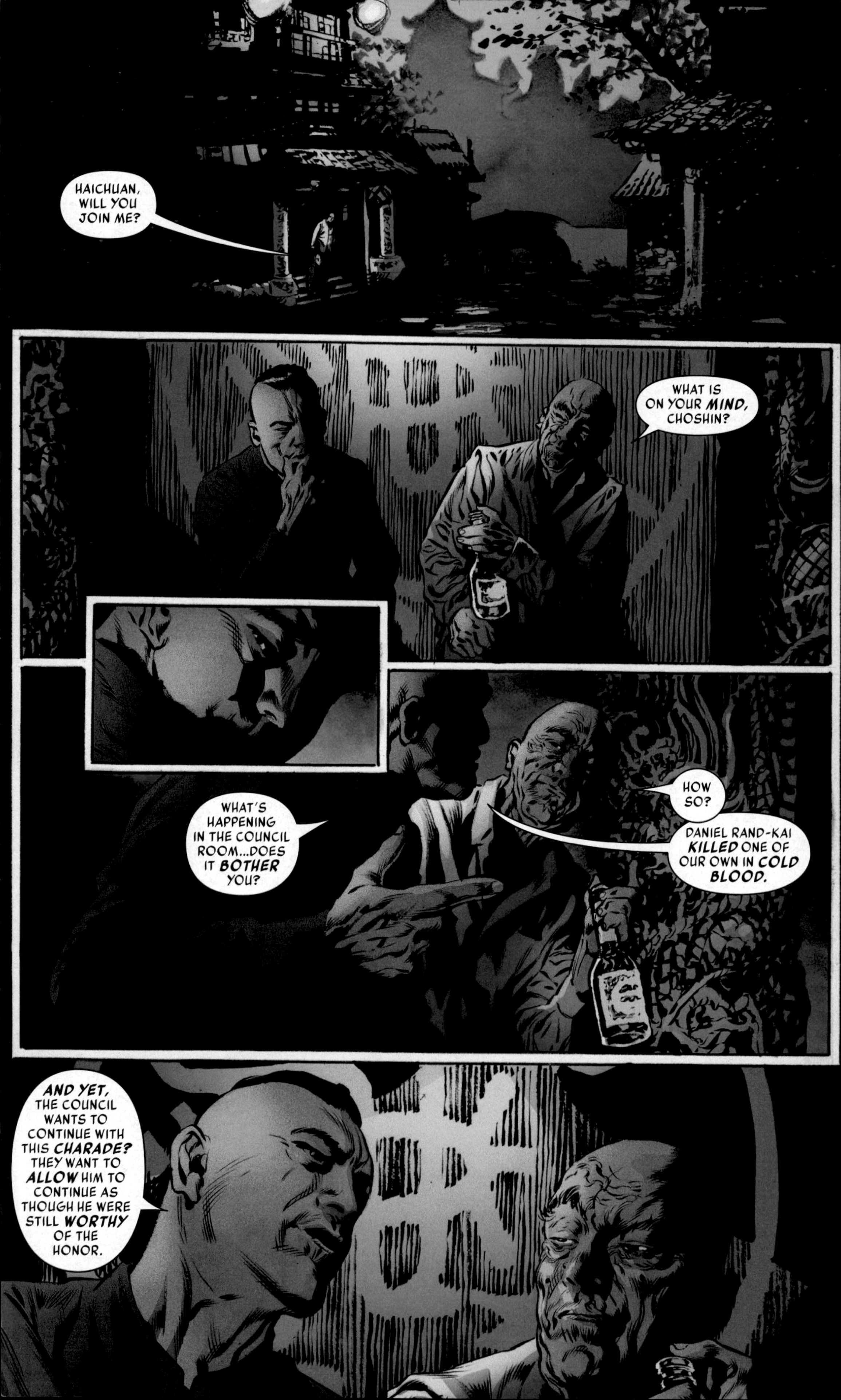
HAICHUAN, WILL YOU JOIN ME?
WHAT IS ON YOUR MIND, CHOSHIN?
WHAT'S HAPPENING IN THE COUNCIL ROOM...DOES IT BOTHER YOU?
HOW SO?
DANIEL RAND-KAI KILLED ONE OF OUR OWN IN COLD BLOOD.
AND YET, THE COUNCIL WANTS TO CONTINUE WITH THIS CHARADE? THEY WANT TO ALLOW HIM TO CONTINUE AS THOUGH HE WERE STILL WORTHY OF THE HONOR.

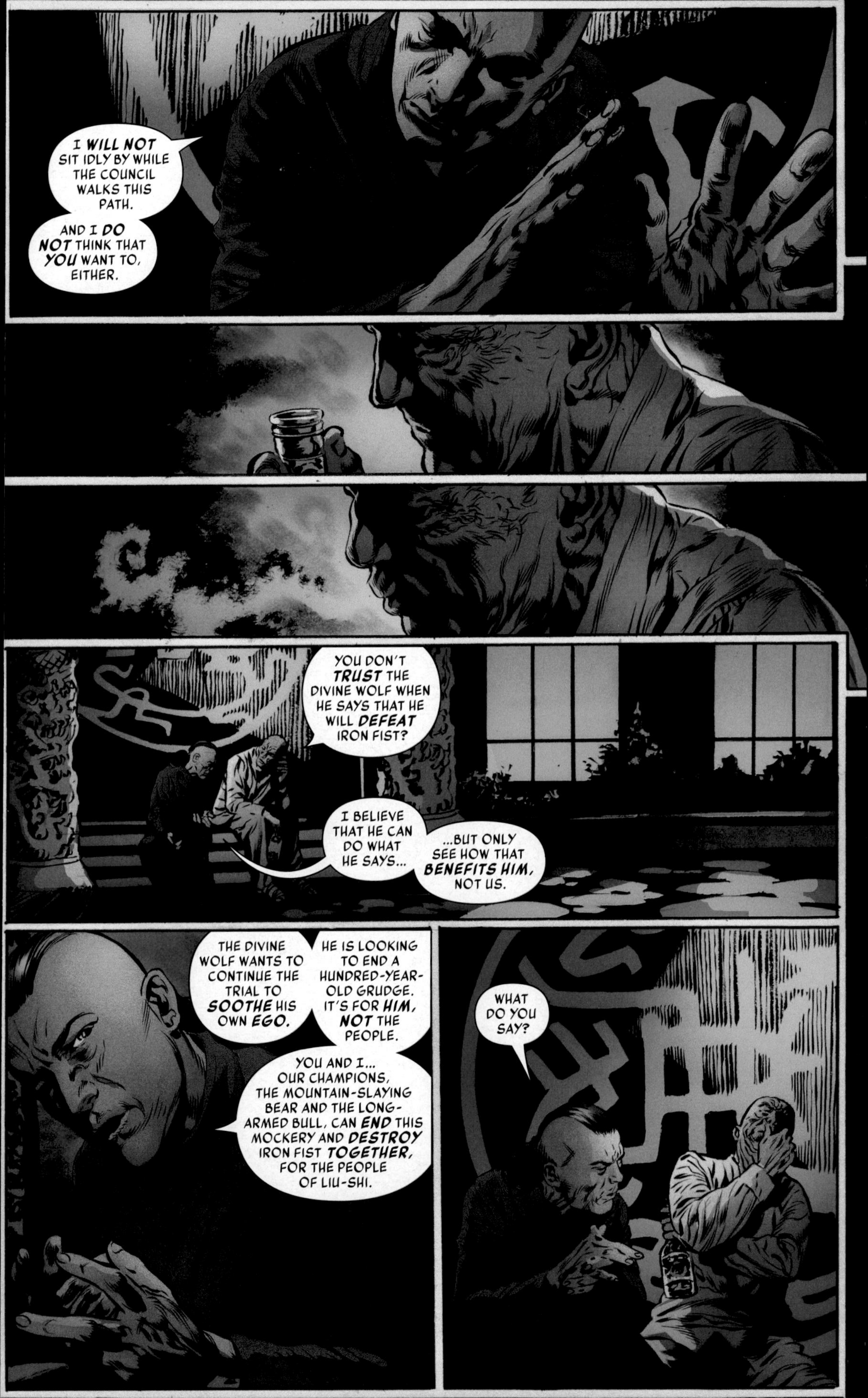

I WILL NOT SIT IDLY BY WHILE THE COUNCIL WALKS THIS PATH.
AND I DO NOT THINK THAT YOU WANT TO, EITHER.
YOU DON'T TRUST THE DIVINE WOLF WHEN HE SAYS THAT HE WILL DEFEAT IRON FIST?
I BELIEVE THAT HE CAN DO WHAT HE SAYS...
...BUT ONLY SEE HOW THAT BENEFITS HIM, NOT US.
THE DIVINE WOLF WANTS TO CONTINUE THE TRIAL TO SOOTHE HIS OWN EGO.
HE IS LOOKING TO END A HUNDRED-YEAR-OLD GRUDGE. IT'S FOR HIM, NOT THE PEOPLE.
YOU AND I... OUR CHAMPIONS, THE MOUNTAIN-SLAYING BEAR AND THE LONG-ARMED BULL, CAN END THIS MOCKERY AND DESTROY IRON FIST TOGETHER, FOR THE PEOPLE OF LIU-SHI.
WHAT DO YOU SAY?

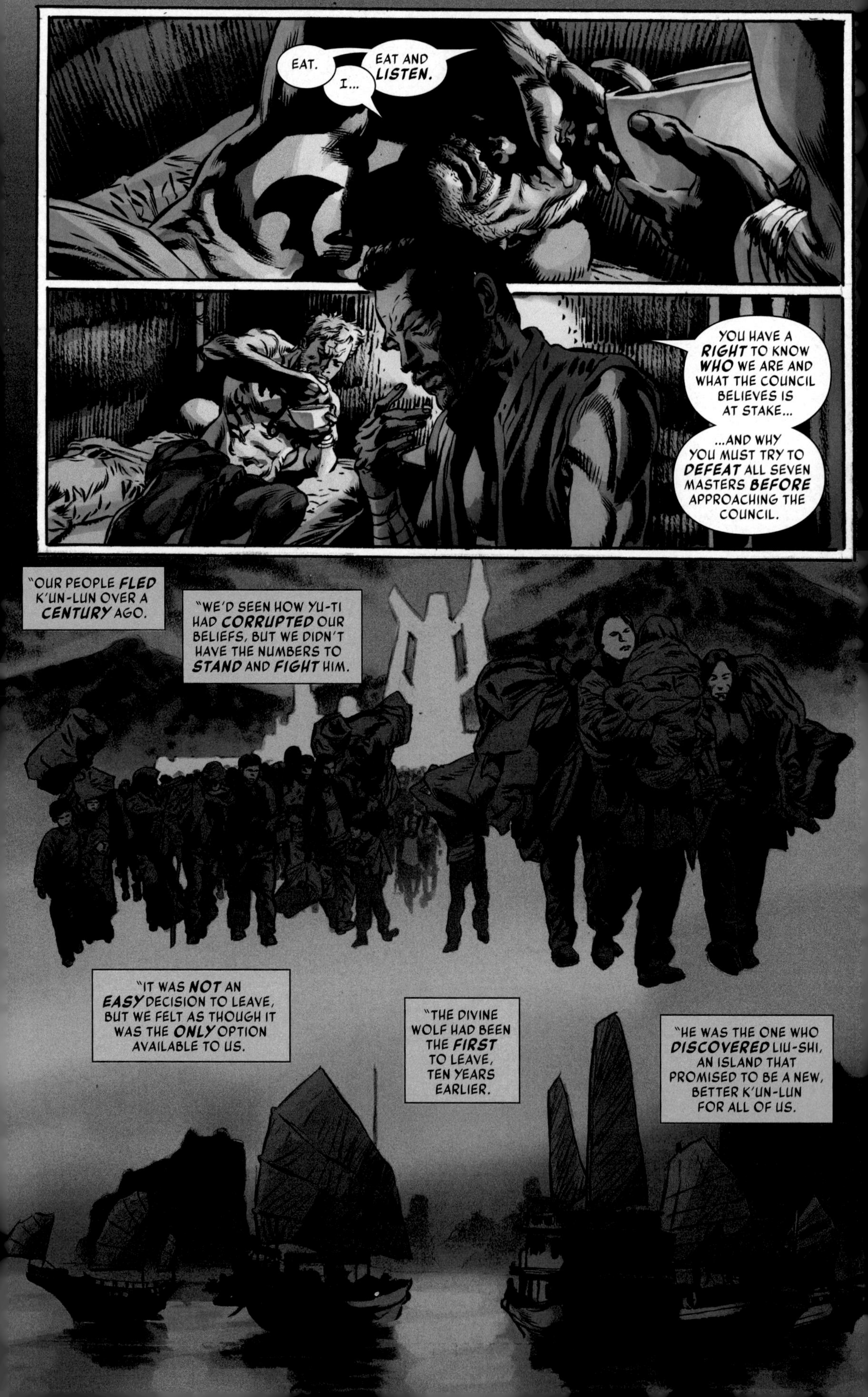
EAT.
I...
EAT AND LISTEN.
YOU HAVE A RIGHT TO KNOW WHO WE ARE AND WHAT THE COUNCIL BELIEVES IS AT STAKE...
...AND WHY YOU MUST TRY TO DEFEAT ALL SEVEN MASTERS BEFORE APPROACHING THE COUNCIL.
"OUR PEOPLE FLED K'UN-LUN OVER A CENTURY AGO.
"WE'D SEEN HOW YU-TI HAD CORRUPTED OUR BELIEFS, BUT WE DIDN'T HAVE THE NUMBERS TO STAND AND FIGHT HIM.
"IT WAS NOT AN EASY DECISION TO LEAVE, BUT WE FELT AS THOUGH IT WAS THE ONLY OPTION AVAILABLE TO US.
"THE DIVINE WOLF HAD BEEN THE FIRST TO LEAVE, TEN YEARS EARLIER.
"HE WAS THE ONE WHO DISCOVERED LIU-SHI, AN ISLAND THAT PROMISED TO BE A NEW, BETTER K'UN-LUN FOR ALL OF US.

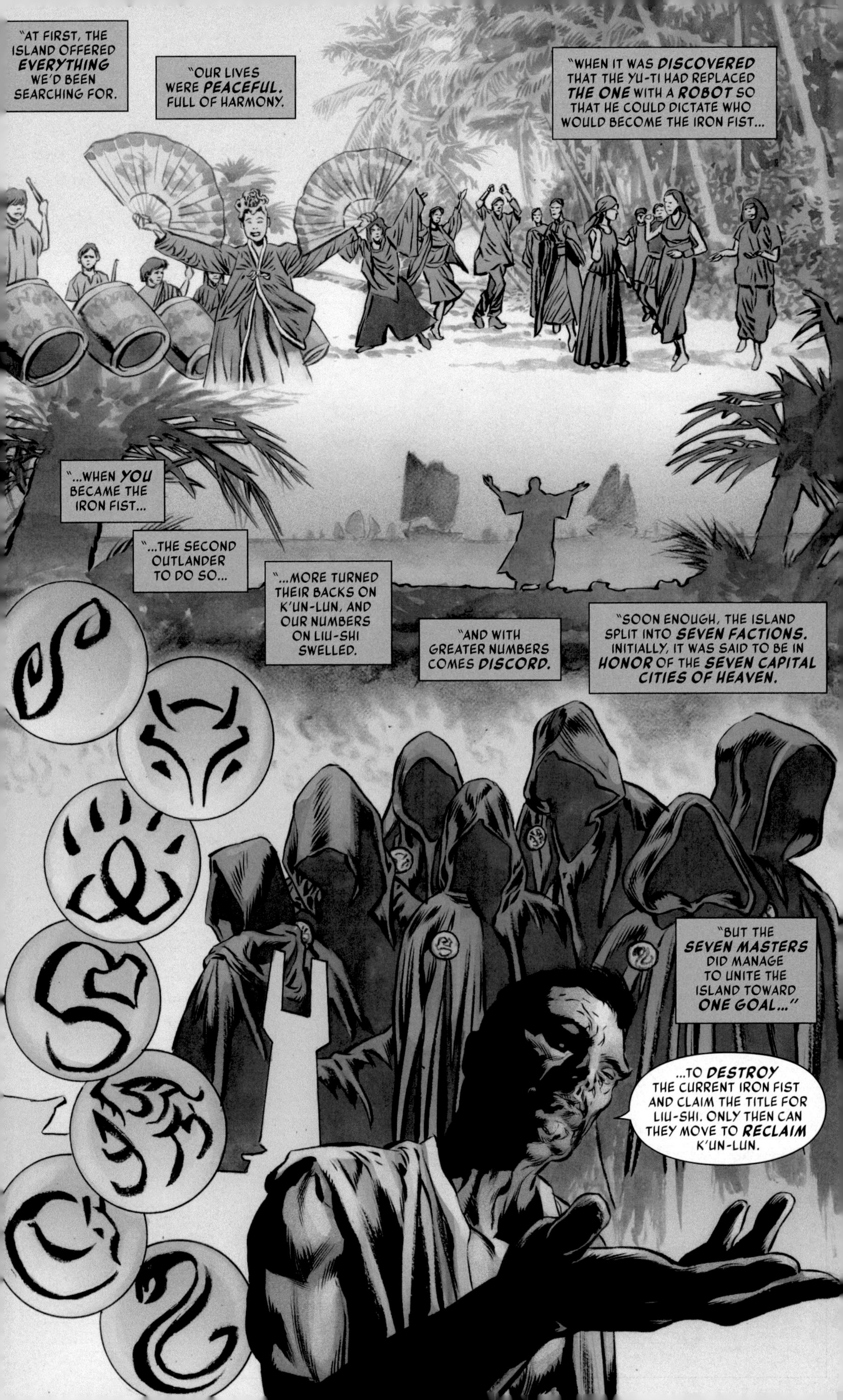
"AT FIRST, THE ISLAND OFFERED EVERYTHING WE'D BEEN SEARCHING FOR.
"OUR LIVES WERE PEACEFUL. FULL OF HARMONY.
"WHEN IT WAS DISCOVERED THAT THE YU-TI HAD REPLACED THE ONE WITH A ROBOT SO THAT HE COULD DICTATE WHO WOULD BECOME THE IRON FIST...
"...WHEN YOU BECAME THE IRON FIST...
"...THE SECOND OUTLANDER TO DO SO...
"...MORE TURNED THEIR BACKS ON K'UN-LUN, AND OUR NUMBERS ON LIU-SHI SWELLED.
"AND WITH GREATER NUMBERS COMES DISCORD.
"SOON ENOUGH, THE ISLAND SPLIT INTO SEVEN FACTIONS. INITIALLY, IT WAS SAID TO BE IN HONOR OF THE SEVEN CAPITAL CITIES OF HEAVEN.
"BUT THE SEVEN MASTERS DID MANAGE TO UNITE THE ISLAND TOWARD ONE GOAL..."
...TO DESTROY THE CURRENT IRON FIST AND CLAIM THE TITLE FOR LIU-SHI. ONLY THEN CAN THEY MOVE TO RECLAIM K'UN-LUN.

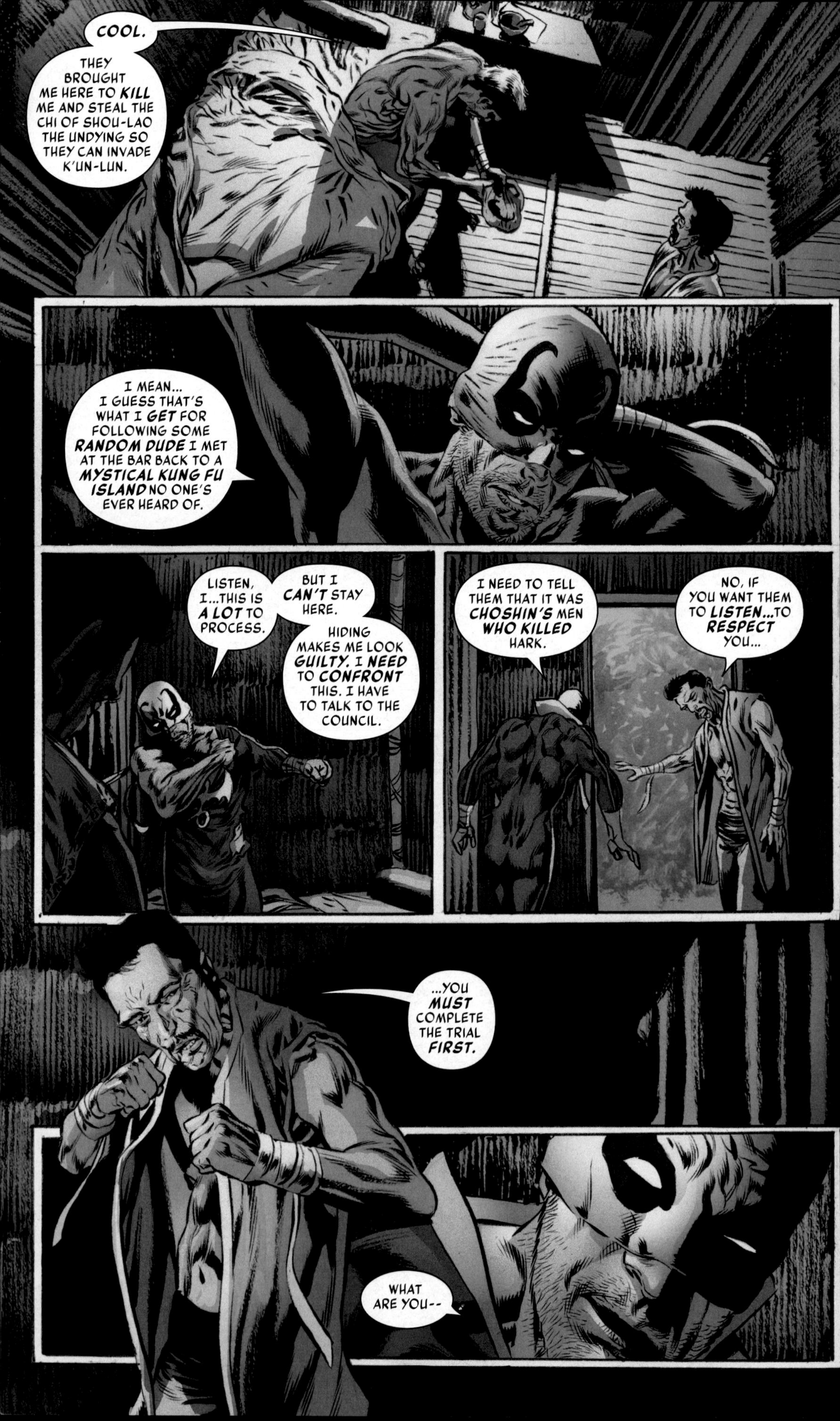
COOL.
THEY BROUGHT ME HERE TO **KILL** ME AND STEAL THE CHI OF SHOU-LAO THE UNDYING SO THEY CAN INVADE K'UN-LUN.
I MEAN... I GUESS THAT'S WHAT I **GET** FOR FOLLOWING SOME **RANDOM DUDE** I MET AT THE BAR BACK TO A **MYSTICAL KUNG FU ISLAND** NO ONE'S EVER HEARD OF.
LISTEN, I...THIS IS **A LOT** TO PROCESS.
BUT I **CAN'T** STAY HERE.
HIDING MAKES ME LOOK **GUILTY.** I **NEED** TO **CONFRONT** THIS. I HAVE TO TALK TO THE COUNCIL.
I NEED TO TELL THEM THAT IT WAS **CHOSHIN'S** MEN **WHO KILLED** HARK.
NO, IF YOU WANT THEM TO **LISTEN**...TO **RESPECT** YOU...
...YOU **MUST** COMPLETE THE TRIAL **FIRST.**
WHAT ARE YOU--

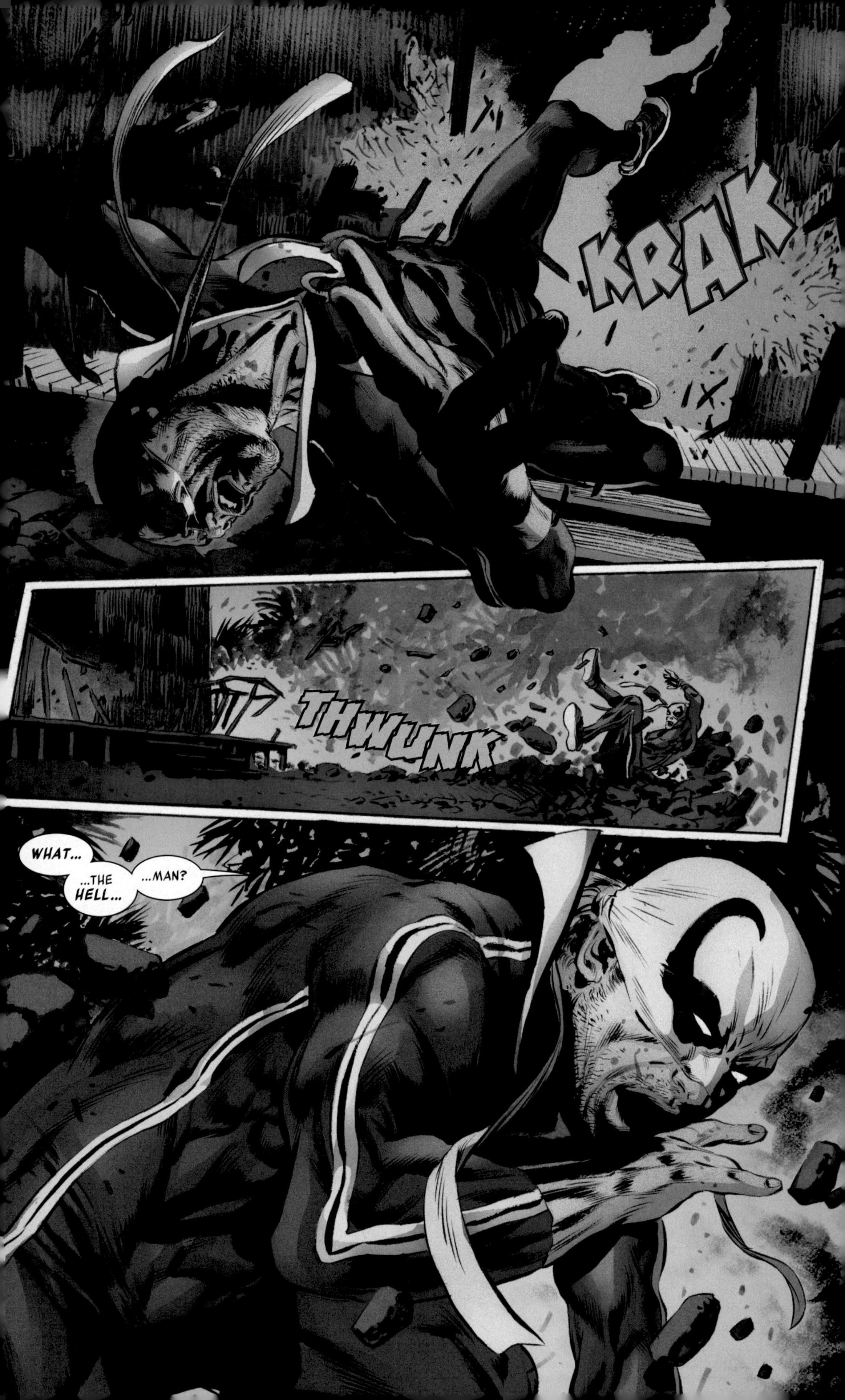

KRAK
THWUNK
WHAT...
...THE HELL...
...MAN?

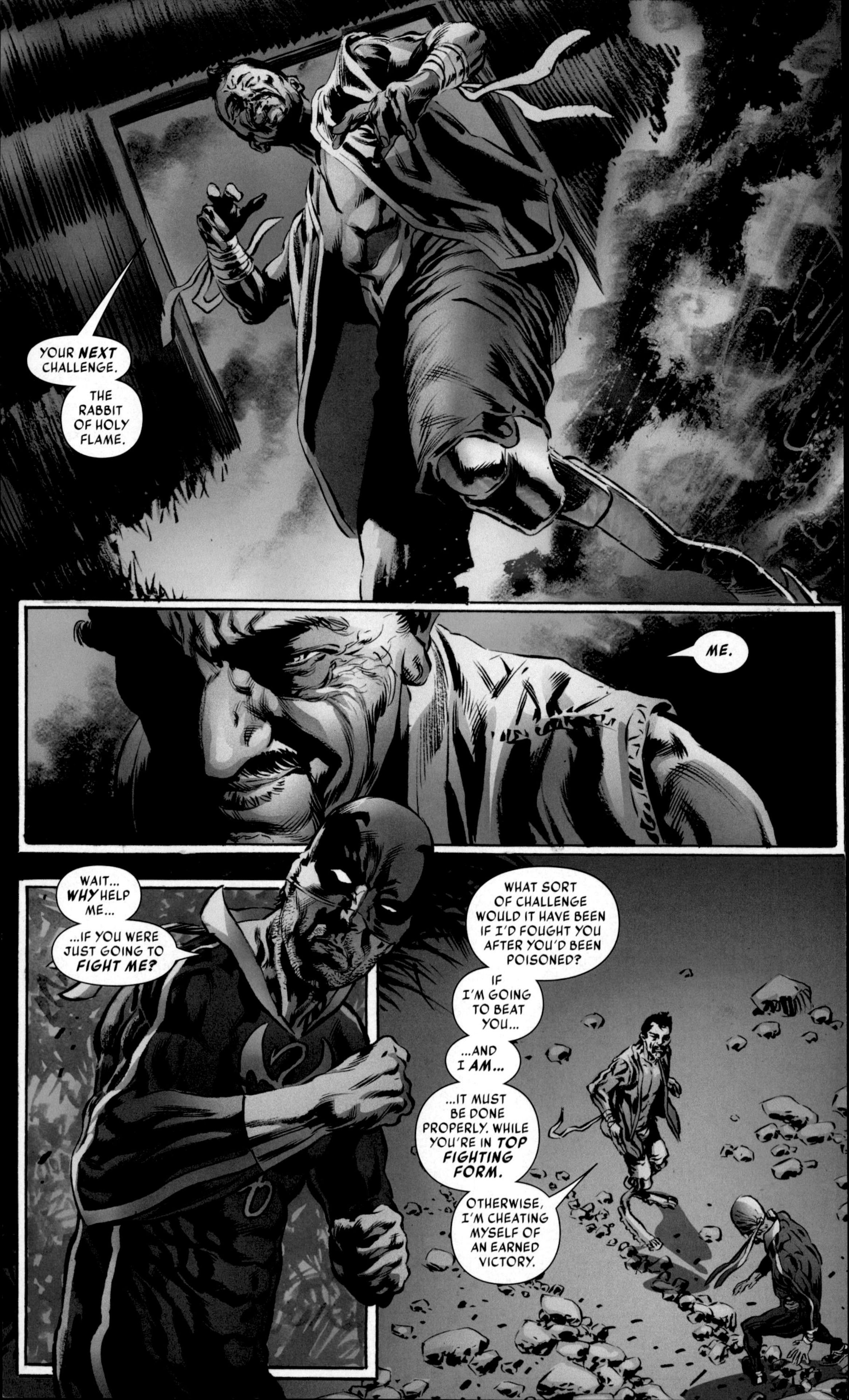

YOUR NEXT CHALLENGE.
THE RABBIT OF HOLY FLAME.
ME.
WAIT... WHY HELP ME...
...IF YOU WERE JUST GOING TO FIGHT ME?
WHAT SORT OF CHALLENGE WOULD IT HAVE BEEN IF I'D FOUGHT YOU AFTER YOU'D BEEN POISONED?
IF I'M GOING TO BEAT YOU...
...AND I AM...
...IT MUST BE DONE PROPERLY. WHILE YOU'RE IN TOP FIGHTING FORM.
OTHERWISE, I'M CHEATING MYSELF OF AN EARNED VICTORY.

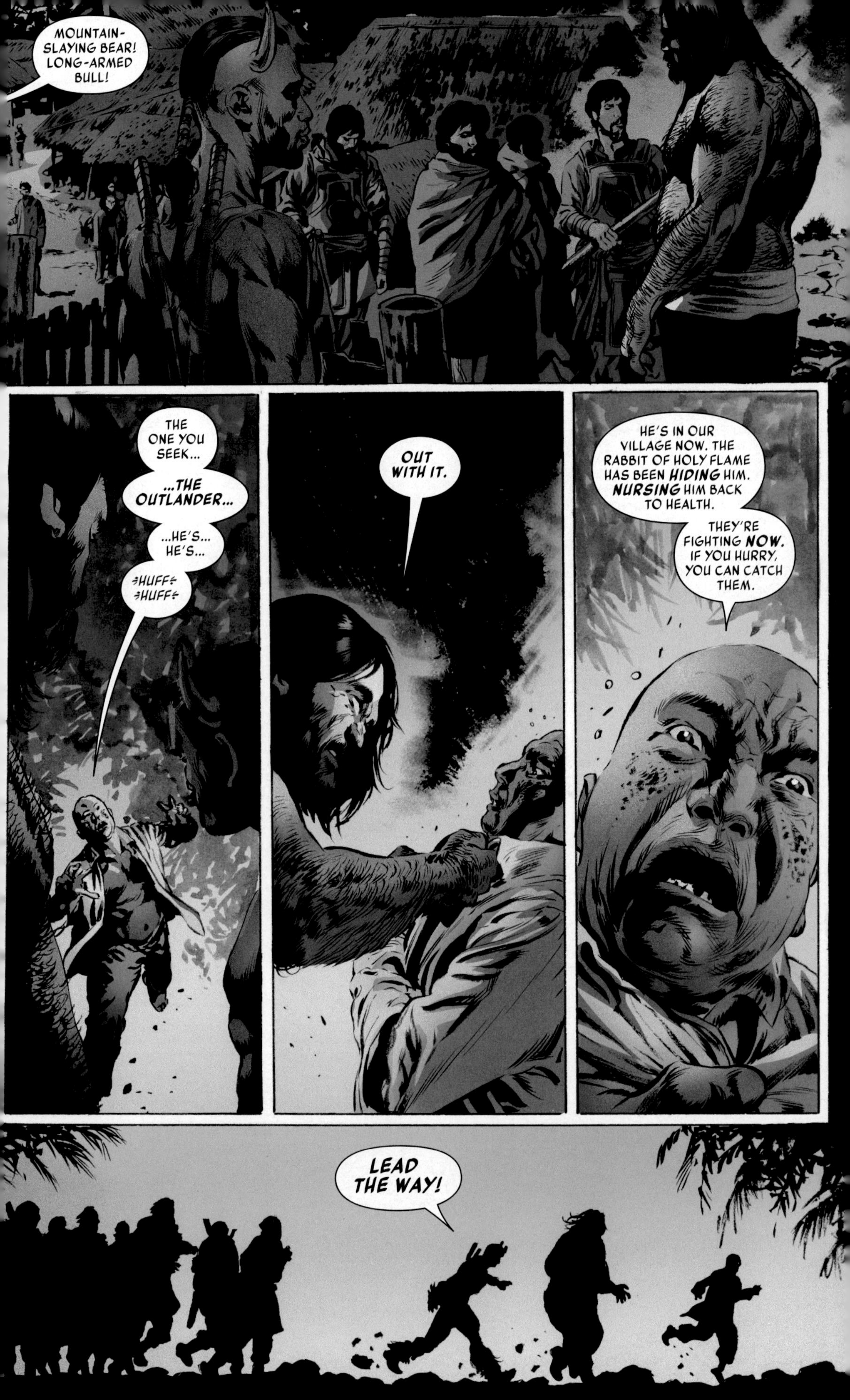
MOUNTAIN-SLAYING BEAR! LONG-ARMED BULL!
THE ONE YOU SEEK...
...THE OUTLANDER...
...HE'S... HE'S...
=HUFF= =HUFF=
OUT WITH IT.
HE'S IN OUR VILLAGE NOW. THE RABBIT OF HOLY FLAME HAS BEEN HIDING HIM. NURSING HIM BACK TO HEALTH.
THEY'RE FIGHTING NOW. IF YOU HURRY, YOU CAN CATCH THEM.
LEAD THE WAY!

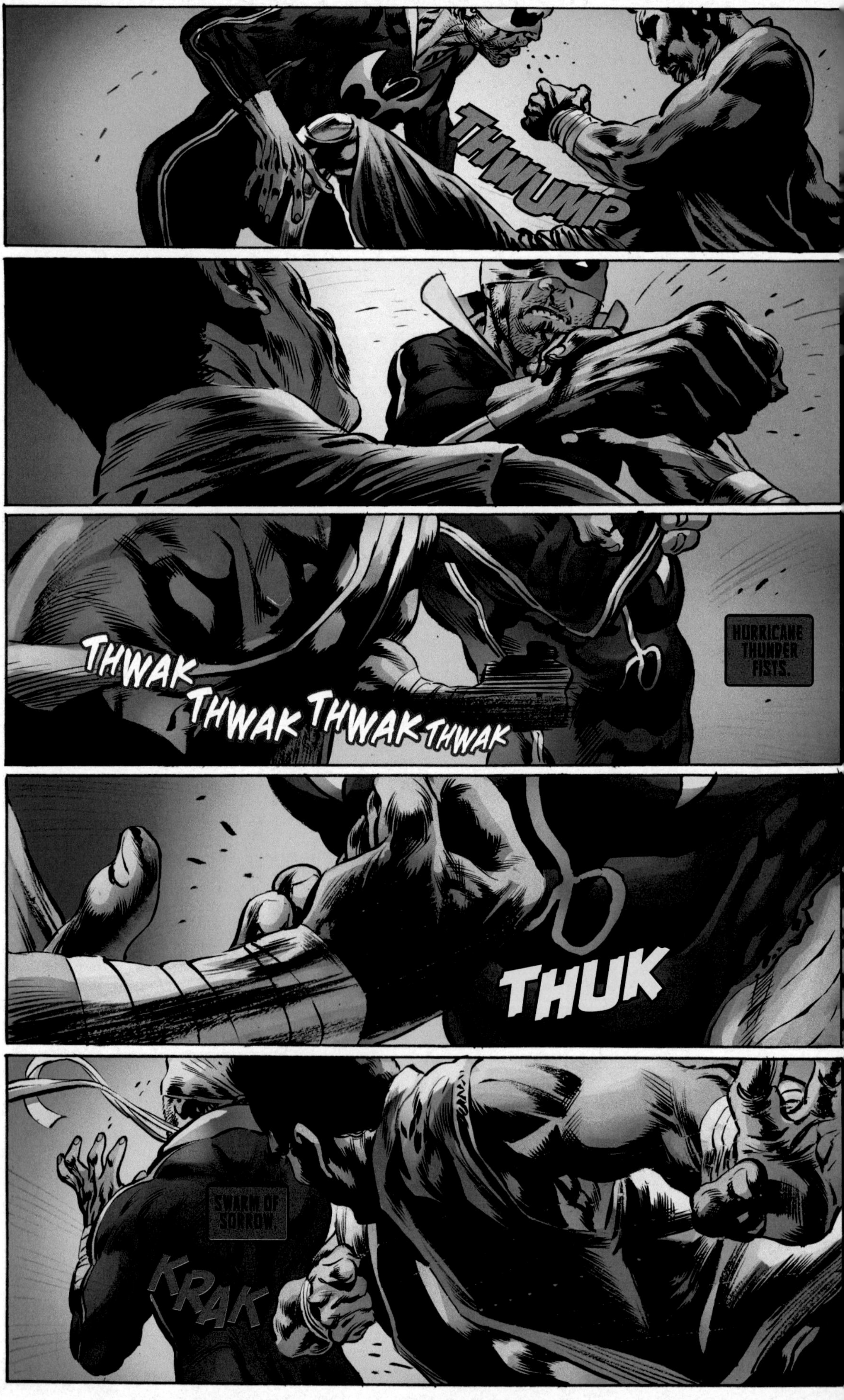
THWUMP
THWAK
THWAK THWAK THWAK
HURRICANE THUNDER FISTS.
THUK
SWARM OF SORROW.
KRAK

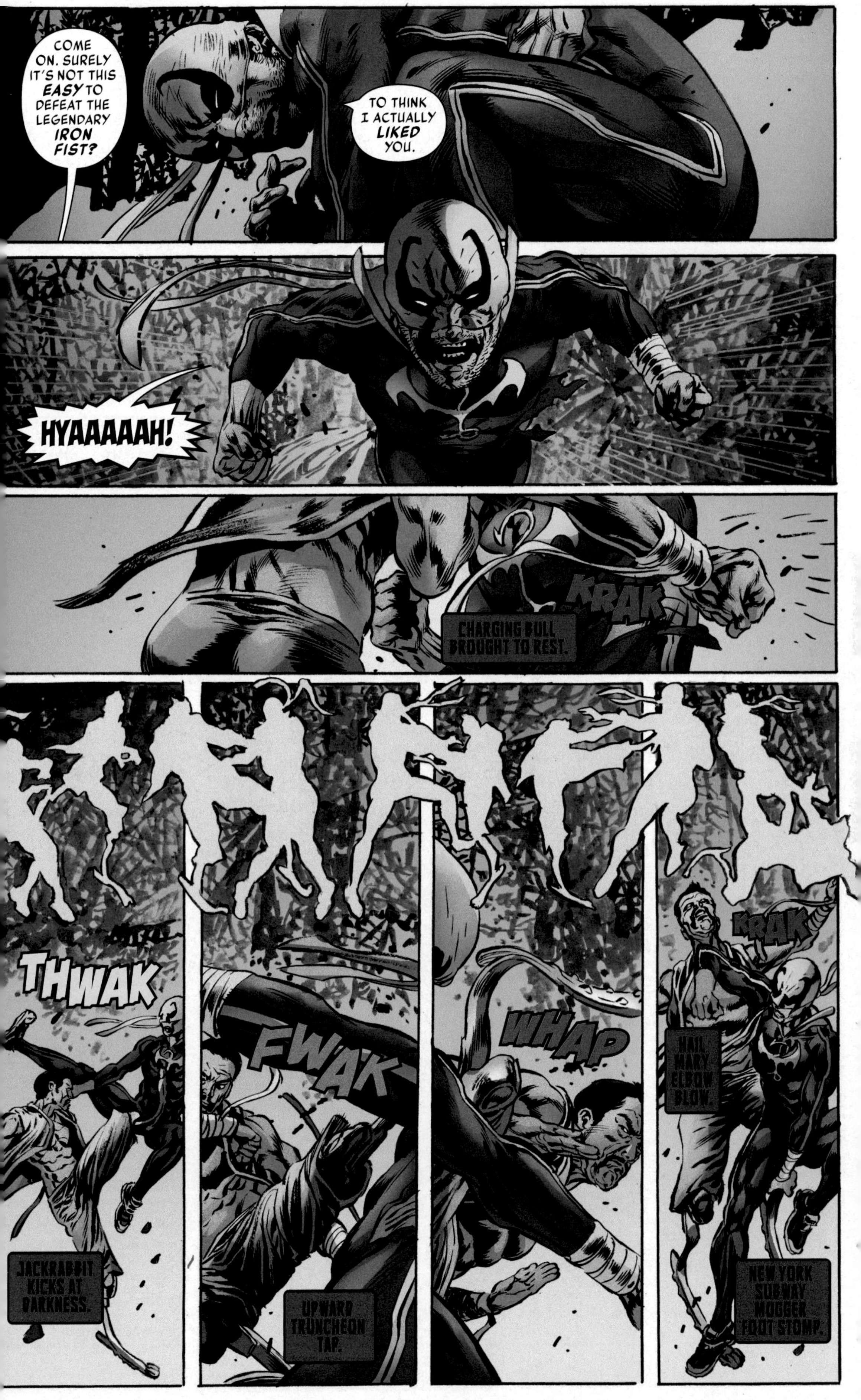
COME ON. SURELY IT'S NOT THIS EASY TO DEFEAT THE LEGENDARY IRON FIST?
TO THINK I ACTUALLY LIKED YOU.
HYAAAAAH!
KRAK
CHARGING BULL BROUGHT TO REST.
THWAK
JACKRABBIT KICKS AT DARKNESS.
FWAK
UPWARD TRUNCHEON TAP.
WHAP
KRAK
HAIL MARY ELBOW BLOW.
NEW YORK SUBWAY MUGGER FOOT STOMP.

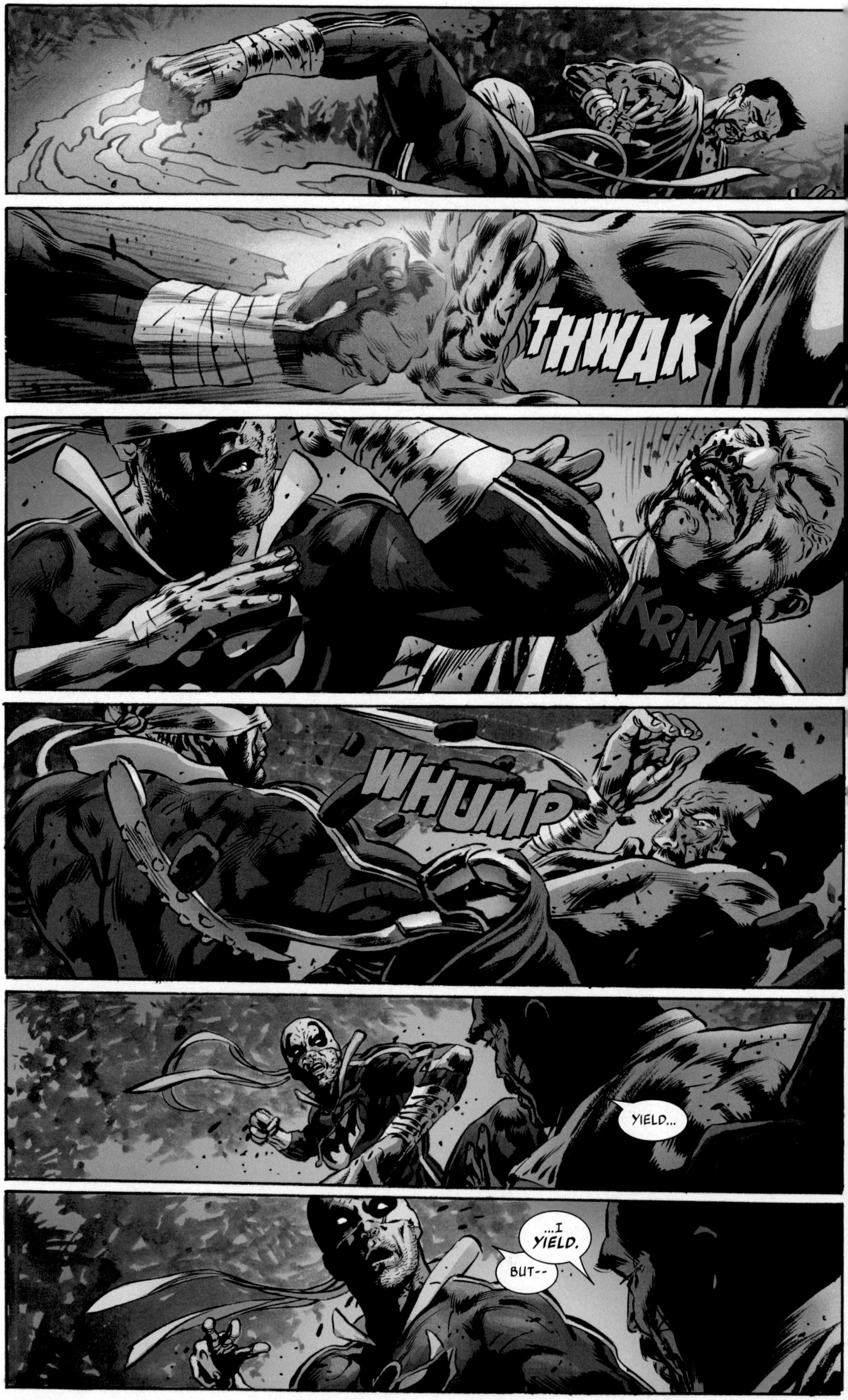
THWAK
KRNK
WHUMP
YIELD...
...I YIELD.
BUT--

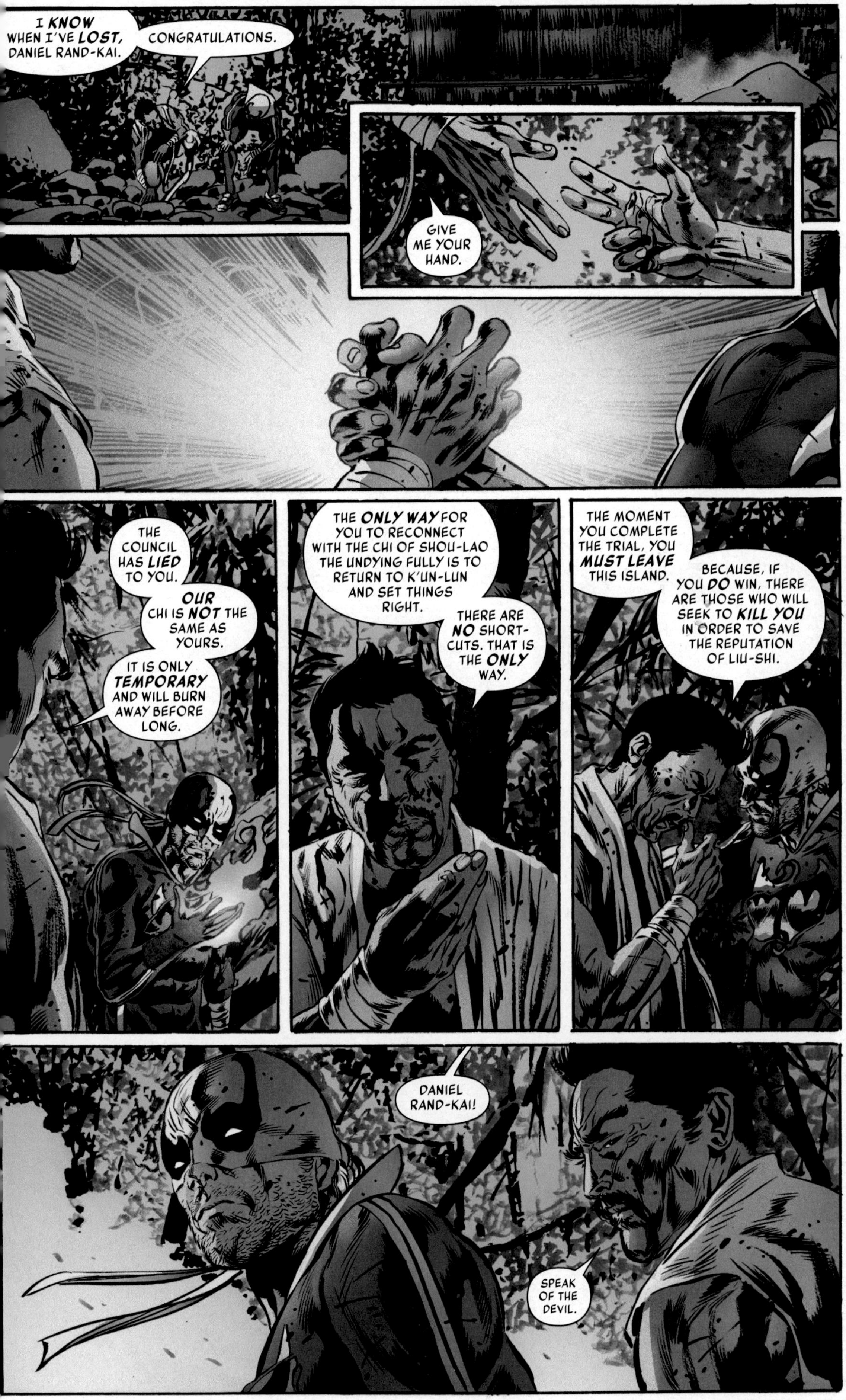
I KNOW WHEN I'VE LOST, DANIEL RAND-KAI.
CONGRATULATIONS.
GIVE ME YOUR HAND.
THE COUNCIL HAS LIED TO YOU.
OUR CHI IS NOT THE SAME AS YOURS.
IT IS ONLY TEMPORARY AND WILL BURN AWAY BEFORE LONG.
THE ONLY WAY FOR YOU TO RECONNECT WITH THE CHI OF SHOU-LAO THE UNDYING FULLY IS TO RETURN TO K'UN-LUN AND SET THINGS RIGHT.
THERE ARE NO SHORT-CUTS. THAT IS THE ONLY WAY.
THE MOMENT YOU COMPLETE THE TRIAL, YOU MUST LEAVE THIS ISLAND.
BECAUSE, IF YOU DO WIN, THERE ARE THOSE WHO WILL SEEK TO KILL YOU IN ORDER TO SAVE THE REPUTATION OF LIU-SHI.
DANIEL RAND-KAI!
SPEAK OF THE DEVIL.

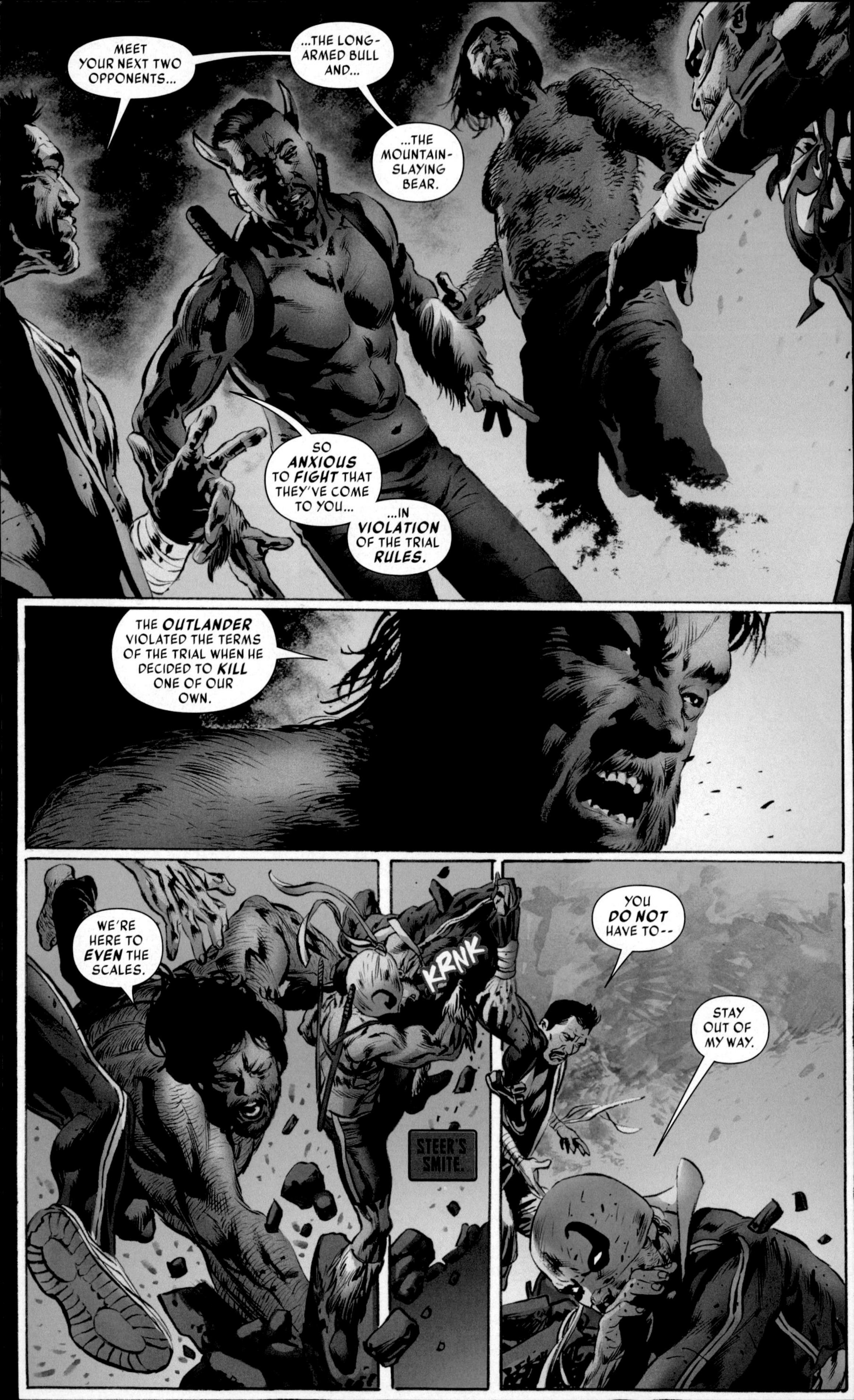
MEET YOUR NEXT TWO OPPONENTS...
...THE LONG-ARMED BULL AND...
...THE MOUNTAIN-SLAYING BEAR.
SO ANXIOUS TO FIGHT THAT THEY'VE COME TO YOU...
...IN VIOLATION OF THE TRIAL RULES.
THE OUTLANDER VIOLATED THE TERMS OF THE TRIAL WHEN HE DECIDED TO KILL ONE OF OUR OWN.
WE'RE HERE TO EVEN THE SCALES.
KRNK
STEER'S SMITE.
YOU DO NOT HAVE TO--
STAY OUT OF MY WAY.

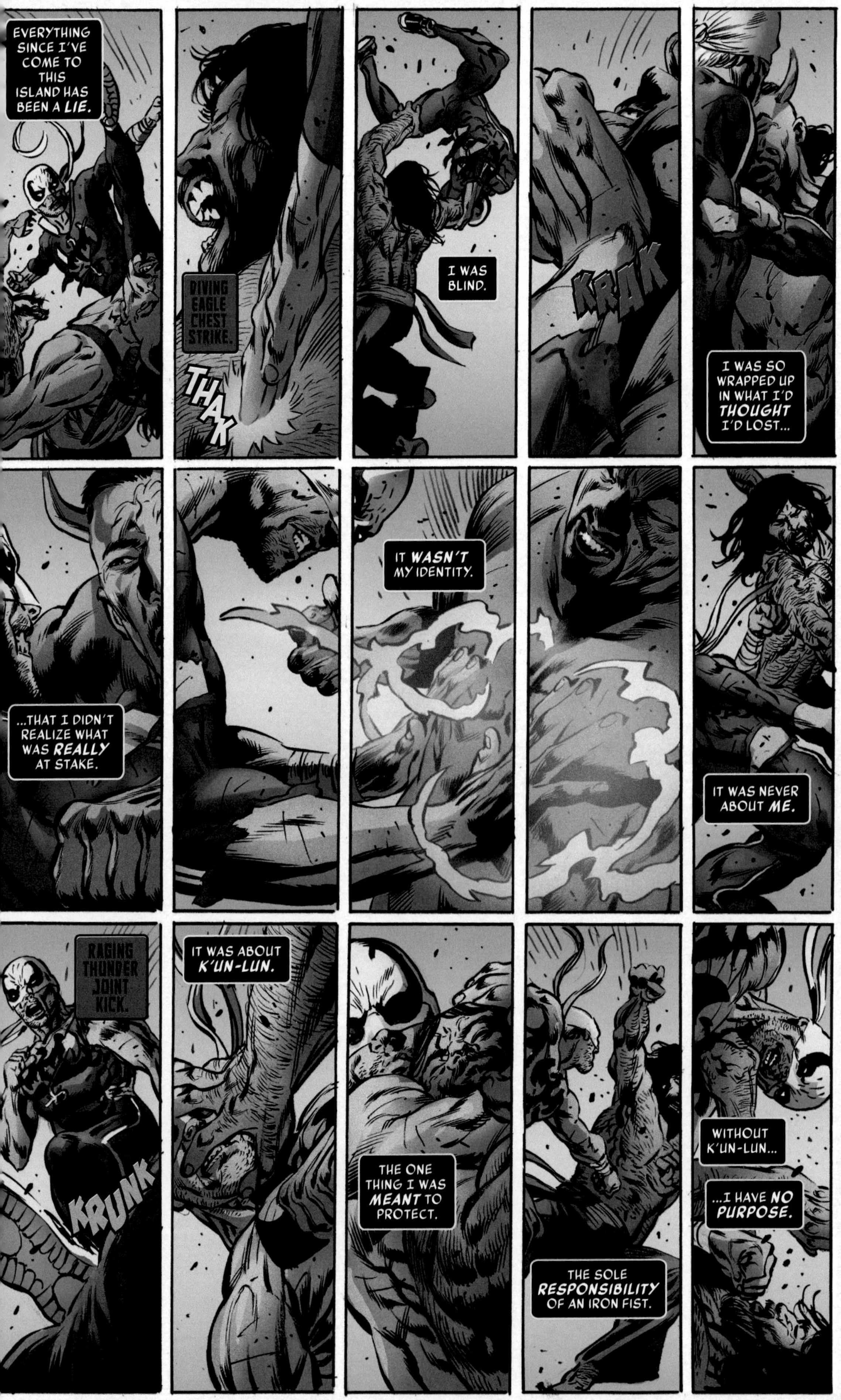

EVERYTHING SINCE I'VE COME TO THIS ISLAND HAS BEEN A LIE.
DIVING EAGLE CHEST STRIKE.
THAK
I WAS BLIND.
KRAK
I WAS SO WRAPPED UP IN WHAT I'D THOUGHT I'D LOST...
...THAT I DIDN'T REALIZE WHAT WAS REALLY AT STAKE.
IT WASN'T MY IDENTITY.
IT WAS NEVER ABOUT ME.
RAGING THUNDER JOINT KICK.
KRUNK
IT WAS ABOUT K'UN-LUN.
THE ONE THING I WAS MEANT TO PROTECT.
THE SOLE RESPONSIBILITY OF AN IRON FIST.
WITHOUT K'UN-LUN...
...I HAVE NO PURPOSE.

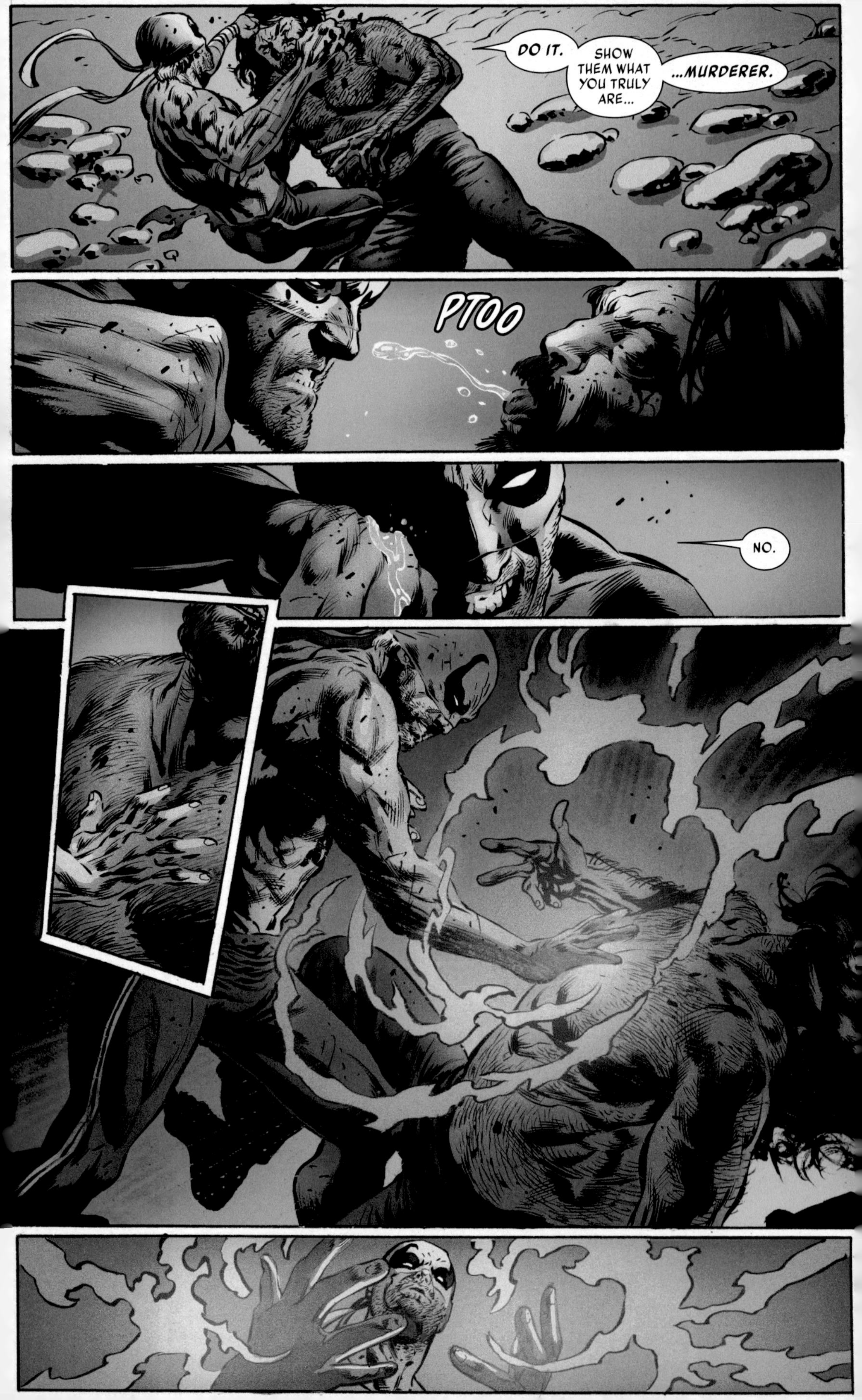
DO IT.
SHOW THEM WHAT YOU TRULY ARE...
...MURDERER.
PTOO
NO.

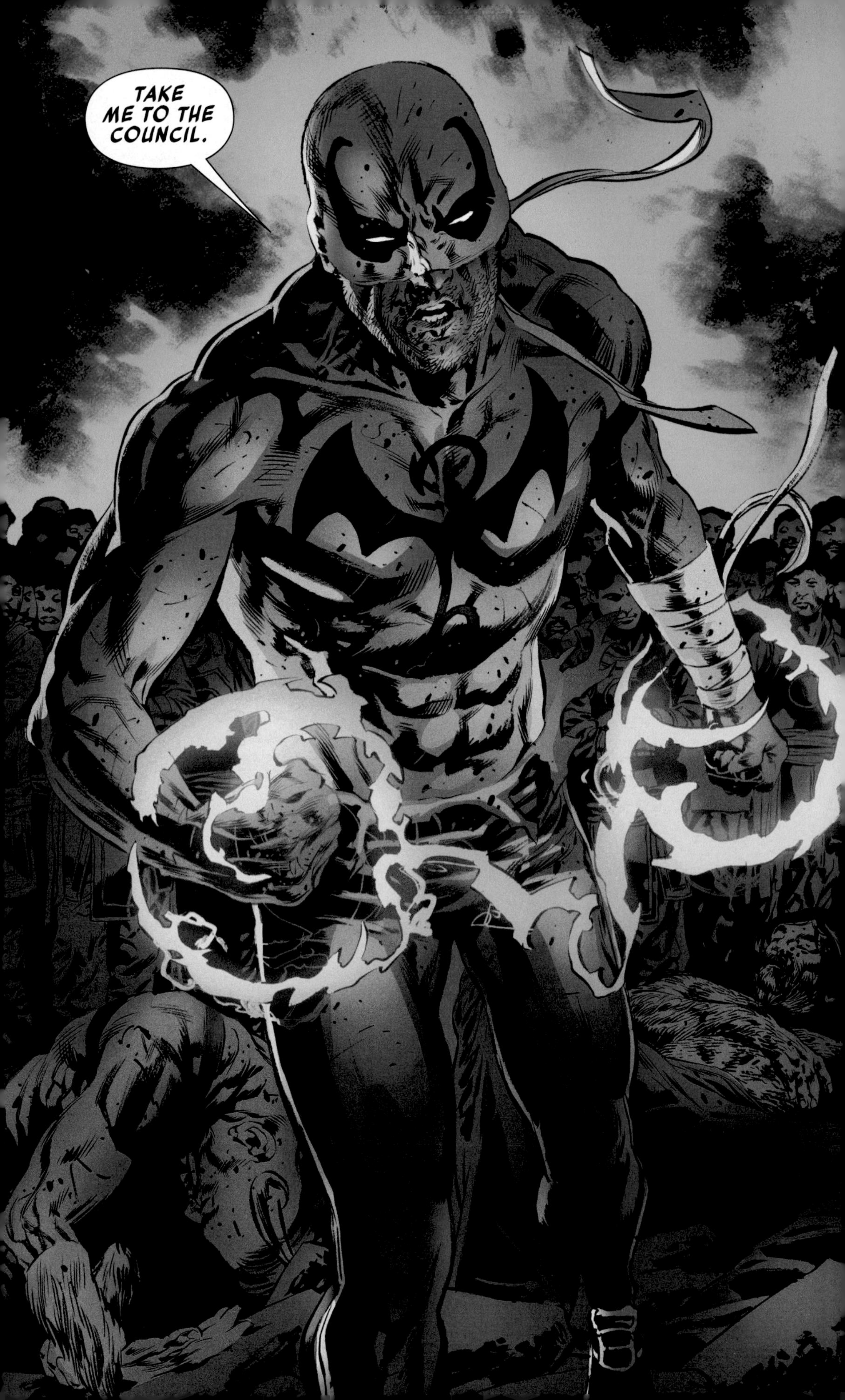
TAKE ME TO THE COUNCIL.

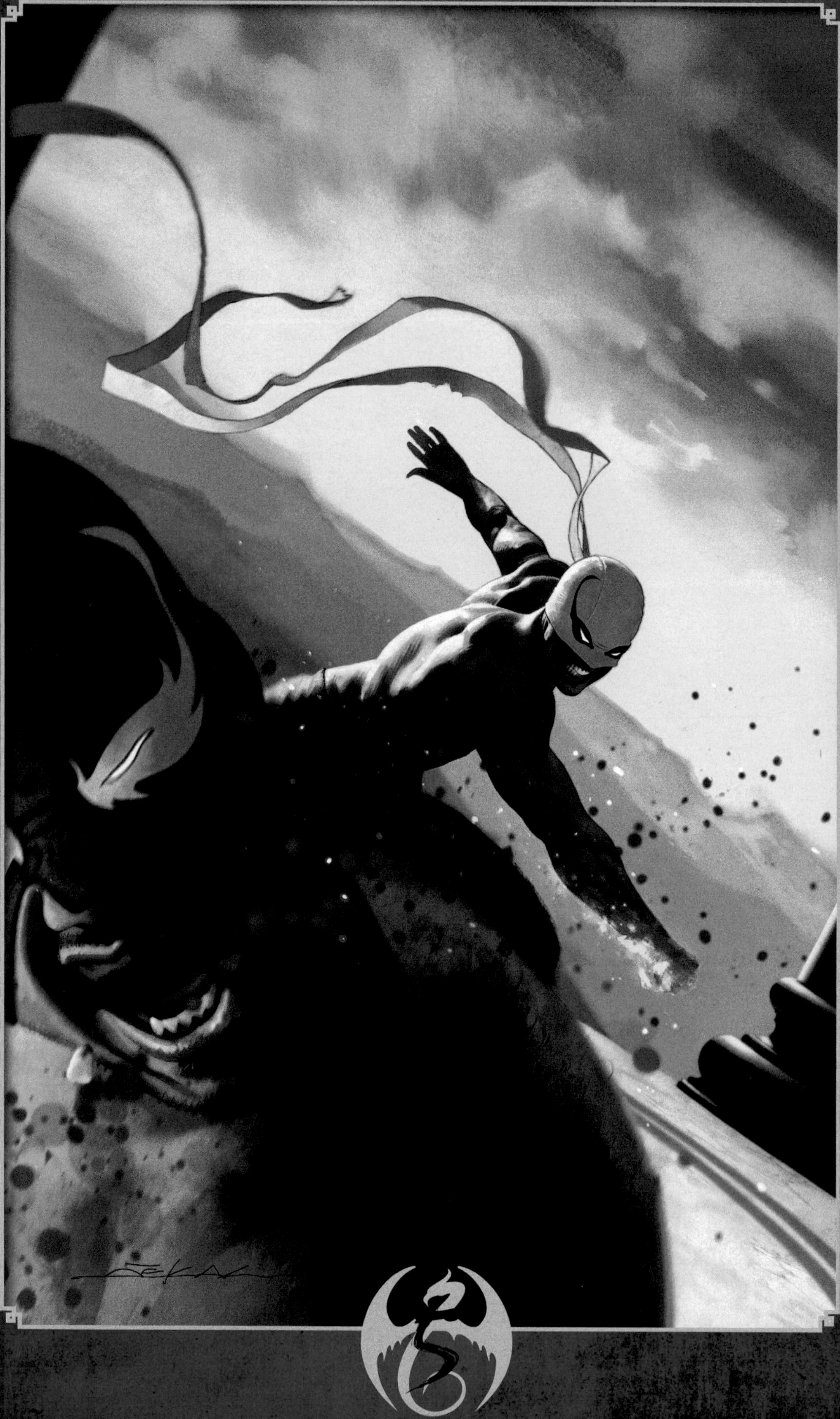

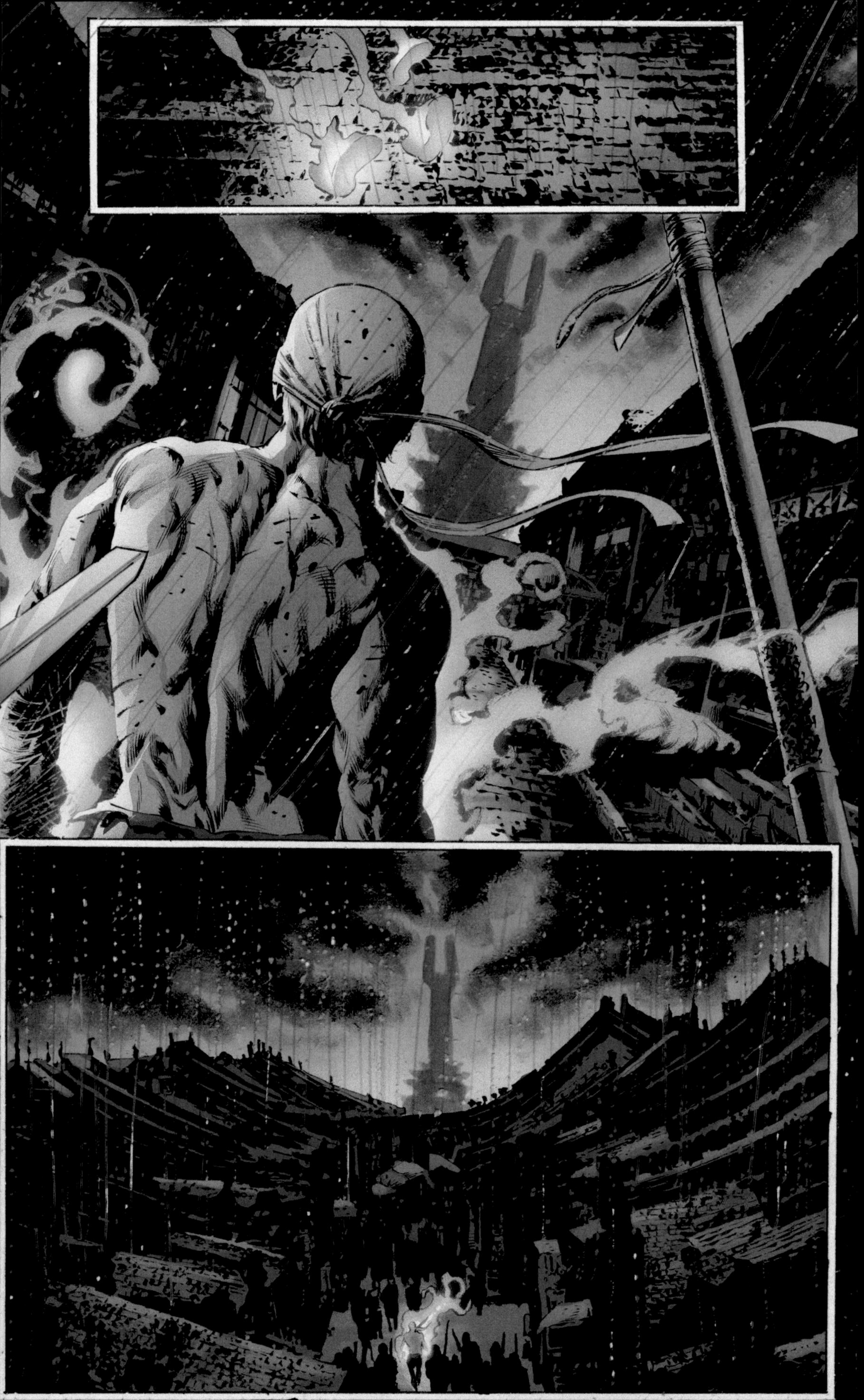

"THE TRIAL OF THE SEVEN MASTERS"

CONCLUSION

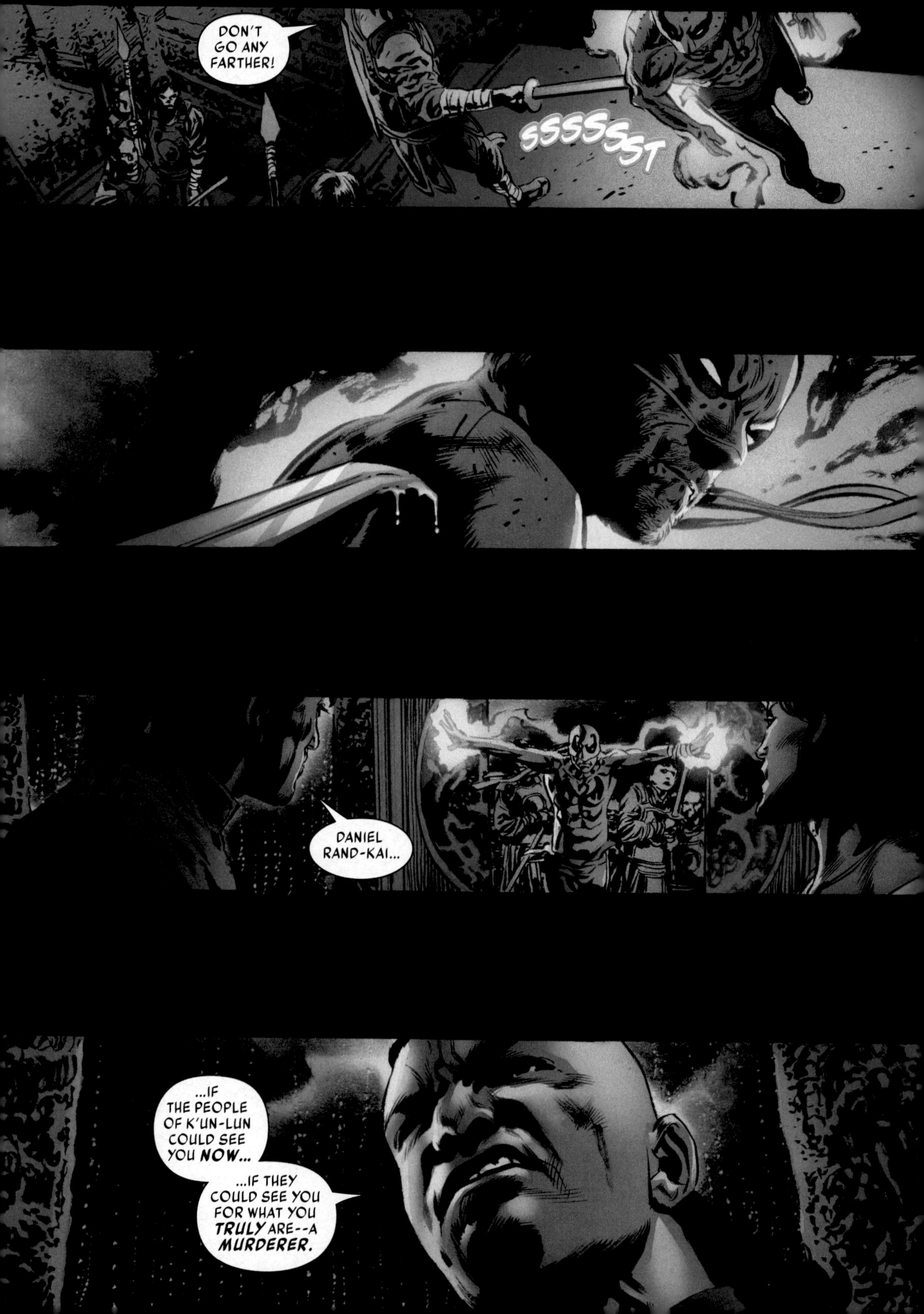
DON'T GO ANY FARTHER!
SSSSSSST
DANIEL RAND-KAI...
...IF THE PEOPLE OF K'UN-LUN COULD SEE YOU **NOW...**
...IF THEY COULD SEE YOU FOR WHAT YOU ***TRULY*** ARE--A ***MURDERER.***

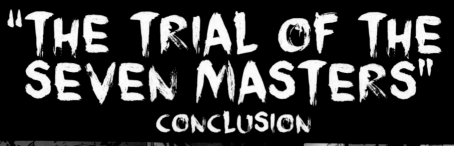

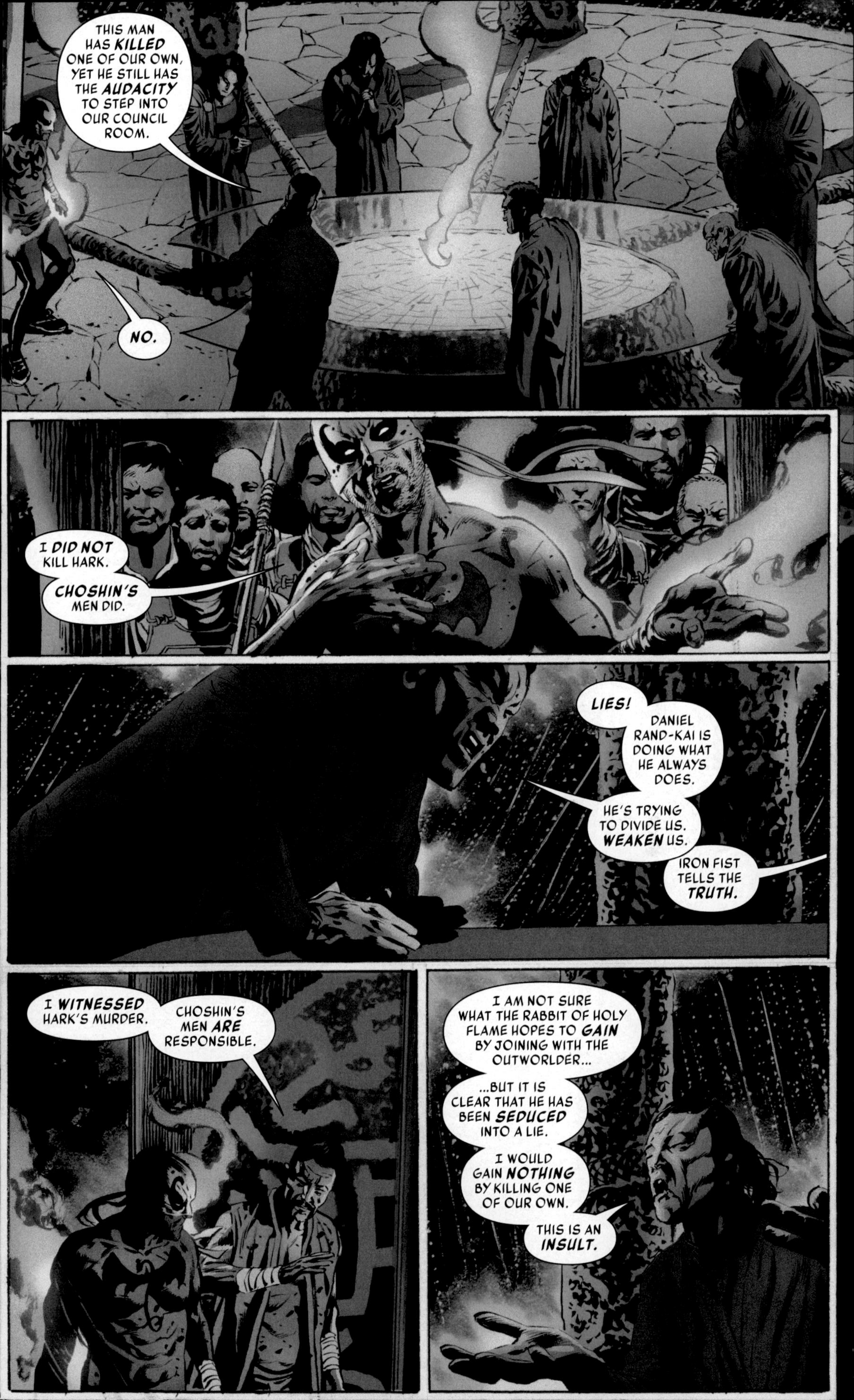
THIS MAN HAS KILLED ONE OF OUR OWN, YET HE STILL HAS THE AUDACITY TO STEP INTO OUR COUNCIL ROOM.
NO.
I DID NOT KILL HARK.
CHOSHIN'S MEN DID.
LIES!
DANIEL RAND-KAI IS DOING WHAT HE ALWAYS DOES.
HE'S TRYING TO DIVIDE US. WEAKEN US.
IRON FIST TELLS THE TRUTH.
I WITNESSED HARK'S MURDER.
CHOSHIN'S MEN ARE RESPONSIBLE.
I AM NOT SURE WHAT THE RABBIT OF HOLY FLAME HOPES TO GAIN BY JOINING WITH THE OUTWORLDER...
...BUT IT IS CLEAR THAT HE HAS BEEN SEDUCED INTO A LIE.
I WOULD GAIN NOTHING BY KILLING ONE OF OUR OWN.
THIS IS AN INSULT.

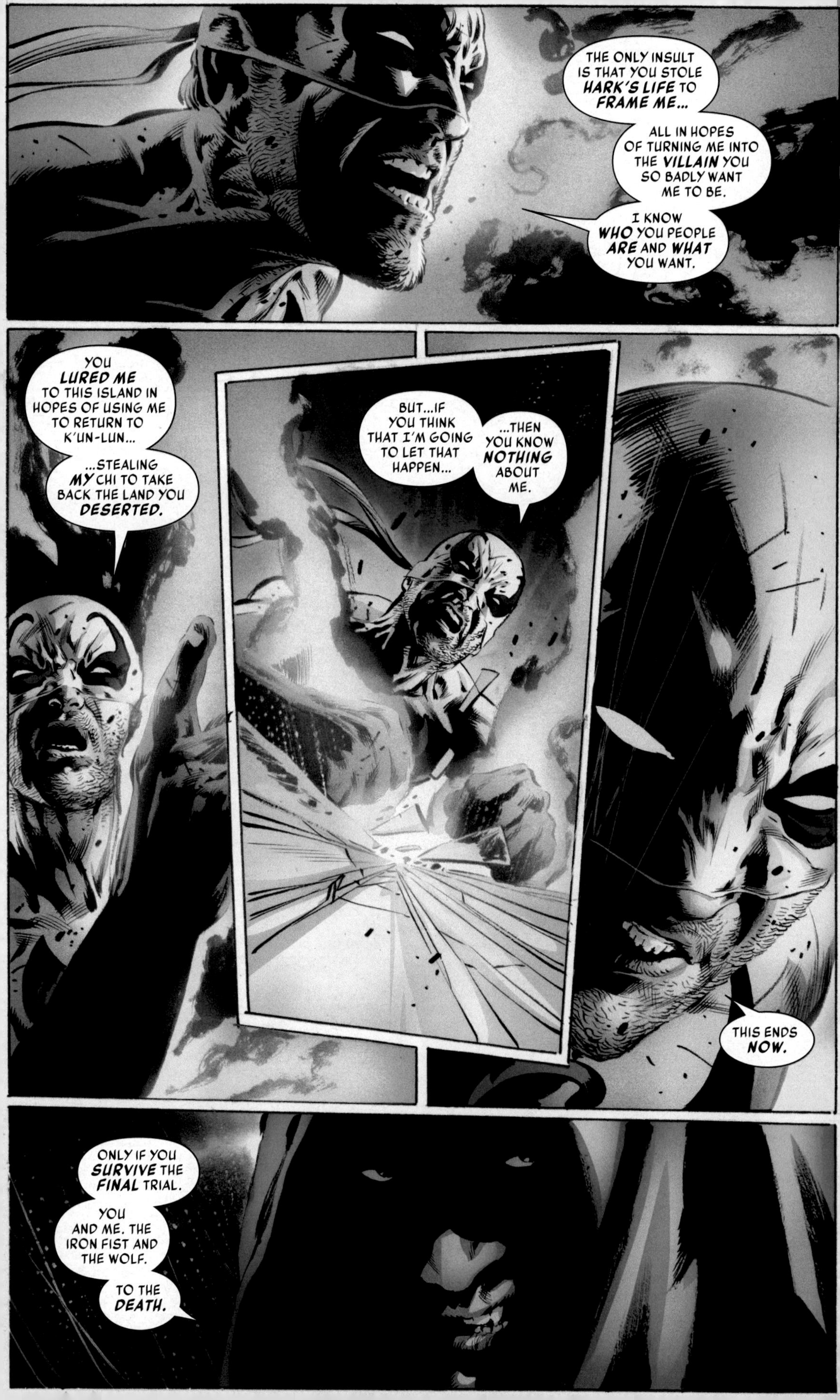
THE ONLY INSULT IS THAT YOU STOLE HARK'S LIFE TO FRAME ME...
ALL IN HOPES OF TURNING ME INTO THE VILLAIN YOU SO BADLY WANT ME TO BE.
I KNOW WHO YOU PEOPLE ARE AND WHAT YOU WANT.
YOU LURED ME TO THIS ISLAND IN HOPES OF USING ME TO RETURN TO K'UN-LUN...
...STEALING MY CHI TO TAKE BACK THE LAND YOU DESERTED.
BUT...IF YOU THINK THAT I'M GOING TO LET THAT HAPPEN...
...THEN YOU KNOW NOTHING ABOUT ME.
THIS ENDS NOW.
ONLY IF YOU SURVIVE THE FINAL TRIAL.
YOU AND ME. THE IRON FIST AND THE WOLF.
TO THE DEATH.

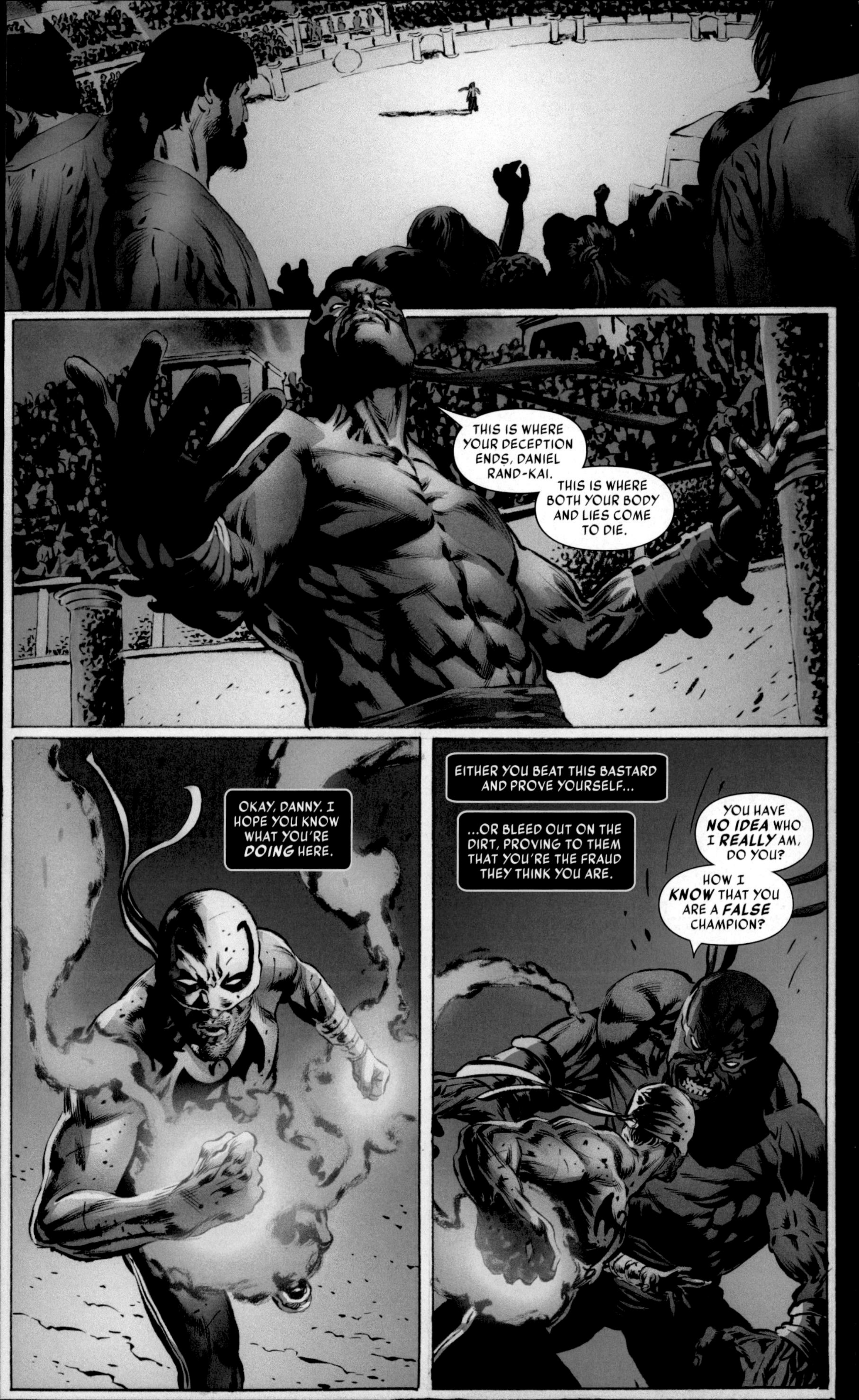
THIS IS WHERE YOUR DECEPTION ENDS, DANIEL RAND-KAI.
THIS IS WHERE BOTH YOUR BODY AND LIES COME TO DIE.
OKAY, DANNY. I HOPE YOU KNOW WHAT YOU'RE DOING HERE.
EITHER YOU BEAT THIS BASTARD AND PROVE YOURSELF...
...OR BLEED OUT ON THE DIRT, PROVING TO THEM THAT YOU'RE THE FRAUD THEY THINK YOU ARE.
YOU HAVE NO IDEA WHO I REALLY AM, DO YOU?
HOW I KNOW THAT YOU ARE A FALSE CHAMPION?

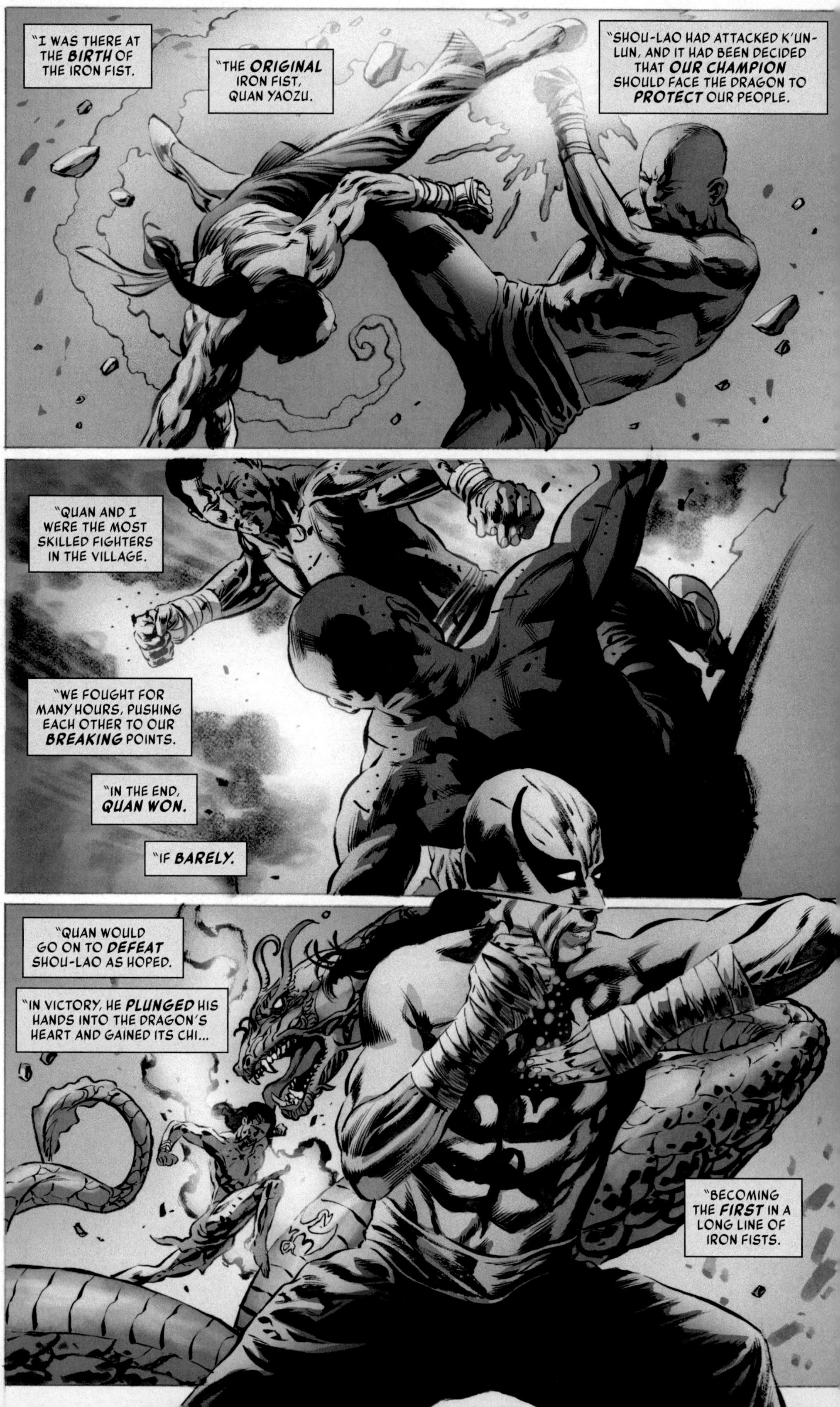
"I WAS THERE AT THE BIRTH OF THE IRON FIST.
"THE ORIGINAL IRON FIST, QUAN YAOZU.
"SHOU-LAO HAD ATTACKED K'UN-LUN, AND IT HAD BEEN DECIDED THAT OUR CHAMPION SHOULD FACE THE DRAGON TO PROTECT OUR PEOPLE.
"QUAN AND I WERE THE MOST SKILLED FIGHTERS IN THE VILLAGE.
"WE FOUGHT FOR MANY HOURS, PUSHING EACH OTHER TO OUR BREAKING POINTS.
"IN THE END, QUAN WON.
"IF BARELY.
"QUAN WOULD GO ON TO DEFEAT SHOU-LAO AS HOPED.
"IN VICTORY, HE PLUNGED HIS HANDS INTO THE DRAGON'S HEART AND GAINED ITS CHI...
"BECOMING THE FIRST IN A LONG LINE OF IRON FISTS.

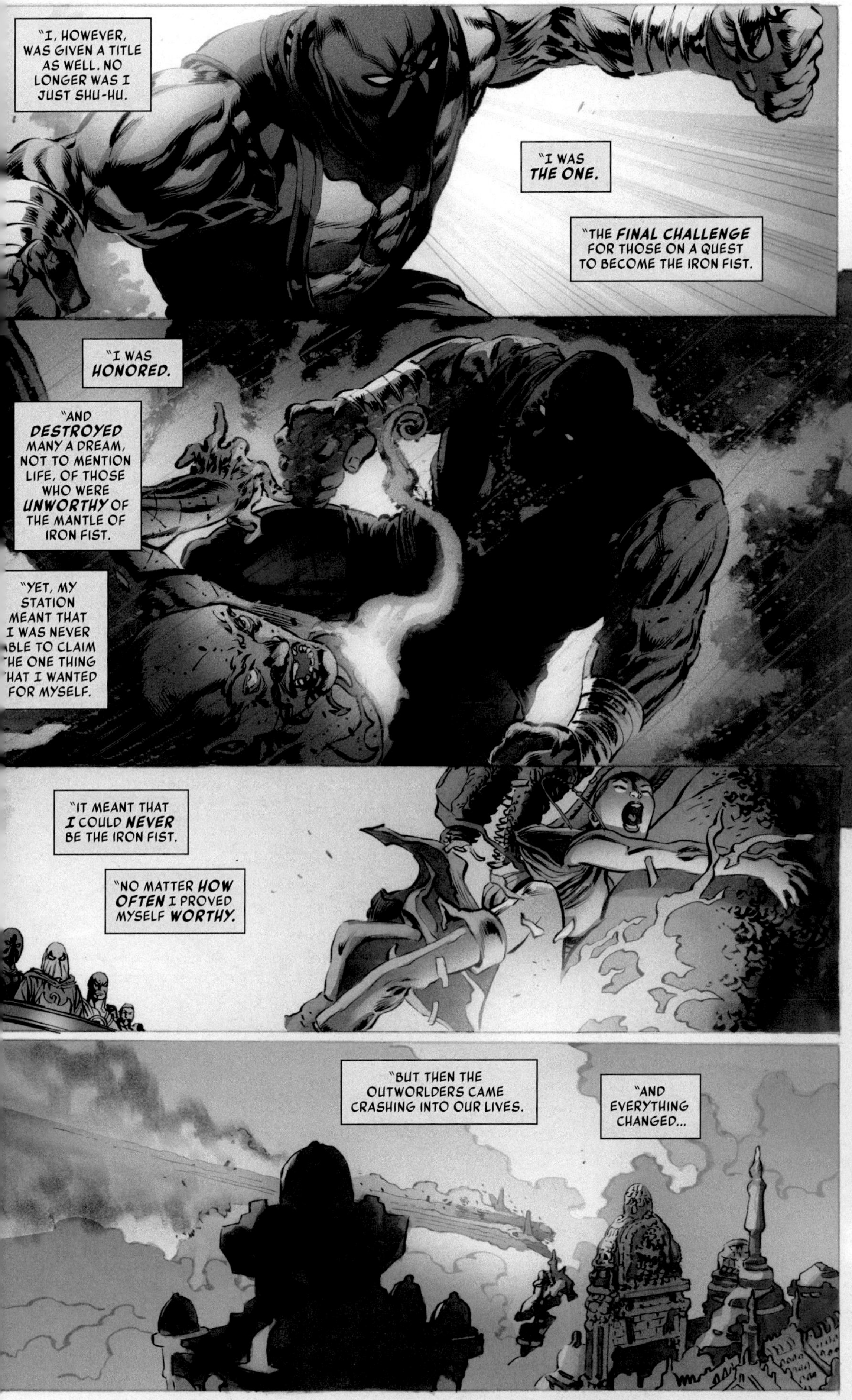
"I, HOWEVER, WAS GIVEN A TITLE AS WELL. NO LONGER WAS I JUST SHU-HU.
"I WAS ***THE ONE.***
"THE ***FINAL CHALLENGE*** FOR THOSE ON A QUEST TO BECOME THE IRON FIST.
"I WAS ***HONORED.***
"AND ***DESTROYED*** MANY A DREAM, NOT TO MENTION LIFE, OF THOSE WHO WERE ***UNWORTHY*** OF THE MANTLE OF IRON FIST.
"YET, MY STATION MEANT THAT I WAS NEVER BLE TO CLAIM HE ONE THING HAT I WANTED FOR MYSELF.
"IT MEANT THAT ***I*** COULD ***NEVER*** BE THE IRON FIST.
"NO MATTER ***HOW OFTEN*** I PROVED MYSELF ***WORTHY.***
"BUT THEN THE OUTWORLDERS CAME CRASHING INTO OUR LIVES.
"AND EVERYTHING CHANGED...

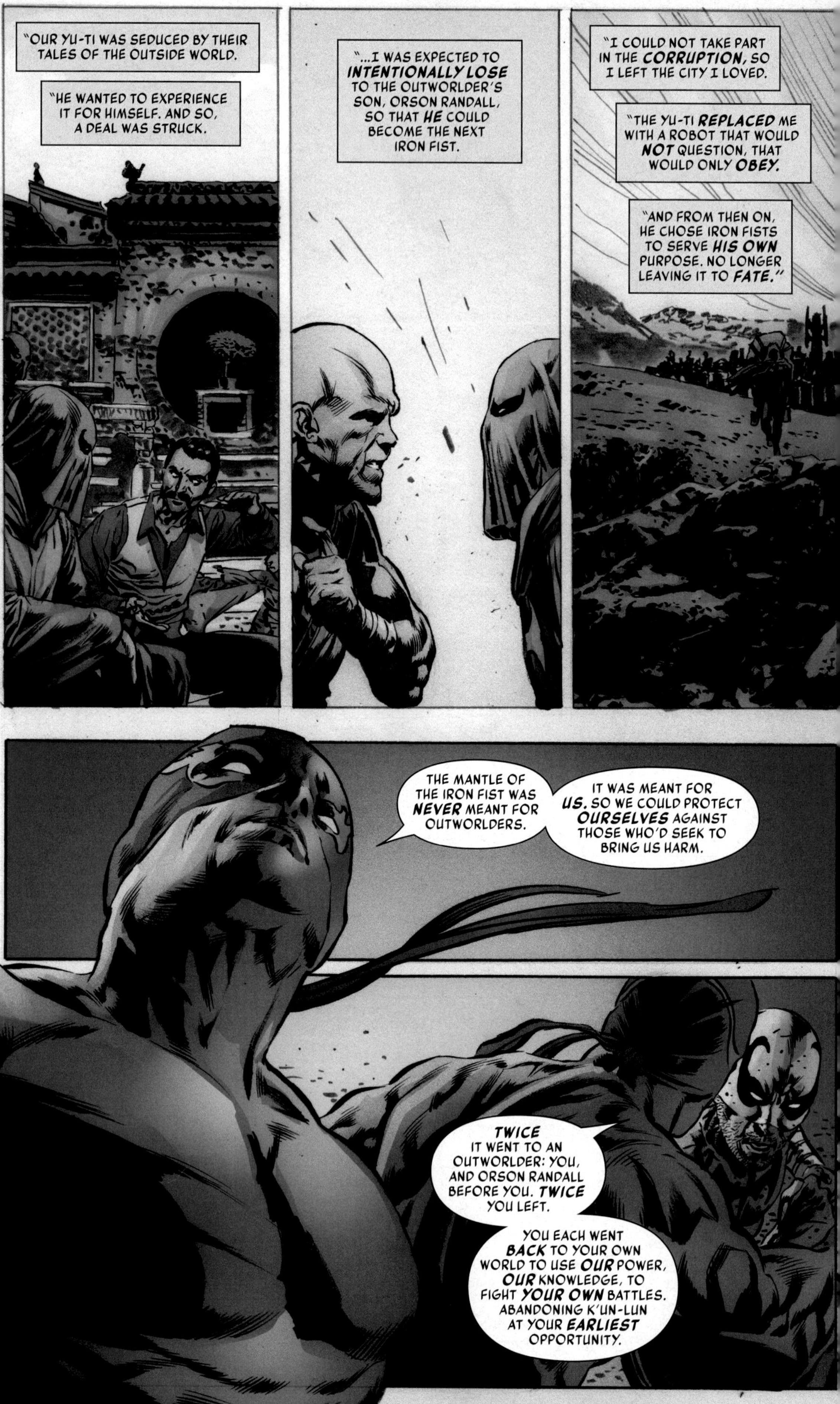
"OUR YU-TI WAS SEDUCED BY THEIR TALES OF THE OUTSIDE WORLD.
"HE WANTED TO EXPERIENCE IT FOR HIMSELF. AND SO, A DEAL WAS STRUCK.
"...I WAS EXPECTED TO INTENTIONALLY LOSE TO THE OUTWORLDER'S SON, ORSON RANDALL, SO THAT HE COULD BECOME THE NEXT IRON FIST.
"I COULD NOT TAKE PART IN THE CORRUPTION, SO I LEFT THE CITY I LOVED.
"THE YU-TI REPLACED ME WITH A ROBOT THAT WOULD NOT QUESTION, THAT WOULD ONLY OBEY.
"AND FROM THEN ON, HE CHOSE IRON FISTS TO SERVE HIS OWN PURPOSE. NO LONGER LEAVING IT TO FATE."
THE MANTLE OF THE IRON FIST WAS NEVER MEANT FOR OUTWORLDERS.
IT WAS MEANT FOR US. SO WE COULD PROTECT OURSELVES AGAINST THOSE WHO'D SEEK TO BRING US HARM.
TWICE IT WENT TO AN OUTWORLDER: YOU, AND ORSON RANDALL BEFORE YOU. TWICE YOU LEFT.
YOU EACH WENT BACK TO YOUR OWN WORLD TO USE OUR POWER, OUR KNOWLEDGE, TO FIGHT YOUR OWN BATTLES. ABANDONING K'UN-LUN AT YOUR EARLIEST OPPORTUNITY.

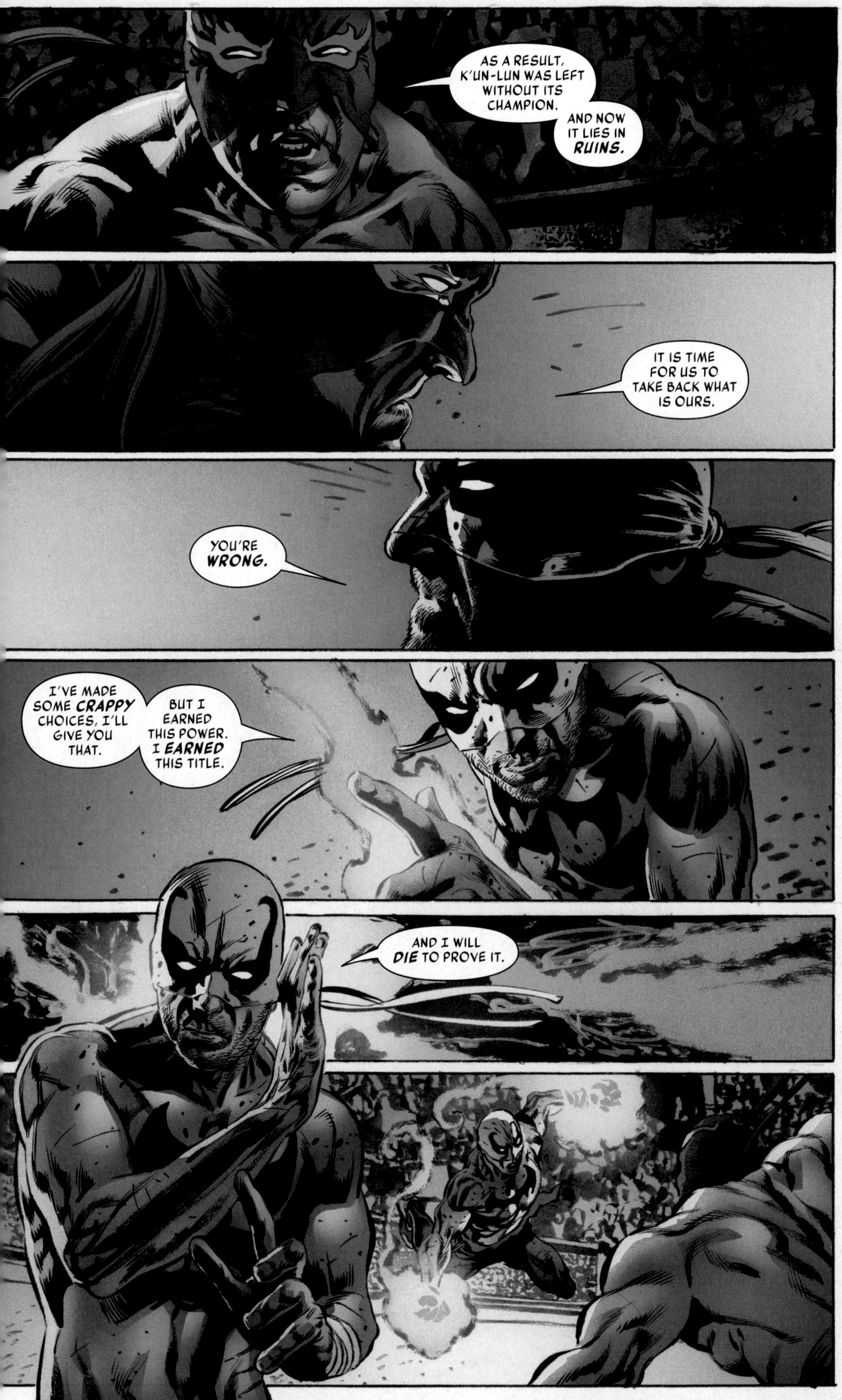
AS A RESULT, K'UN-LUN WAS LEFT WITHOUT ITS CHAMPION.
AND NOW IT LIES IN RUINS.
IT IS TIME FOR US TO TAKE BACK WHAT IS OURS.
YOU'RE WRONG.
I'VE MADE SOME CRAPPY CHOICES, I'LL GIVE YOU THAT.
BUT I EARNED THIS POWER. I EARNED THIS TITLE.
AND I WILL DIE TO PROVE IT.

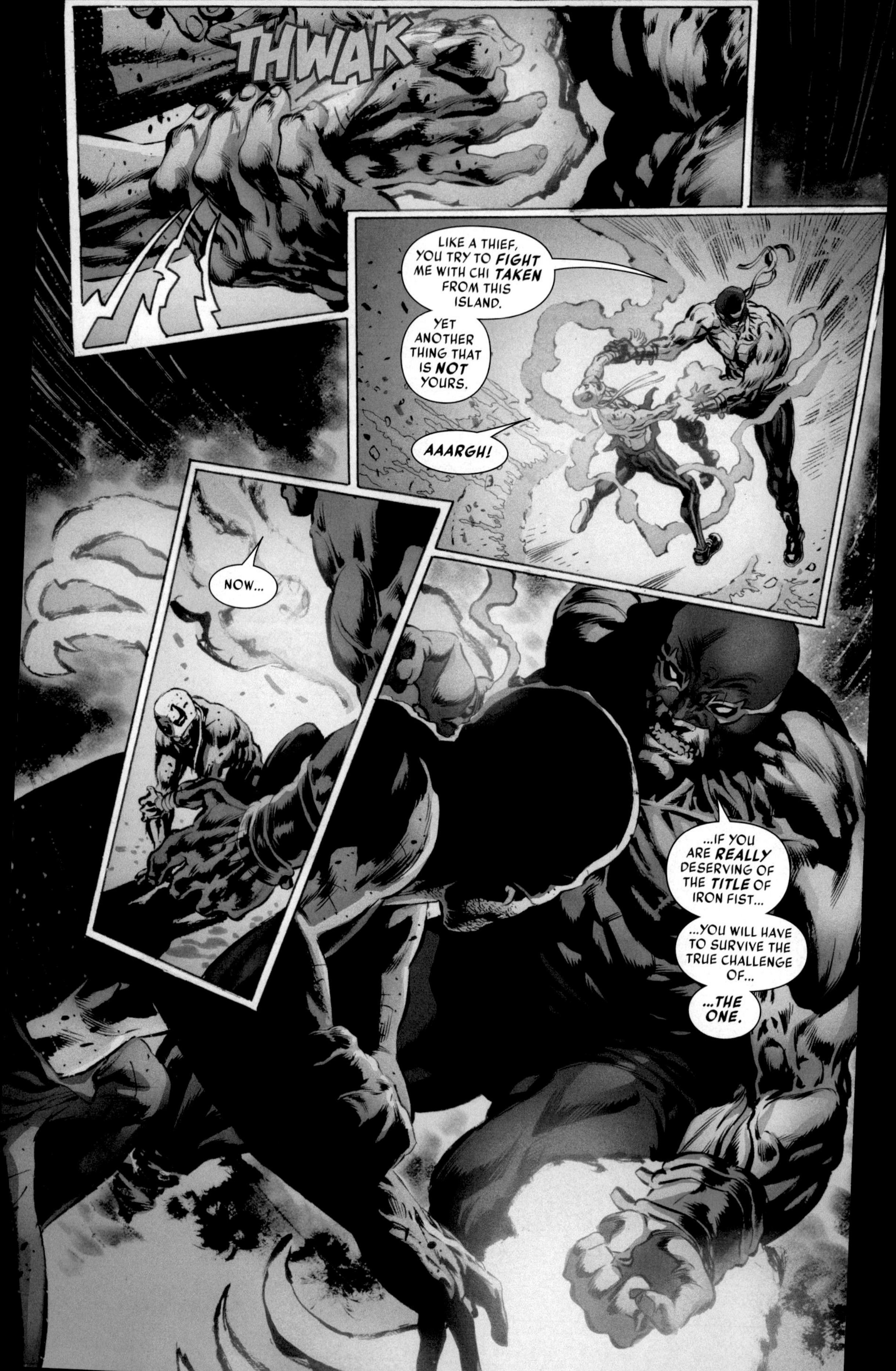
THWAK
LIKE A THIEF, YOU TRY TO FIGHT ME WITH CHI TAKEN FROM THIS ISLAND.
YET ANOTHER THING THAT IS NOT YOURS.
AAARGH!
NOW...
...IF YOU ARE REALLY DESERVING OF THE TITLE OF IRON FIST...
...YOU WILL HAVE TO SURVIVE THE TRUE CHALLENGE OF...
...THE ONE.

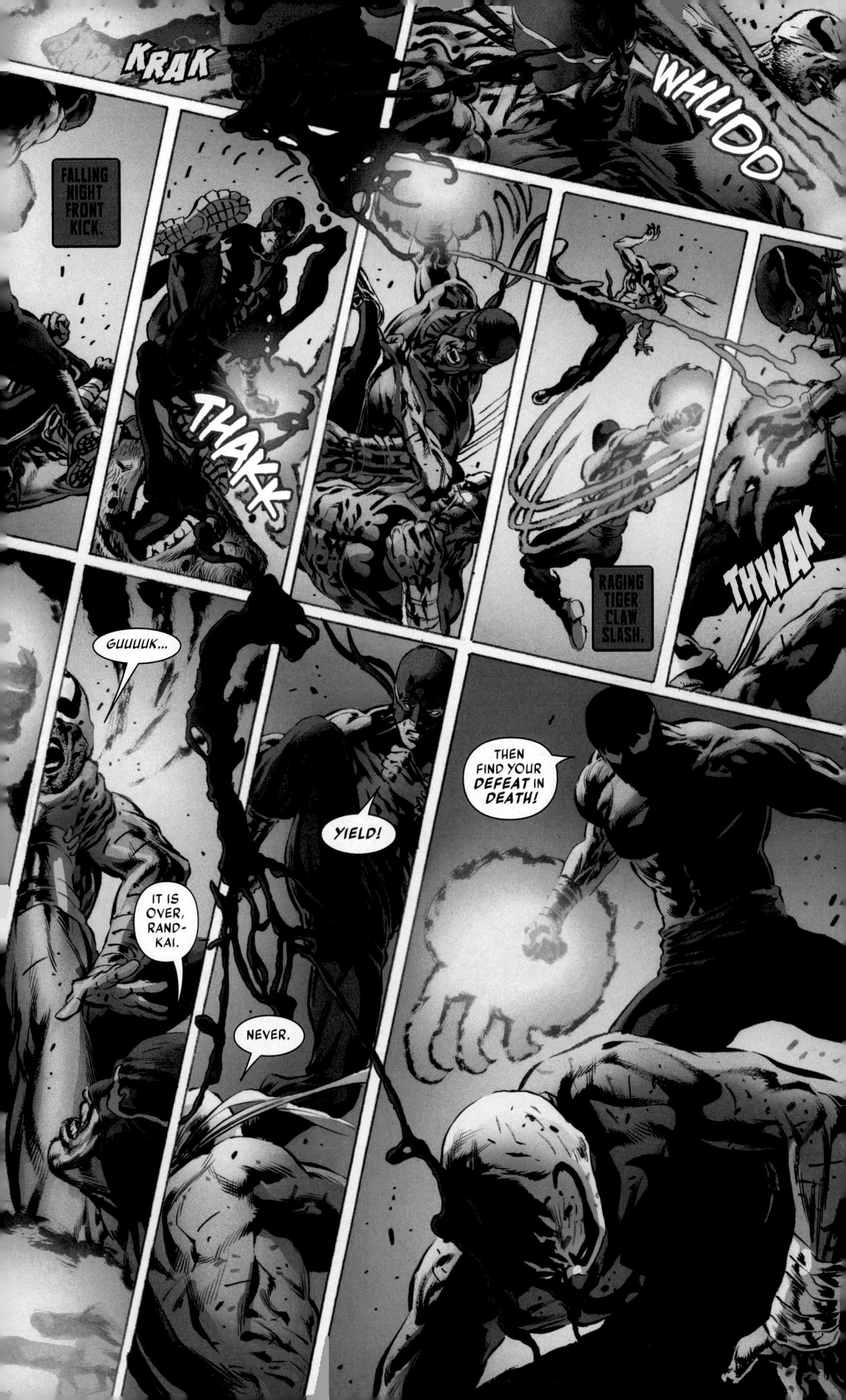

KRAK
WHUDD
FALLING NIGHT FRONT KICK.
THAKK
RAGING TIGER CLAW SLASH.
THWAK
GUUUUK...
IT IS OVER, RAND-KAI.
YIELD!
NEVER.
THEN FIND YOUR DEFEAT IN DEATH!

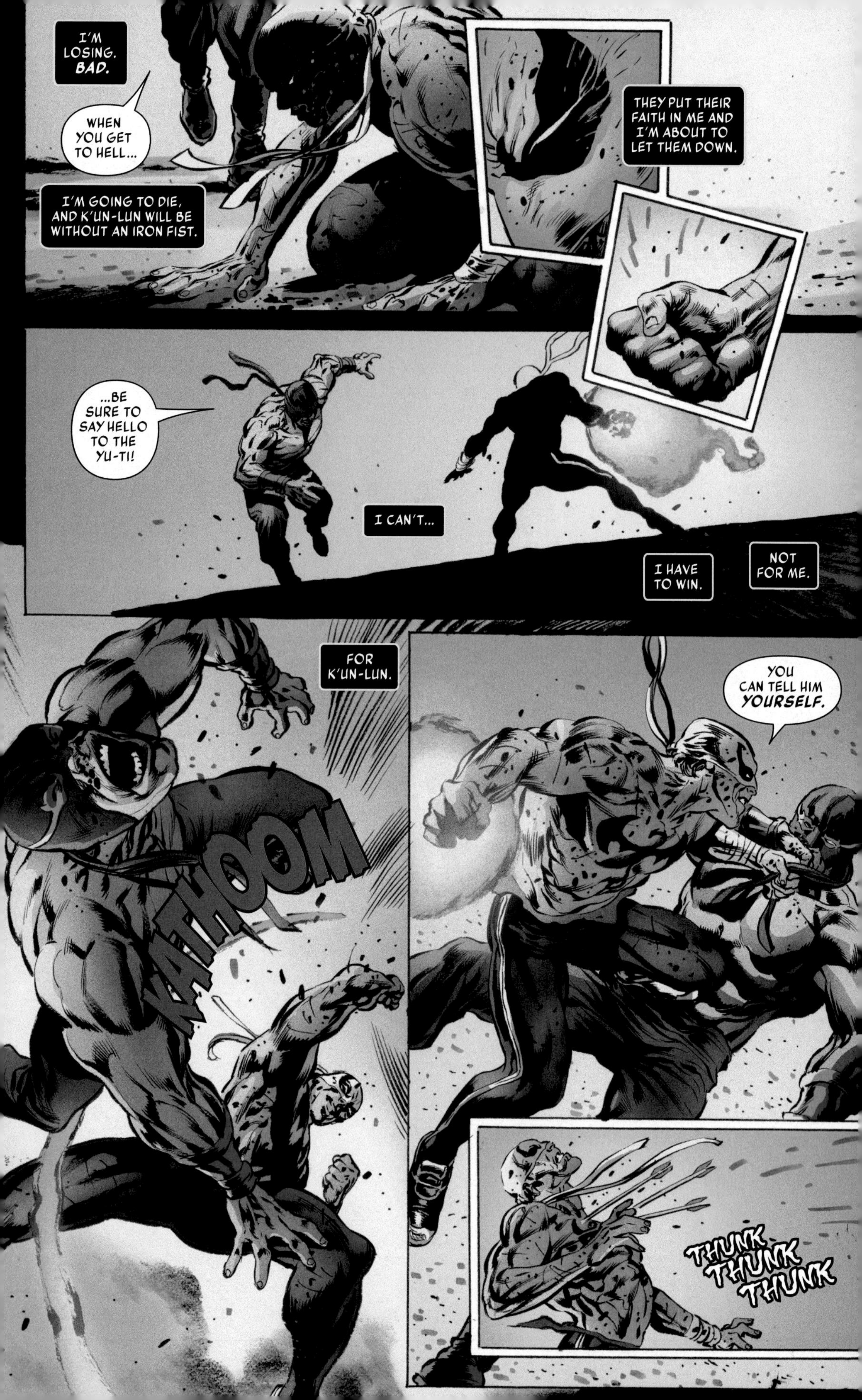
I'M LOSING. BAD.
WHEN YOU GET TO HELL...
I'M GOING TO DIE, AND K'UN-LUN WILL BE WITHOUT AN IRON FIST.
THEY PUT THEIR FAITH IN ME AND I'M ABOUT TO LET THEM DOWN.
...BE SURE TO SAY HELLO TO THE YU-TI!
I CAN'T...
I HAVE TO WIN.
NOT FOR ME.
FOR K'UN-LUN.
KATHOOM
YOU CAN TELL HIM YOURSELF.
THUNK THUNK THUNK

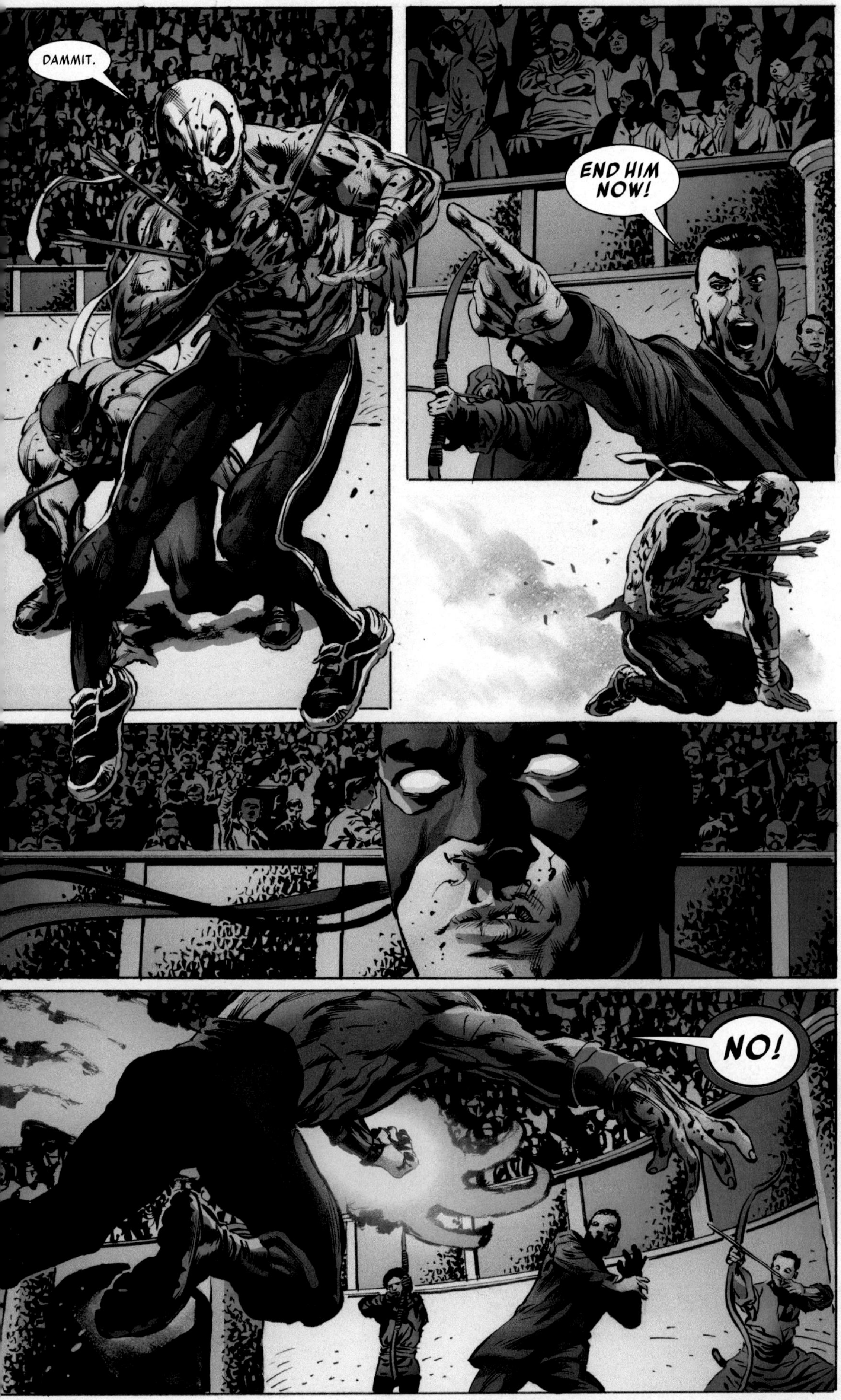
DAMMIT.
END HIM NOW!
NO!

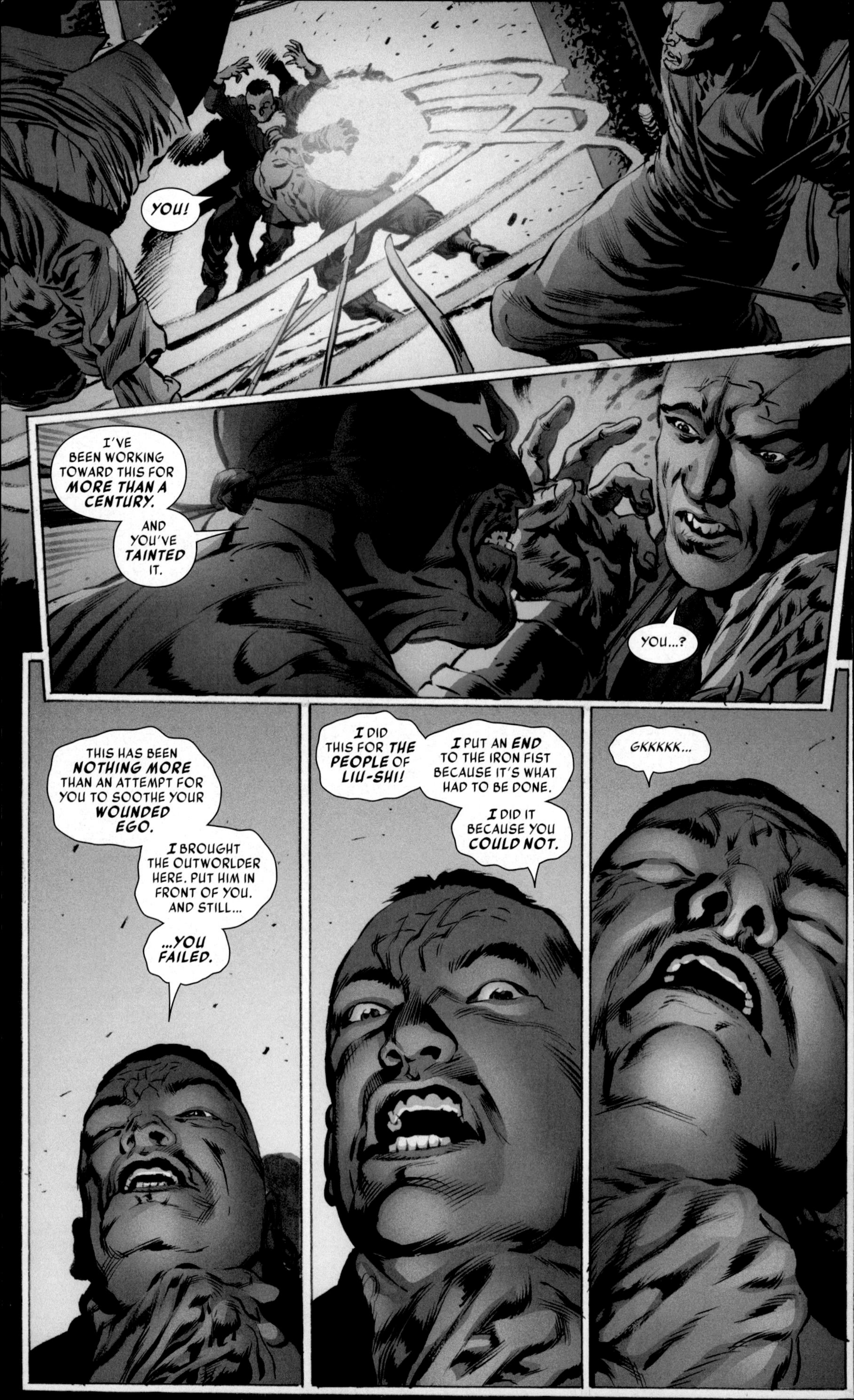
YOU!
I'VE BEEN WORKING TOWARD THIS FOR MORE THAN A CENTURY.
AND YOU'VE TAINTED IT.
YOU...?
THIS HAS BEEN NOTHING MORE THAN AN ATTEMPT FOR YOU TO SOOTHE YOUR WOUNDED EGO.
I BROUGHT THE OUTWORLDER HERE. PUT HIM IN FRONT OF YOU. AND STILL...
...YOU FAILED.
I DID THIS FOR THE PEOPLE OF LIU-SHI!
I PUT AN END TO THE IRON FIST BECAUSE IT'S WHAT HAD TO BE DONE.
I DID IT BECAUSE YOU COULD NOT.
GKKKKK...

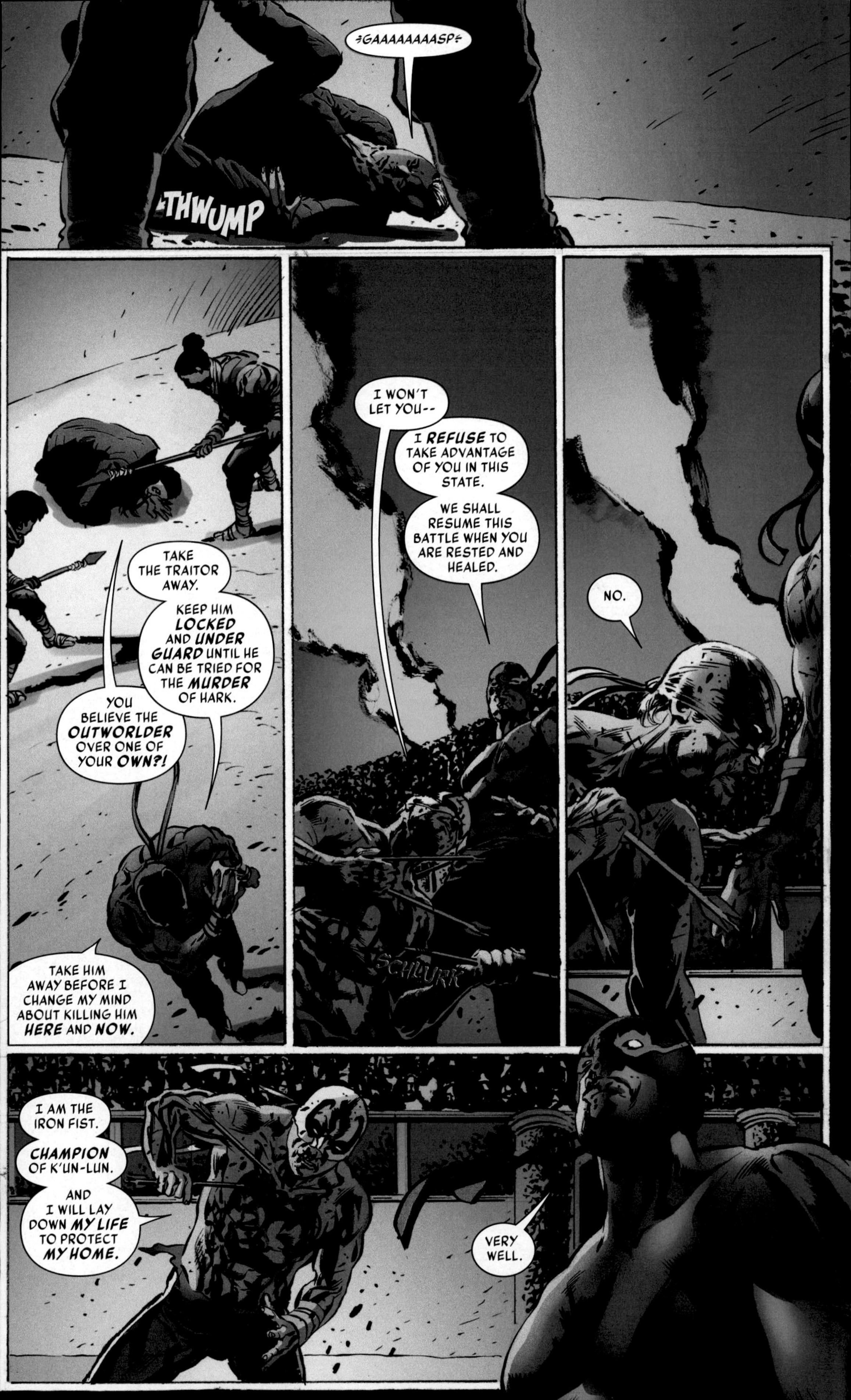

GAAAAAAAASP
THWUMP
TAKE THE TRAITOR AWAY.
KEEP HIM LOCKED AND UNDER GUARD UNTIL HE CAN BE TRIED FOR THE MURDER OF HARK.
YOU BELIEVE THE OUTWORLDER OVER ONE OF YOUR OWN?!
TAKE HIM AWAY BEFORE I CHANGE MY MIND ABOUT KILLING HIM HERE AND NOW.
I WON'T LET YOU--
I REFUSE TO TAKE ADVANTAGE OF YOU IN THIS STATE.
WE SHALL RESUME THIS BATTLE WHEN YOU ARE RESTED AND HEALED.
SCHLURK
NO.
I AM THE IRON FIST.
CHAMPION OF K'UN-LUN.
AND I WILL LAY DOWN MY LIFE TO PROTECT MY HOME.
VERY WELL.

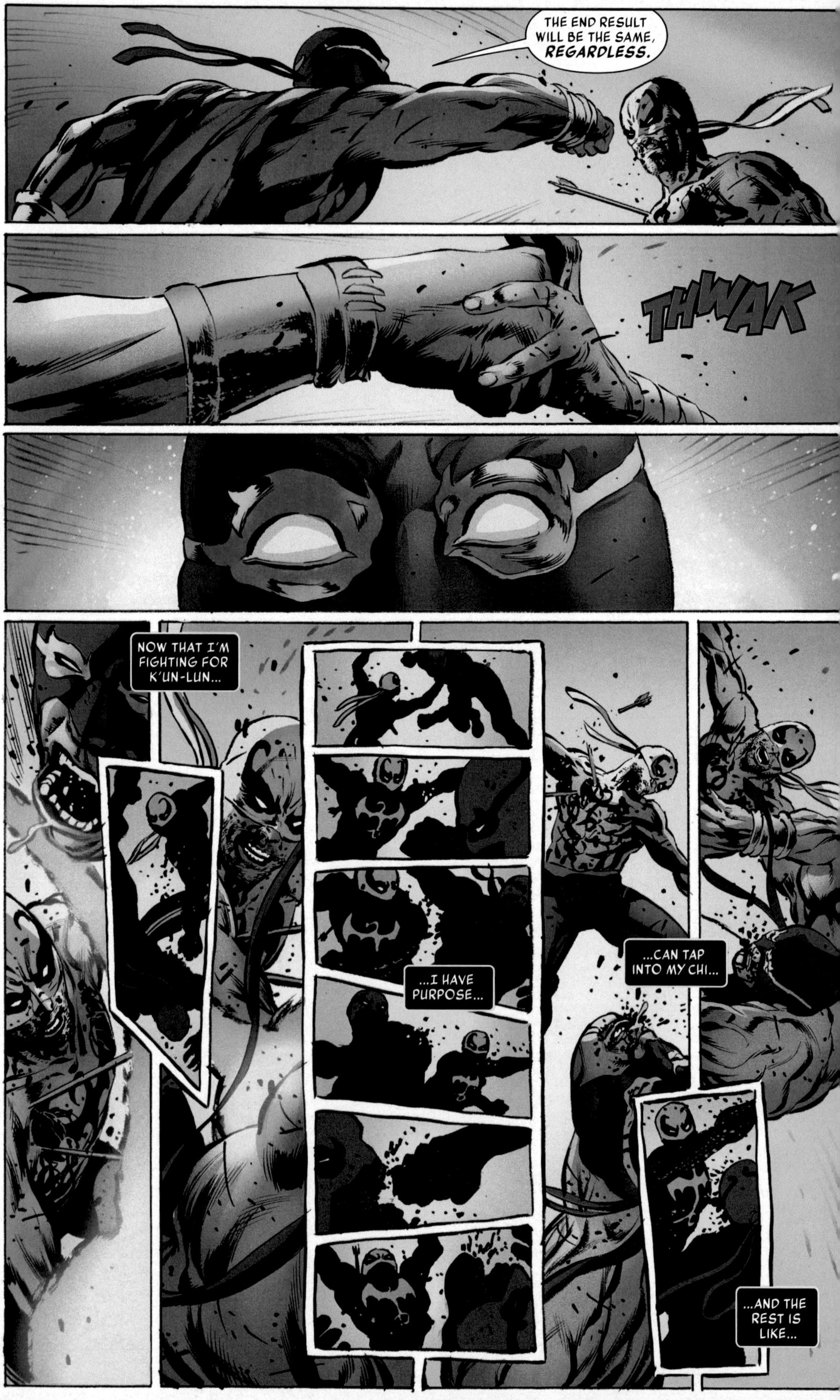
THE END RESULT WILL BE THE SAME, *REGARDLESS.*
THWAK
NOW THAT I'M FIGHTING FOR K'UN-LUN...
...I HAVE PURPOSE...
...CAN TAP INTO MY CHI...
...AND THE REST IS LIKE...

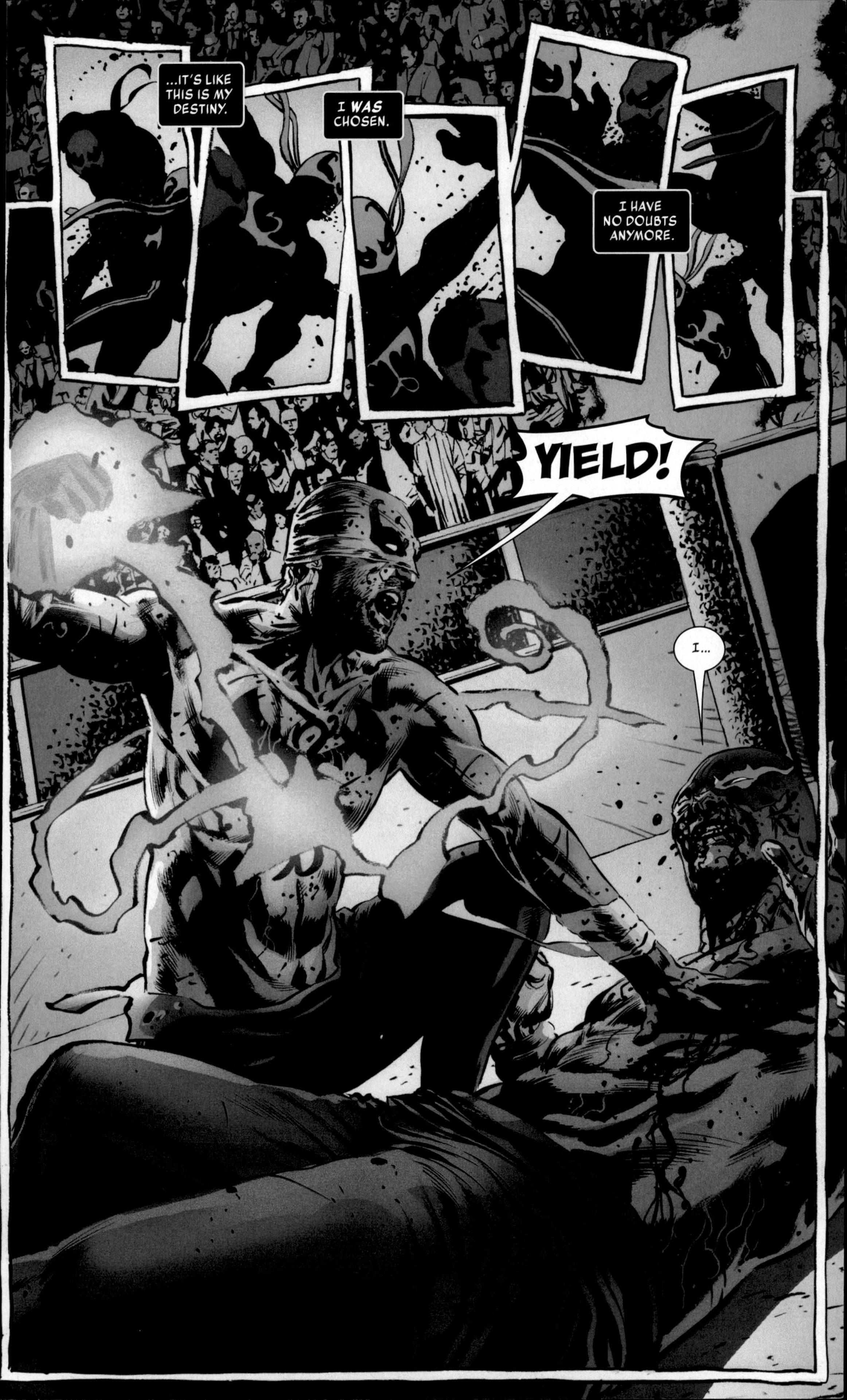
...IT'S LIKE THIS IS MY DESTINY.
I WAS CHOSEN.
I HAVE NO DOUBTS ANYMORE.
YIELD!
I...

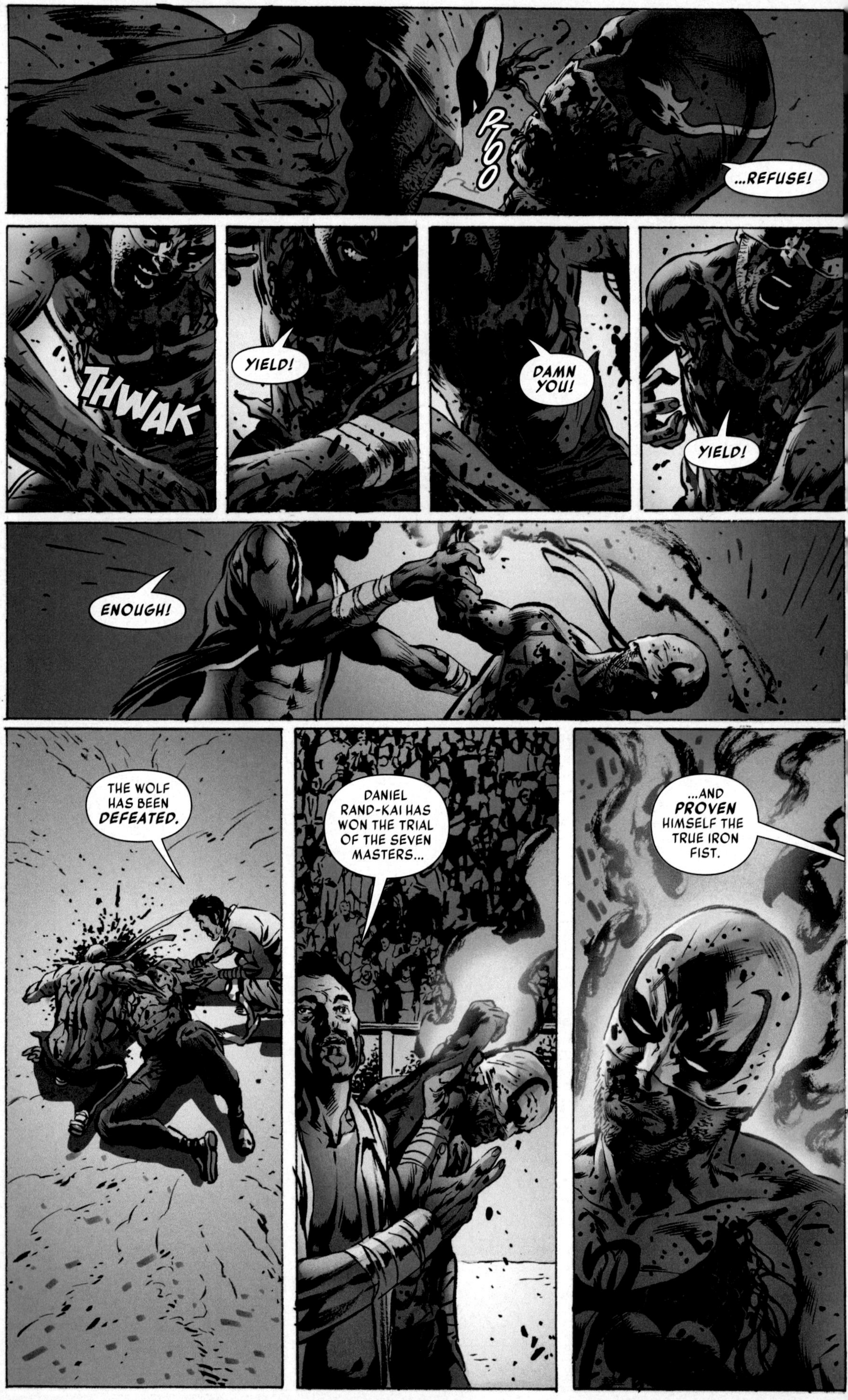
PTOO
...REFUSE!
THWAK
YIELD!
DAMN YOU!
YIELD!
ENOUGH!
THE WOLF HAS BEEN DEFEATED.
DANIEL RAND-KAI HAS WON THE TRIAL OF THE SEVEN MASTERS...
...AND PROVEN HIMSELF THE TRUE IRON FIST.

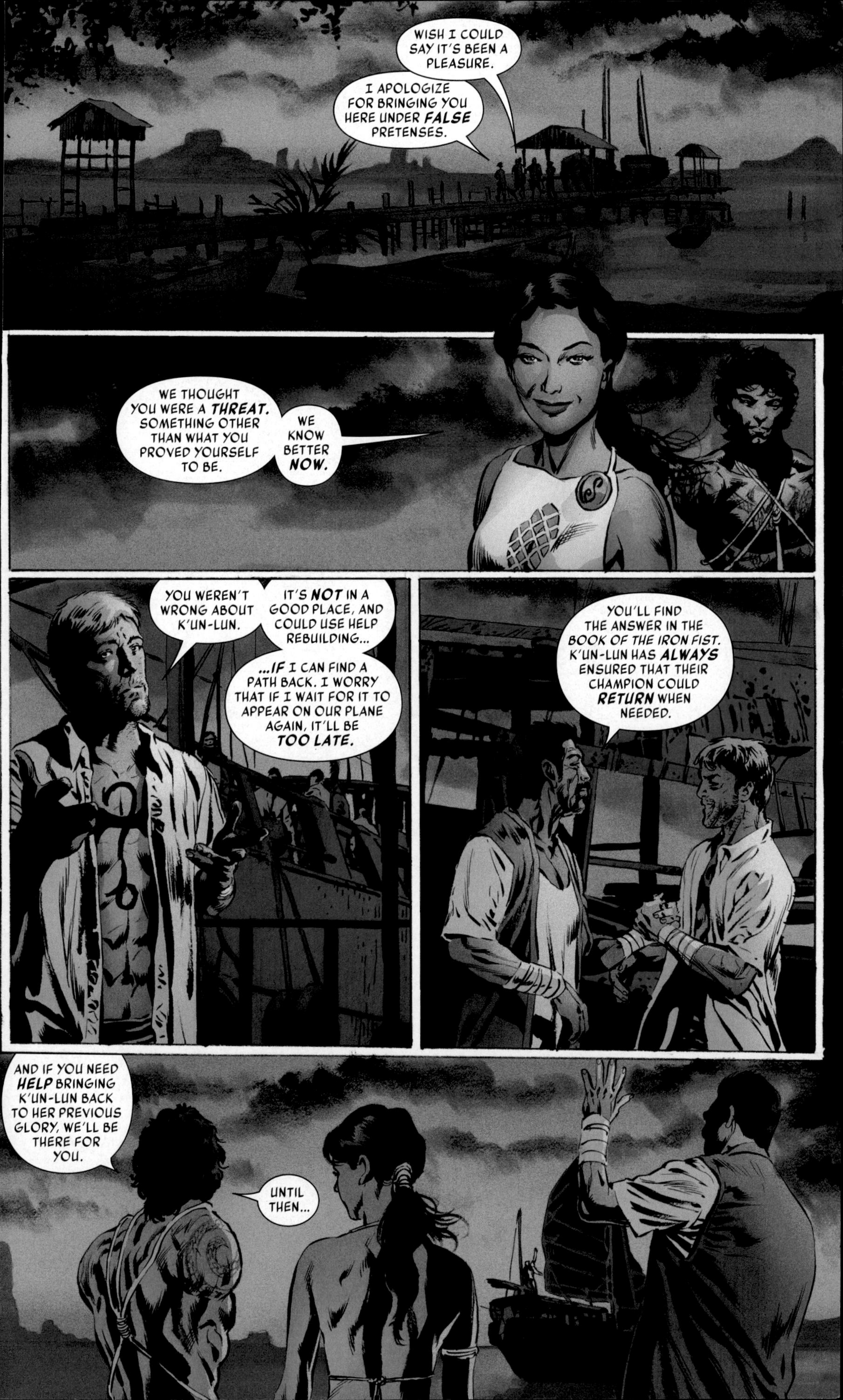
WISH I COULD SAY IT'S BEEN A PLEASURE.
I APOLOGIZE FOR BRINGING YOU HERE UNDER FALSE PRETENSES.
WE THOUGHT YOU WERE A THREAT. SOMETHING OTHER THAN WHAT YOU PROVED YOURSELF TO BE.
WE KNOW BETTER NOW.
YOU WEREN'T WRONG ABOUT K'UN-LUN.
IT'S NOT IN A GOOD PLACE, AND COULD USE HELP REBUILDING...
...IF I CAN FIND A PATH BACK. I WORRY THAT IF I WAIT FOR IT TO APPEAR ON OUR PLANE AGAIN, IT'LL BE TOO LATE.
YOU'LL FIND THE ANSWER IN THE BOOK OF THE IRON FIST. K'UN-LUN HAS ALWAYS ENSURED THAT THEIR CHAMPION COULD RETURN WHEN NEEDED.
AND IF YOU NEED HELP BRINGING K'UN-LUN BACK TO HER PREVIOUS GLORY, WE'LL BE THERE FOR YOU.
UNTIL THEN...

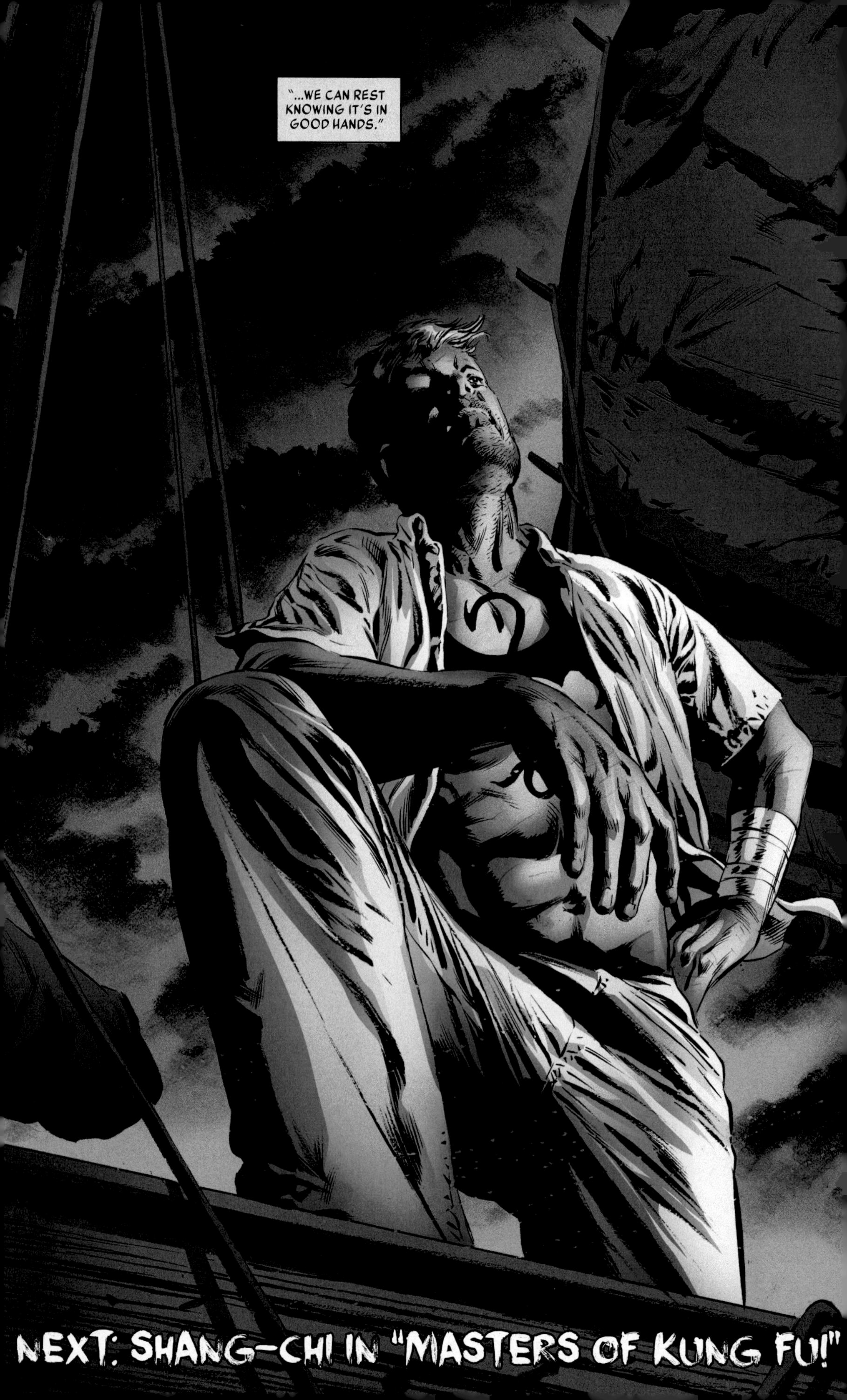
"...WE CAN REST KNOWING IT'S IN GOOD HANDS."
NEXT: SHANG-CHI IN "MASTERS OF KUNG FU!"

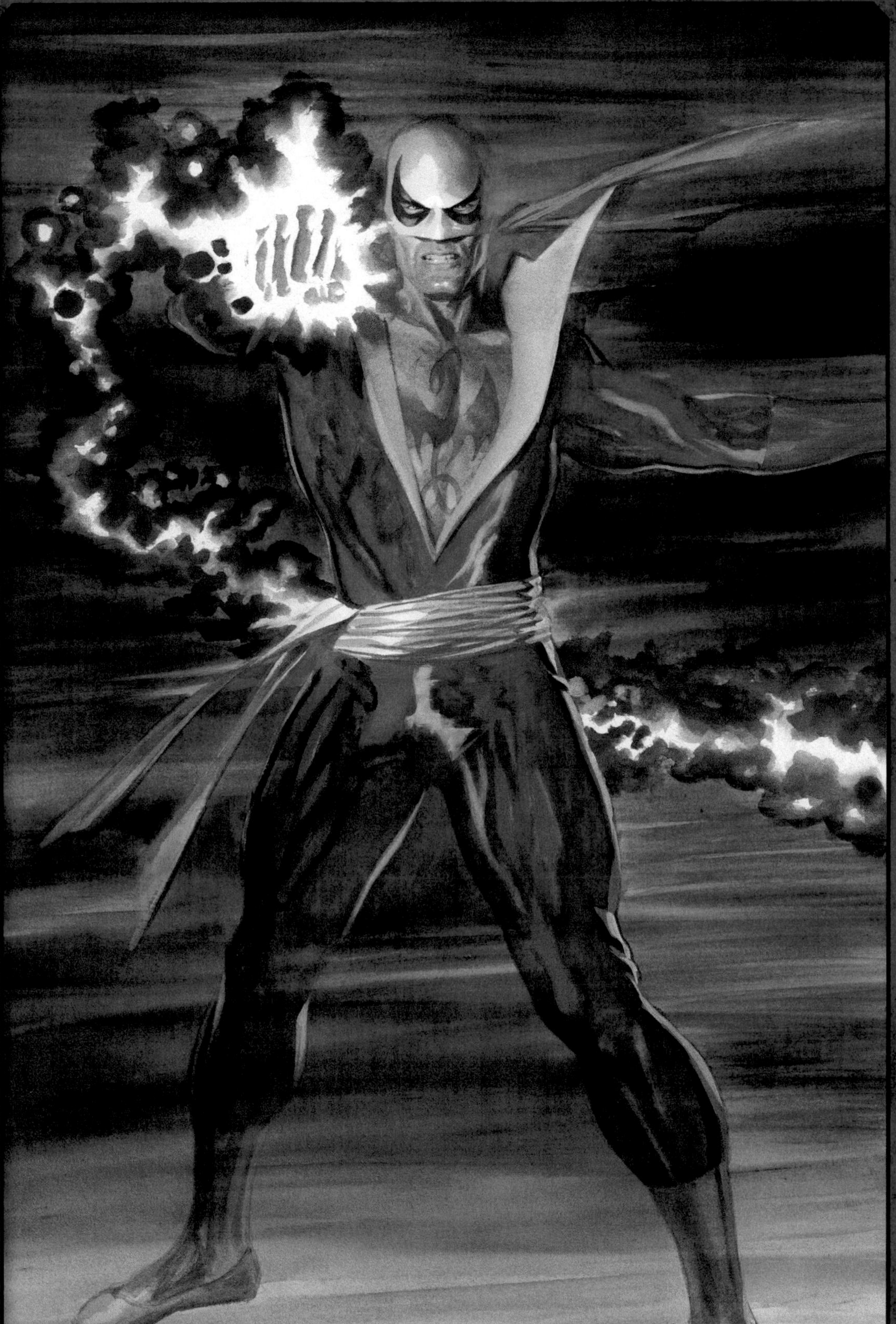

Alex Ross
No. 1 variant

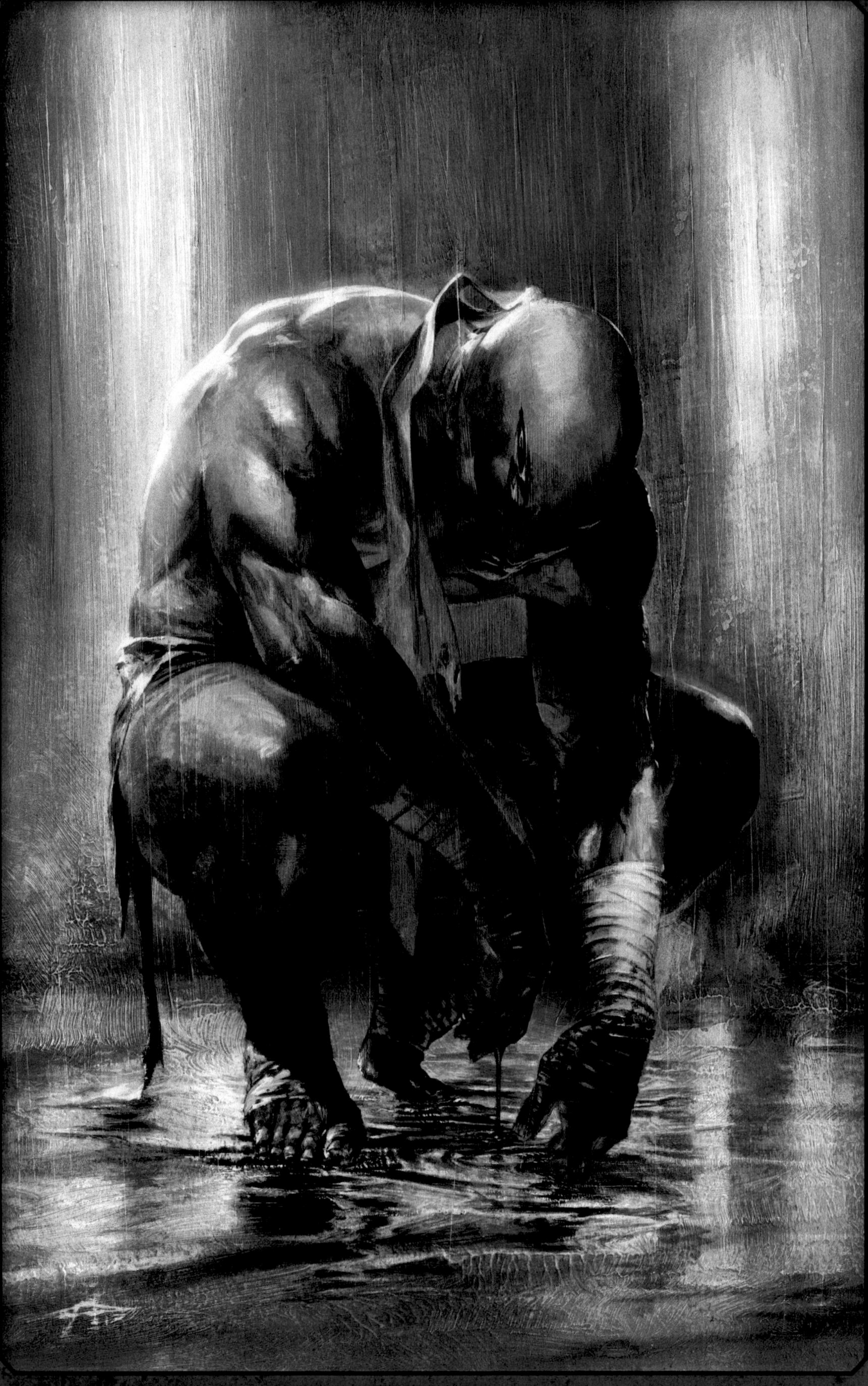

Gabriele Dell'Otto

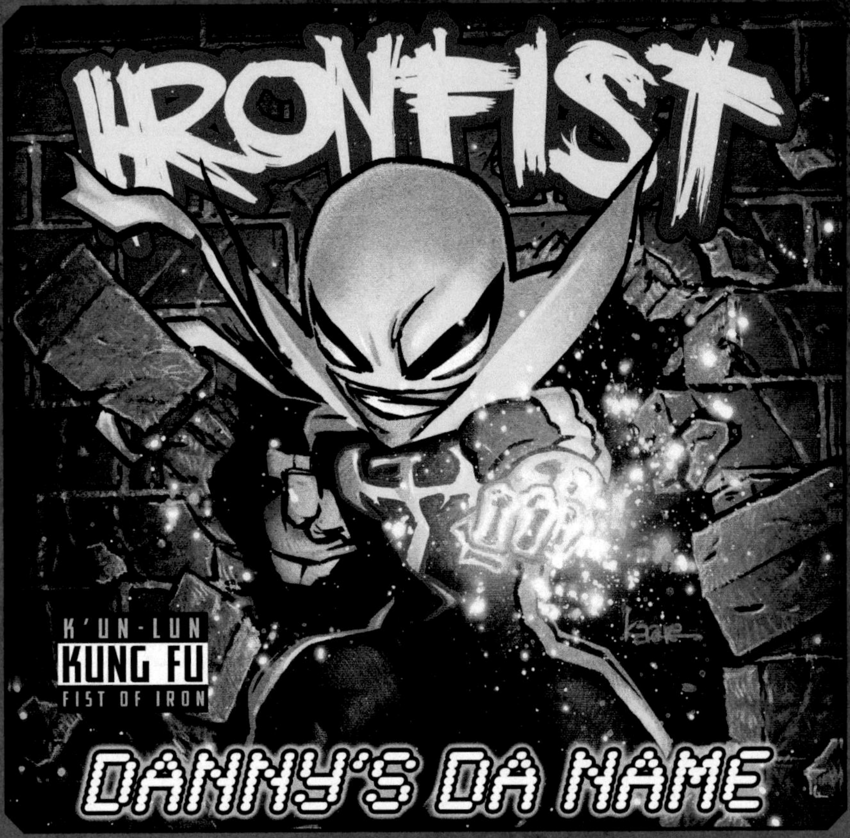
IRON FIST
K'UN-LUN
KUNG FU
FIST OF IRON
DANNY'S DA NAME

Kaare Andrews
No. 1 hip-hop variant

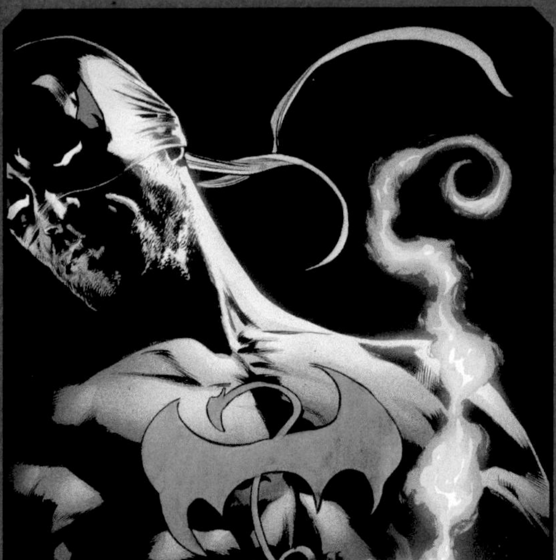

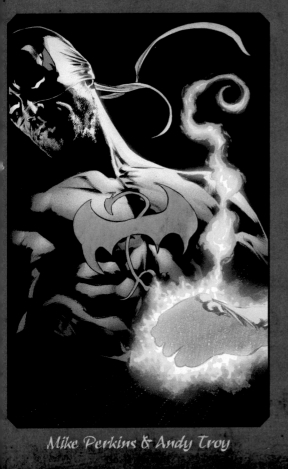

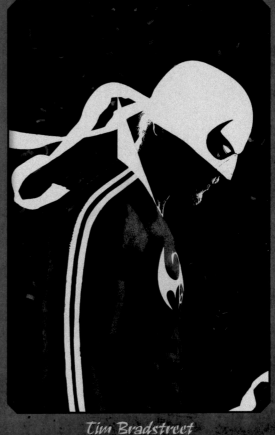

Mike Perkins & Andy Troy

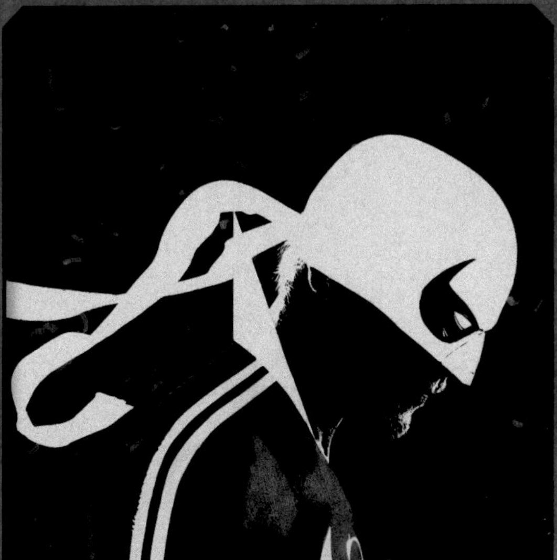

Tim Bradstreet

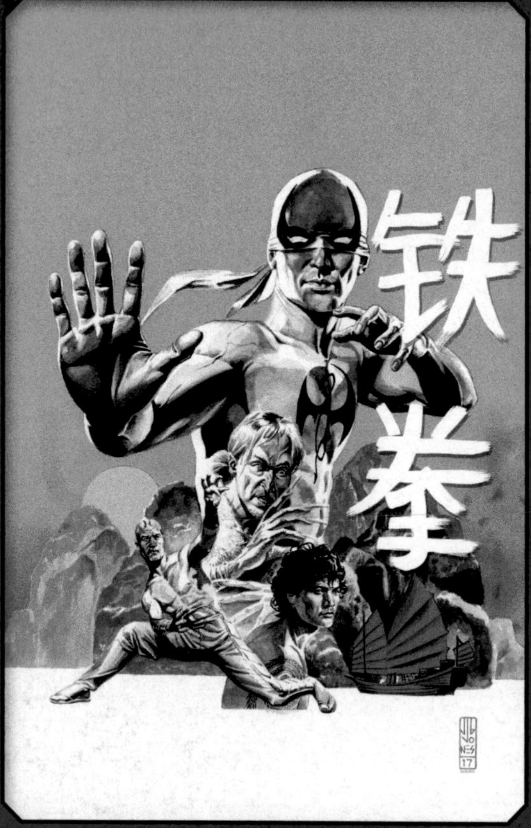
铁
拳

J.G. Jones & Paul Mounts

No. 3 variant

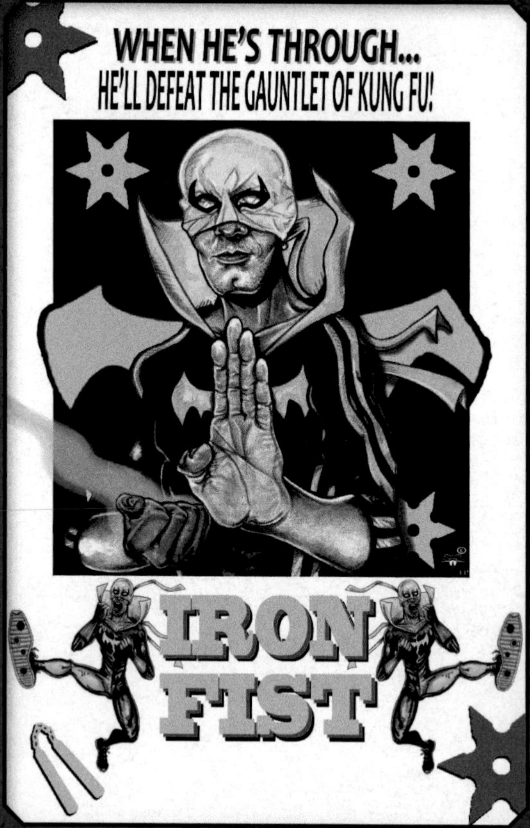
WHEN HE'S THROUGH...
HE'LL DEFEAT THE GAUNTLET OF KUNG FU!
IRON FIST

André LeRoy Davis

No. 4 variant

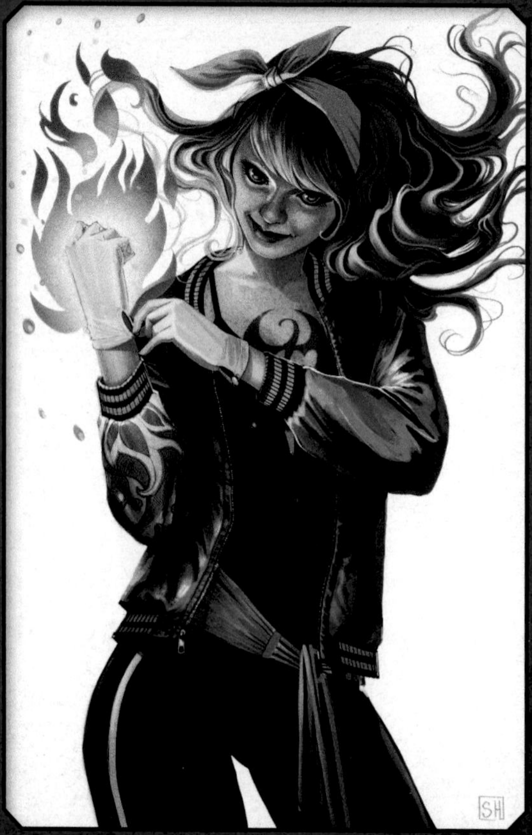

Stephanie Hans